# SEX AND SENSIBILITY

*A Parent's Guide to
Talking Sense About Sex*

## DEBORAH M. ROFFMAN

PERSEUS PUBLISHING
*Cambridge, Massachusetts*

A CIP record for this book is available from the Library of Congress
ISBN: 0-7382-0293-2
Copyright © 2001 by Deborah M. Roffman

Perseus Publishing is a member of the Perseus Books Group.

Text design by Jeff Williams
Set in 11.5-point Adobe Garamond by the Perseus Books Group

1 2 3 4 5 6 7 8 9 10—03 02 01 00 99
First printing, December 2000

Perseus Publishing books are available at special discounts for bulk purchases in the United States by corporations, institutions, and other organizations. For more information, please contact the Special Markets Department at HarperCollins Publishers, 10 East 53rd Street, New York, NY 10022, or call 1–212-207-7528.

Find us on the World Wide Web at http://www.perseuspublishing.com

# Contents

*To my two families*
*David, Josh, and Adam*
*and*
*The Park School of Baltimore*

# Acknowledgments

This book would never have been written without the guidance and support of four special women. First, the late Annette Filtzer Lieberman, who headed the education department at Planned Parenthood of Maryland in the 1960s and early 1970s, and for whom I first worked as a sexuality educator. When Netsie—as she was affectionately known by all—later moved on to become the first development officer at The Park School, it was she who invited me to come teach in 1975. Netsie was a brilliant and dynamic leader and a deeply moral and courageous person. Her dedication to excellence, and to the belief that each of us is obliged in our own way to work toward enhancing social justice, has inspired and informed my work for thirty years.

Second is Peggy Brick, a born educator and enabler. In her work as Director of the Center for Family Life Education in Hackensack, New Jersey, she created a steady stream of quality educational materials and training opportunities that immediately became the gold standard for the profession. Peggy has always been a wonderful source of encouragement and support for all of us in the "trenches"; her boundless enthusiasm, encyclopedic knowledge, and sharp intellect have been indispensable to whatever progress we have made. As I have told her, I wouldn't dare think of writing a book about sexuality education without her looking over my shoulder. And that she has done; she has read every word and made dozens of suggestions that have improved the work immeasurably.

It was Louise Mehta, Associate Head of The Park School of Baltimore, who first encouraged me to undertake the process of writing a book proposal. As the administrator who ably oversees the F. Parvin Sharpless Faculty and Curricular Advancement program at Park, she suggested one year that I follow my heart and apply for funds for an individual summer writing project, rather than the group curricular project that I felt I ought to do. Louise, too, is a marvelous enabler of people and ideas, always extending her support to the individual and the institution in equal measure. Like Peggy, she has made the time to read the entire manuscript and to make insightful and important comments.

Finally, to Gail Ross, my literary agent, I will be indebted always for sticking with me and this project throughout its development. As I followed her through the hallways of the various publishing houses we visited just a year ago in New York, I marveled at the respect and affection she garnered from all who passed by. As we walked along, people would spot her and come out of their offices to greet us, excited and happy to have the chance to chat and catch up. Gail *really* knows her job, and it shows in everything she does. I am privileged to have her in my corner and also indebted to my friend and colleague Catherine O'Neill Grace for introducing us.

Gail in turn introduced me to Marnie Cochran, my editor at Perseus. Marnie has been a joy to work with from our first meeting—warm, forthright, perceptive, and wise. She's been my head cheerleader every step of the way, and has read and responded helpfully from many perspectives—editor, "average reader," and new, first-time mom. Each role has been enormously helpful in refining the text. She has indeed made the experience as painless and enjoyable as possible.

Several other readers have made a huge difference in the final product, and I am deeply grateful for their insights about specific chapters: Zella Adams, Ellen Barth, Howard Berkowitz, Rachel Edelman, Patti Flowers-Coulson, Alex Eifler, Margarita Gurri, Shira Lander, Searle Mitnick, Jessica Rowe, and Dave Tracey. Both Joanne Mason and Kathy Levin Shapiro helped shape the chapters on gender in important ways, and both have been wonderful advisers to me throughout the entire project, from proposal to publication. Hillary Jacobs, Director of Advancement at Park, has also been a constant source of wisdom and support.

Most teachers throughout their careers work with only a handful of school heads and administrators. Because I work with so many different schools, and usually within more than one division, I've had the good fortune of working with dozens of them. Many I've known for years and count among my most respected colleagues: Betty Brown, Barbara Buck, Aurelia Burt, Arnie Cohen, Bo Dixon, Cornelia Donner, Janet Edwards, Merrill Hall, Margi Hoffman, David Jackson, Betsy Leighton, Noreen Lidston, Patti Lyall, Mike McGill, Evelyn McClain, Alice Mering, Ceil Millar, Cammie Peterson, Dick Peyton, Bonnie Rosenblatt, Paul Schneider, Zipora Schorr, Ken Seward, Carla VanBurkum, Abigail Weibenson, and Brian Wright. I thank each of these colleagues for his or her support of our programs over the years. Thanks as well to friends or colleagues who go even farther back and were among my earliest and most important mentors: Shirley Handelsman, Judy Richter, Stan Mazer, Paul Ephross, Priscilla Huff, Deborah Mitnick, Jack Osman, Phyllis Ensor, and Nancy Kennedy.

The Baltimore/Washington metropolitan area is blessed with many fine independent schools, and I have had the privilege of working with students, faculty, parents, and boards of trustees at many of these wonderful institutions. In addition to Park School, I've enjoyed long-term associations in Baltimore at the Bryn Mawr School, Roland Park Country School, McDonogh, St. Timothy's, Calvert, Friends School of Baltimore, Beth T'filoh, Krieger Schechter Day School; and in or near Washington, at the Barrie School, Green Acres, Capitol Hill Day School, and at Langley, Sheridan, St. Stephens and St. Agnes, and Potomac Schools. Each of these experiences has enriched my life and work and taught me much about teaching.

Finally, to my husband, David, and my two sons, Josh and Adam, I express my deepest gratitude for their excitement and support during this wonderful and amazing experience. They have made it all possible, in every possible way.

# Preface

## My Mother Always Wanted Me to Be a Sex Educator, and Other Myths

Life is full of unpredictable twists, but in my case it made a full hairpin turn. I don't know anyone less destined than I for a career in sex education. In one recurring nightmare, I run into an old boyfriend from college. When he learns what I do for a living, he can be heard laughing uncontrollably. They finally have to sedate him to get him to stop. It is very embarrassing. In real life, my mother and I barely discussed anything as sensitive as periods, so if she had hopes or dreams about my becoming a sex educator when I grew up, she never mentioned them.

So how did I turn up in this most unlikely of professions? Totally by accident, I can assure you. It was the early 1970s, and I needed a new job. On a tip, I interviewed for a community educator's position at a local family planning agency. To this day, I still wonder why I was hired. Sometimes I think the director simply wanted to demonstrate that you literally could take anybody off the street and make her into a sex educator (thereby proving that there is hope for us all!). But, nonetheless, within two weeks, I was traveling the state of Maryland talking to people I had never met before about sex and birth control, and waving diaphragms, IUDs, and condoms in front of them.

No one was more astonished than I that I could do just that. Up until then, I had not uttered the words "penis" or "vagina" more than three times during the previous twenty-three years. (That is only once every seven and a half years or so, and not a lot of practice). Suddenly, I was having to say these words, and plenty more like them, for a living—in front of Girl Scouts, garden clubs, rap groups, college kids, foster parents, social workers, nursery school teachers, armed forces personnel, Rotarians, prison inmates, and just about any other category of folks you could name.

It was fun, adventurous even. Though the sixties had passed me by as a naive high school and college student, I was catching up in a hurry as a young professional working in a "child of the sixties" movement. The family planning and sexuality education fields were in their infancy, and my agency was at the cutting edge of both. With family planning declared a national priority, clinical and educational facilities were being funded all over the United States.

Consequently, shortly after I was hired, the agency was awarded a federal grant to train newly hired personnel throughout the mid-Atlantic region. The challenge was scary and exciting. I myself had barely learned the rudiments of teaching, and before I could blink, I was being asked to show others. There were so few of us, and precious few good resources. We had to learn quickly (mostly by trial and error), and then teach the next guy how to do it. As a result, from practically the first day I've walked into a classroom, I've brought a triple layer of questions: What's the best and quickest way to get this lesson across? Exactly what's working, what isn't, and why? What did I learn today about teaching, and how can I most effectively pass it on?

After all these years of fallopian tubes, I am even more excited to be in the classroom today than I was thirty years ago. I'm still asking the very same questions and discovering new answers every day. I'm still constantly teaching about teaching and trying hard to impart whatever I'm learning as quickly as possible. Over the years, I've worked with thousands of students, parents, teachers, counselors, administrators, health care professionals, and youth workers of all kinds; my sense of urgency has only increased as a new list of topics and problems—HIV, gender, sexual harassment, date rape, the special needs of sexual minority youth—has entered the picture.

It is my concern over these and other issues, and my frustration at not being able to impart my learning quickly enough, that have motivated me to write this book. I wrote it fully committed to the proposition that what children and adolescents need most are not sexuality "experts," but wider and wider circles of everyday adults available to them for open dialogue about sexual matters. Otherwise, my work and the work of all of us in the classroom, no matter how skillful, become isolated, out-of-context learning experiences with, ultimately, very limited impact.

All our work as professionals is severely limited unless the role of parents—our children's primary and most important sexuality educators—can be strengthened. Consistently, research documents that children who grow up in families where sexuality is openly discussed grow up healthier, a finding that should cause no great surprise. Moreover, when parents do not take positive, conscious, and proactive roles, much of the work in the classroom becomes remediation—helping children *unlearn* inaccurate information and destructive attitudes—before new learning can even begin to take place.

I believe that these truths about the sexual learning process create a mandate for all of us who work as sexuality educators: To be truly effective, we must—as an essential component of our work, never as a sideline, an afterthought, or a defensive measure—encourage and support parents. Unless we work with parents as full partners, no matter how skilled and successful we may be as teachers, we may well be sabotaging our own efforts. Unless we constantly define and highlight the complementary but unique and critical role of parents, we risk encouraging a false sense of relief for them and a false sense of reliance on us. By allowing the perception that we are giving children all that they need, we may inadvertently disempower the very adults who can help them the most.

Although I have worked in a great variety of settings over the years, the independent school community is where I have learned most of what I know about children and adolescents, development, and teaching. In the many fine, independent schools in the Baltimore/Washington area and throughout the country where I have worked as a teacher and consultant, I have been struck most by the ongoing commitment to identifying and meeting real developmental need. Whether the school considers itself very "traditional" or one that is more on the "progressive" end of the continuum, adults in all these institutions consistently try to tell children the truth about the world around them, and the children, in turn, are allowed and encouraged to tell us the truth about themselves and their world. As simple as this may sound, in the midst of a culture that operates out of denial about so many sensitive issues, most especially sexuality, institutions like these provide children an oasis of honesty, openness, and directness. And for adults, these schools are veritable laboratories for learning about children and their needs as they grow up in this very complex world. Consequently, in my work as a sexuality educator in the independent school community, I have always been encouraged, and in fact implicitly expected, to be in touch with and accommodate the real needs and interests of children.

I began teaching in independent education in 1975, having both attended and taught classes in many other schools where caution, not accommodation, was the primary operative. I was, therefore, a little slow at first to fully catch on. Then one day I came to work and was greeted by someone asking a rather unusual question: "Hey, Deb, have you seen the Womb Room?"

"Womb Room? What's a womb room?" I asked sheepishly, because if indeed there was such a place, then I, the resident "sex lady," as the kids called me, should certainly be able to speak about it intelligently.

"It's upstairs at the end of the upper school hallway," I was matter-of-factly informed.

A short flight up, and I could hardly believe my eyes. The senior drama class had decided to put on as its final project an avant-garde play about a serious contemporary issue. The topic they had chosen, after research and deliberation, was sexually transmitted disease—venereal disease, as it was called at the time. Their teacher had helped them locate a play about Gonorrhea and Syphilis, quite literally, as these were the names of its central characters. The third and only other player was—who else?—Penicillin. (You can tell how long ago this was by the absence of any other actors; there wasn't even so much as a Penicillin-Resistant Gonorrhea character, let alone someone named Herpes, Chlamydia, or HIV.)

To achieve maximum dramatic effect, the class had obtained permission to turn their classroom into a suitable stage. They accomplished this feat by transforming the entire space into the inside of a uterus! Using various shades of crepe paper, with lots of reds and pinks, they had lowered the ceiling to create a truly womblike setting. To enter the womb room, the audience walked single file through a long tunnel, constructed from dark, folded blankets strung from above. After a sharp, anatomically correct right turn, a brief walk through the cervical canal brought the audience center stage, or rather center uterus, where they sat on benches and watched the performance. In the background, a faint, rhythmic, swooshing sound (fetal heart beat? menstrual sloshing?) pervaded the cavity.

On the way out, audience members were handed a pencil and a brief true/false quiz about gonorrhea and syphilis, complete with latest statistics, appropriate admonishments, and a list of places to go for help. The entire upper school, including students, faculty, and parents, was invited to attend one of the numerous performances offered throughout the day, and even middle schoolers were welcome. After some thought, though, and with help from the middle school principal, the students decided to discourage sixth-graders. As consummate concrete thinkers, the sixth-graders may have drawn some pretty strange conclusions about how human bodies—or upper school classrooms—are actually constructed!

As amazing as all this was to me, the most remarkable part was the casual reaction of the school community. No student was surprised, no teacher got nervous, no parent got outraged, no administrator got so much as a phone call. What's most important, nobody got, or gave, the message, either directly or indirectly, that there was anything special or unusual about this topic. Human sexuality was just another interesting and important subject—like all the others addressed during the course of a normal school day—to think, learn, wonder, and ask about.

In fact, the only person who seemed unglued at all was me, the sex lady. I stood in the corner, silently taking it all in and trying hard not to let on that anything remarkable was happening—for fear of spoiling it!

Tragically, what is expressly permitted and encouraged at schools like this one is a revolutionary concept in U.S education: that children can and should be trusted to say spontaneously what they really think about and experience regarding sexuality, and that teachers can and should be trusted to respond in kind in whatever ways they feel are necessary and appropriate. In contrast, in most U.S. schools, when sexuality is dealt with at all, what is typically covered are the subjects that the adults in the building are most comfortable talking about or least afraid to teach about—or subjects permissible according to some distant mandate, prescriptive policy, or airtight, controversy-free curriculum finalized long before the first real live student enters the classroom. Somewhere in the midst of meeting all those adult needs, the real needs of the children and adolescents inevitably become lost, if they truly are ever considered at all.

Partially because they are more able than schools in the glare of the public eye, independent schools are willing to take the risks necessary to meet real student need. However, this incongruity is not fundamentally a public/private issue or dichotomy. There are many fine individual public schools and whole school districts that, despite real or perceived community opposition, insist on programs that are honest, inclusive, and relevant. What's more, many independent schools remain blind to the real needs of their students or cave in at the slightest hint of controversy. The critical difference lies in a realistic understanding and acceptance of developmental need, and an unshakable commitment to meeting it.

In an environment where children are not permitted to learn what they need and want to learn about sexuality, they lose. So do the adults in that environment. If students are not permitted to grow, neither are their teachers. When students are allowed to ask, stretch, and test, they teach, because they reveal themselves and their needs. When teachers are permitted to listen, respond, change course, take risks, make mistakes, and change course again, only then can they really teach.

We may decide, finally, that the stakes are now too high, and that our children and our teachers should be trusted to learn from and teach one another. But both students and teachers have already lost many opportunities to learn and to teach, and much precious time. Many of us are novices in territory that is foreign and dangerous.

Over these many years, I have been privileged to teach, to listen, to respond, to take risks, to make many mistakes, and to change course as often as I have needed. My hope is to help reclaim some of that lost time for others, by sharing what I have learned back from my students, who have taught me well.

## PART 1

*New Ways of Thinking and Talking*

# 1

# Starting Over:
# We Can't Get There from Here

Some time ago, I was invited to teach a brand new sexuality program for fourth-graders at a nearby independent school. I was excited. Each time I've added a new grade level to my teaching, it's been a marvelous opportunity to learn something fresh and important about how kids think, feel, and learn. I go in knowing that for the first year, at least, I most definitely will learn more than my students.

That year, the student who taught me the most about teaching fourth grade was a burly, socially savvy young boy who had seated himself at the left end of the very last row, a great vantage point for observing his peers. On the third day of the class, he raised his hand with slight hesitation and posed a wonderful question.

"Why is sex supposed to be cool?" he asked.

"What makes you think that?" I asked him.

"Well, I don't know exactly. I just sort of get that idea watching older kids, like teenagers, talk about it. Boys, mainly."

His comment sparked at least twenty minutes of discussion, and as many questions. Did we think those boys meant that sex was cool, or that having sex made the person seem cool? Do boys seem to think that way more than girls? At what age do kids start talking about sex in this way? Why then? And what does the word *cool* mean, anyway? Is sex cool, and, if so, what's cool about it?

I was charmed and amazed by the maturity of these fourth-graders, as they tried to sort it all out. We talked a lot about teenage posturing and what that might be about, and about how easy it is to use sex, or even talking about it, to try to make yourself look grown-up. We reasoned that since girls may face more potential consequences than boys, it's understandable that they seemed sometimes to take the issue more seriously. Since parents and other adults had tried to communicate that sex was supposed to be about things like love, marriage, caring, and closeness, we struggled, with a lot of confusion, to put those ideas together with the word *cool*. As another boy finally put it, it seemed to him that sex was about warm, not cool, and that those teenagers had somehow gotten it backward.

## Getting There First

As I told the fourth-grade parents not long after, it was one of those golden teachable moments you hope and pray for. To be sure, fourth-graders are decidedly still children. But make no mistake, they nonetheless are paying close and constant attention to how the larger world works, including the teenage and adult social and sexual worlds. They have already surmised, from their exposure to thousands and thousands of cultural messages, that sex and romance are supposed to be ultra-important in grown-up life, and they understand intuitively that they too will need to master the rules of sexual and social interaction—just as surely as they will need to master the rules of grammar, math, and science. So, continually and subconsciously, they listen, they watch, they build and test theories. They may check out their ideas with a convenient peer or, if we're lucky, with a trusted adult, but eventually they will come to their own conclusions about what is true and false, important and unimportant, cool and uncool. And, if the source is deemed particularly credible, they may simply take what they see and hear at face value, absorbing it unconsciously as absolute and unquestioned truth.

"Don't we adults want to be the ones to get to our children first, with the right way to look at things—with *our* truths—before they get it backwards from someone else?" I asked the parents. Even when our children are in the fourth grade—and younger—we need to be right there next to them, watching what they are watching, asking what they're thinking, listening to their ideas, making ourselves available as often as possible as credible sources of information, attitudes, and values.

## Slender Windows of Opportunity

In truth, that's not exactly what I learned from the fourth-grade boy that day. I'd already known for a very long time that unless we become more proactive in reaching out to our children about the topic of sexuality—probably a great deal earlier than we may erroneously believe is the age-appropriate time—they most assuredly will learn about it first from someone else. And that someone else, more than likely, will be offering a different kind of message from the one we would like them to have.

What I did learn that day was not really from the boy's question at all or from the earnest and endearing way the class dealt with it, but from his asking it in the first place. I realized immediately that later on, as a more self-conscious fifth-grade boy (especially one so socially savvy), he would most likely have kept the question to himself, fearing that he might be the only boy in the room not to know the answer. And, not having asked the question in the fifth grade, the same boy as a sixth-grader would most likely not even think to ask it: After two more years of confirmation, watching and listening to older boys, he might well have simply concluded that, yes, sex *was* supposed to be cool.

How slender is the window of opportunity for adults who want to be there for children and adolescents at just the right moment, and yet how frequently we don't know how, when, why, or even that the window is open. There is no mystery as to how those older teenager boys—the ones whom fourth-grade boys are watching so carefully—"somehow" got it backward: Someone or something else had seized their attention during an earlier, critical window of opportunity and shaped their views of sex, perhaps for the rest of their lives.

## The Crucial but Unfulfilled Role of Parents

The year 1998, the time of the Clinton/Lewinsky debacle, will long be remembered as a watershed year in the history of American sexual attitudes. A nation awash in sexual scandal and sensationalism, fearing for its children's innocence and its own credibility, finally reached the outer limits of its sexual sensibilities. As adults everywhere fixated on the continual debasement of our society's standards regarding sex, privacy, integrity, media, and government itself, the nation ultimately seemed to exclaim a resounding and collective "Enough!"

Despite the power and intensity of the year-long wake-up call, adults—parents in particular—are still unsure about how and what to change. As dozens of studies show, when it comes to discussing sexuality with their children, most parents don't even know when they should begin talking, let alone what they should be talking about. According to one survey, 60 percent of parents have not talked to their early adolescent children about how to prevent pregnancy or avoid sexually transmitted diseases, even though a majority of young teens have made it clear that they want more information about these and other topics. And nearly half of parents of ten- to twelve-year-olds have not discussed peer pressure and sex with their children. A similar percentage of parents have not even considered when it is appropriate for their children to become involved in sexual activity.

Young people in the United States have paid a terrible price for adult confusion and evasion. U.S. teen pregnancy rates, for example, are twice as high as they are in England or Canada, and nine times as high as in Japan or the Netherlands. One out of every fifteen of our teenage boys will father a child; four in ten teenage girls will become pregnant at least once. Add to these statistics the widespread incidence of child sexual abuse, sexual harassment, rape, date rape, and violence against gay youth, and it is clear that the sexual health of our young people is in a virtual state of crisis. Moreover, we haven't yet mentioned the specter of HIV infection. Though presently at relatively low levels in the overall teenage population, HIV infection looms just over the horizon as a ticking time bomb for an age group already engaged in exactly the same unprotected risk behaviors that have led to the rapid spread of the virus elsewhere.

Most of our troubling youth problems—drug use, dropouts, crime, school violence, eating disorders—are baffling, have multiple causes, and are frustratingly intractable. However, unlike many of these other tragedies, researchers have already identified our first and most important line of defense against adolescent sexual health problems: parents. The most consistent finding in sex education research over the past quarter century confirms what should be intuitively obvious: Children who grow up in families where sexuality is openly discussed grow up healthier. In broad human terms, the implications for the lifelong sexual health of these youngsters are probably inestimable. But even in the most concrete and immediate terms, the research findings are dazzling: As a group, these youngsters tend to delay first intercourse and, if and when they become involved, act with greater forethought and protection. In other words, children who grow up with an atmosphere of openness about sexuality *grow up more slowly and more responsibly.*

Clearly, as families and as a nation, we cannot afford to continue ignoring the singularly important role of parents in supporting our children's healthy development. Yet, despite decades of consistent research, we have done precisely that. Look around. Where are the national, state, and local initiatives to support parents in this role? Where is the funding for parent classes and educational materials? Where are the ubiquitous billboards, bus placards, public service announcements, and political speeches? Where are the school and community-based programs to highlight and supplement what parents can contribute? Where are the concerned religious leaders, in all denominations, and across the entire spectrum of religious belief? Where is the clamoring public? What stops us?

## A Culture Stuck in the Seventies

When I first became a community health educator in the early 1970s, I recall making several visits to one high school in particular. The school was part of a district in which a variety of sexual health topics, including the subject of birth control, were explicitly barred from the curriculum. Since the topic I was asked to speak about was in fact contraception, I was allowed by my agency to accept the invitation only with written permission from the school's principal. Troubled by the high number of pregnancies among the students every school year, he always agreed without hesitation.

It was the classroom teacher, Mrs. Thomas, who was most nervous about my visits—even though it was she who extended the invitation in the first place, out of genuine concern for her students' welfare. After all, it was her neck that would be on a very public block if parents were to complain to the school board or if a community controversy blew up, and she knew it. I felt bad for her, every time I came to speak. She was so overtly anxious and worried that her hands shook and her voice quivered.

I'll never forget how she would explain the reason for my visit whenever she introduced me to her classes: "This is Mrs. Roffman," she'd say to the girls, in a clumsy but forgivable attempt to cover herself. "She has come here today to discuss methods of birth control. Those of you who are behaving morally do not have to listen. The rest of you, well, you'd had better pay *close* attention!" She had felt a little safer, I guess, knowing that if anything untoward were to happen, she'd at least be on record as being definitively opposed to "immorality."

What had Mrs. Thomas so intimidated was the political climate in her home county. Throughout the 1950s and 1960s, many schools and school districts across the United States had become targets of outspoken individuals or highly organized community-based or religious groups opposed to sex education in the public schools. By the 1970s, through unrelenting and often uncompromising participation in local family life education advisory boards, these groups had succeeded in taking de facto control of the sex education curricula in Mrs. Thomas's home county and several others in the state. What that meant, essentially, was an enforced litany of topics that could not be discussed or mentioned in any classroom or under any circumstance, even at the high school level. As we'll see in Chapter 7, this dangerous legacy persists throughout the United States even today, even in the age of AIDS, even in the midst of a vastly different and highly sexualized society.

## Parents Are Stuck as Well

Mrs. Thomas's anxiety was far overblown. I don't recall that parents ever expressed opposition to our work in the schools. Sadly, they were most often just plain relieved and grateful that somebody else was doing this uncomfortable job for them.

When it comes to their children's sexual upbringing, the average parent is often just as "stuck" as the average school district. Lacking anything even approaching comprehensive sex education when they were growing up—either within their family or in their formal schooling—most of today's parents have never seen what the possibilities might be for their children. Parents consequently have few criteria with which to judge what might be best for them.

For those schooled in the 1950s, 1960s, and 1970s, sex education—more accurately, "reproduction education"—was either nonexistent or a didactic "organ recital" or perhaps a film about the workings of the reproductive system, menstruation, or puberty. The typical course often placed heavy emphasis on hygiene and acne and had a strong spoken or unspoken message about the perils of premature or premarital sexual involvement. Characteristically, it was taught by an unsure, unwilling, or deeply embarrassed teacher to an equally embarrassed, fidgety, and very quiet—or very rowdy—group of youngsters. Both were greatly relieved when the bell rang and the torture was finally over.

I'm not sure what any of us learned in those classes about reproduction, hygiene, or fallopian tubes. But sadly and perhaps tragically for some of us, we did learn one thing for sure: *This was a topic far too scary and uncomfortable to talk, learn, or even think about.* Quite a message for what was supposed to have been an "educational" experience!

Conversations at home, if they occurred at all, were typically no more helpful or comfortable. Stereotypical images of stammering parents and squirmy children engaged in the archetypal giving and receiving of the "facts of life" are fairly close to actual memory for many of us.

What adults tend to remember from their early sexual learning experiences, both in schools and in families, is not so much the content of the lessons or conversations themselves, but the feelings they evoked. In her book *When Sex Is the Subject,* Pam Wilson describes this concept of conversational tone metaphorically as the background "music" that accompanies the "lyrics," or words, that are spoken to us. This "melody" lingers on long after the particulars of conversations have been forgotten, influencing some of our most fundamental attitudes and beliefs about the whole topic of sexuality.

For most of us, the background music accompanying even our earliest sexual learning was filled with anxiety. Whenever the subject of sexuality surfaced in my own family, there was always an abrupt shift in the atmosphere around me. The change was subtle, but immediately discernible. Suddenly someone would blush, crack a joke, become tense, lower his eyes, clear her throat, darken her voice, or try to change the subject altogether. Whereas moments before we all might have been conversing naturally and comfortably, suddenly there was a feeling of threat in the air, and the background music of my family no longer felt cozy and safe. I didn't like the way that felt at all. I made the decision, as many children do, probably quite unconsciously at first and then quite deliberately later on, to help keep my family environment "safe" by avoiding the subject as much as possible, and enabling my parents to do the same. We became partners in a childhood-long conspiracy of silence, as a defense mechanism against the great big elephant in the corner that was far too anxiety-provoking for any of us to mention.

With these kinds of associations from the past, no wonder that when we are asked today to participate in sex education, either as teachers or as parents, our first reaction is to perspire, gulp, and head out the back door. Many of us, especially those who consciously think of ourselves as children of the sexual revolution, ironically have an even harder time with all this than did our parents' generation. Since we are supposed to have been liberated from these ways of the past, we tend to feel very confused, and often guilty, about the overwhelming lack of confidence we experience whenever we have to confront our adult role as sex educators. As concern about HIV infection has grown, these feelings of inadequacy—fueled by rising expectations regarding parental roles and increasing panic regarding our children's health—have only escalated.

In my work with tongue-tied parents and teachers from all over the country, I am constantly amazed by the near universality of these compounded reactions of discomfort, anxiety, confusion, fear, guilt, and vulnerability. I have found that no matter what our socioeconomic, religious, racial, or ethnic background or level of education, the topic of sexuality is one of the great equalizers of U.S. culture. Everywhere, it seems, adults are feeling more motivated, but less capable.

## Schools Are Faring No Better

Even in this age of HIV risk, despite mandates for sexuality and AIDS education in more than half the states across the nation, an estimated fewer than 10 percent of school-age children receive anything approximating comprehensive, K–12 education about human sexuality. With the increasing emphasis in recent years on "abstinence-only" programs (in many districts, financed by matching grants from the federal government), even districts that previously may have taken a more comprehensive approach now teach curricula that are narrow and restricted. Combined with a widespread lack of effective parental guidance, this institutionalized evasion continues to help create a dangerous educational vacuum in our children's lives.

Research conducted in other countries culturally and technologically similar to our own bears out the overriding importance of education, parental involvement, and community-wide support—as well as the folly of the U.S. approach. In several European countries, for example, where sexuality education is institutionalized uniformly, the status of teenage sexual health is astoundingly better than that in the United States (especially where the European programs are accompanied by easy access to preventive medical services). With rates of teenage pregnancy two to nine times lower, the incidence of some sexually transmitted infections (STIs) from four to twenty-five times lower, and teen abortion levels approximately half of U.S. levels, any one of these foreign health indicators puts U.S. efforts to shame. And, perhaps most shamefully, while we in the United States continue to actively, even self-righteously, resist the kind of open and comprehensive approach adopted in nations such as the Netherlands, Germany, and France, teens in these countries actually delay the experience of first sexual intercourse for up to two full years longer than do their American peers!

## Lack Of Cultural Integrity

These same studies also reveal in U.S. society some deep societal factors that do not exist elsewhere. What seems to make the real difference abroad is a kind of cultural integrity and consistency about sexual values and decision making that is completely lacking in the United States; teens in other countries are told in no uncertain terms that sexual behavior, especially sexual intercourse, is a very serious matter, and that they *must* learn to take personal responsibility for the ethical choices and considerations involved. In the United States, instead, they are barraged constantly with sexual ideals and values that are vague and hopelessly contradictory. At one extreme are ubiquitous mass media messages, which project an endless stream of indiscriminate and consequence-free nonmarital and extramarital sexual scenarios. At the other is the official public posture of U.S. society's major institutions, which idealizes sexual restraint, extreme caution, and nonmarital chastity. Our children, without the help of skillful adults to carve out a more realistic framework for decision making, and developmentally unable as yet to rely on an internally based values system, are dangerously caught in the middle of this "Do It Now!"/"Just Say No!" crossfire. As a result, they are more likely to act out, to test, and to experiment with risk-taking behaviors far beyond their developmental capabilities.

Beyond the need to address these critical issues is the important realization that comprehensive sexuality education is not simply a matter of damage control, that is, a matter of raising our children to be disease-, pregnancy-, and exploitation-free. As will become clear, the notion of sexuality and sexuality education, as distinguished from sex and sex education, centers on the much broader goal of supporting our children's development and growth toward healthy sexual adulthood in *all* aspects—not just the physical, but the emotional, social, and ethical as well.

If we are to make real progress in improving our children's sexual education and health status, we will need to resolve the anxieties within ourselves and within the American culture about sexuality. To start, we will need to make our adult need for denial and avoidance subordinate to our children's need for honesty and directness. How we have chosen to educate and protect our young does not fit the realities of their lives; the old ways do them great harm and must be replaced. We must commit ourselves as a community of caring adults to defining and articulating for young people a set of messages about human sexuality that is clear, unified, realistic, and humanistically based.

If we succeed, we will change the background music in our children's lives and in our own about the topic of sexuality. We will know this has happened because a palpable shift will occur in the atmosphere of our families and in our classrooms. We will recognize it as a pleasant hum in the air whenever the topic of sexuality surfaces; people around us will remain physically and emotionally relaxed. There will be an underlying feeling of safety and security. People will share openly and honestly, and ask the questions they really want to ask. They will laugh a lot, not out of nervousness, but because it will be enjoyable and fun. Everyone will want to continue the conversation, even after the bell has rung or it's time for bed. Far from feeling torturous, it will feel joyous, because sexuality *is* wonderful and joyous, and because it is a wonderful and joyous subject for children and adults to discuss together.

## Reclaiming Our Common Sense

I once ran into a woman who recently had attended a presentation I often give for parents of middle school youngsters. A fine clinical psychologist, the wife of a pediatrician, and the mother of two terrific daughters, she was someone I had known and respected for several years.

"I'm so glad to see you," she said. "I want you to know that you have changed my life!"

Flattered, but dubious, I asked her what she was talking about. "After I heard you speak that night, about the kinds of things that children at different ages want to know and are capable of understanding," she confessed, "I decided that I had been letting my daughter down all of these years, ever since she was a very little girl. So, as soon as I got home, I woke her up! I said to her, 'When you were four, I could have told you this. And when you were five, I could have told you that.' And so on, and so on, and so on. I don't think she liked my waking her up very much, but we haven't stopped talking since!"

Then the woman added the part of the story I liked the best, because she sounded so happy and elated when she said it: "Thank you. It's been so much fun!"

Much as I might like to take credit for this and other life changing "miracles," I know, alas, that all I did was enable a very simple phenomenon: The woman had merely rediscovered her own good common sense.

The United States is a nation of people who somewhere along the way misplaced common sense and replaced it with common nonsense about sex education. I first realized this years ago when I began to work with professionals in training to be sex educators—all seasoned teachers, administrators, social workers, nurses, doctors, and counselors. Despite their varied backgrounds, unquestioned competence, and many years of training and experience, they had one thing in common: They hadn't a clue about how to pull this off, not even a shred of an idea about where to start. Without a lot of help, they were simply unable to apply to this issue what they already knew so unfailingly about so many other topics.

This selective incompetence, I have always suspected, results from a kind of culturally induced short circuit in how we think about sexuality. An experience working with a British school several years ago convinced me that I was right.

Invited to give a talk about sex education to teachers and parents, I accepted with great anticipation but also a fair amount of trepidation, since I had grown up with traditional stereotypes of British propriety. I recall asking nervously for guidance about what to expect.

"We're a lot more conservative over here, you know," cautioned an equally nervous-sounding school head.

As it all turned out, the cultural joke was on us both. Culture shock set in all right, but in a double-edged form that neither of us, misled by our mutual stereotypes, could have anticipated.

What ensued was perhaps the most open and productive two hours I have spent with any group, anywhere. Although I found some reticence, actually just a kind of sweet shyness, about open discussion of sex, I was greeted by an audience only too willing to tackle this very sensitive subject head-on. Sensibility took clear precedence over embarrassment, responsibility over reservation. In the age of AIDS, especially, these parents and educators, unlike so many American adults with whom I work, did not intend to let mere discomfort tie their tongues, certainly not to the detriment of their children.

In the midst of my astonishment, I suddenly recalled that it had been the "conservative" British who inaugurated the nationwide "Don't Die of Ignorance" campaign when England had tallied only several hundred cases of AIDS. In contrast, it took a U.S. president six years and thousands upon thousands of cases to even utter the word in public. My mind flashed to my last visit to the London Airport, where disembarking travelers were greeted by a giant billboard promoting careful condom use, and I tried to imagine such a sight at Dulles or JFK.

My audience was also in for a serious jolt. Like many other foreigners, they had acquired a gross misperception of sexual liberation in the United States, fostered primarily, we decided, by American television. Those who watch American TV conclude that because Americans are seen either having sex or talking about it all day long on television (and in our films, rock videos, music, advertisements, etc.), we must, therefore, be comfortable with it.

Ha! After decades of work in this sexually bipolar culture, I was only too willing to blow the stereotype of a sexually liberated United States, with vivid accounts of the real world here. My audience was utterly aghast over the sorry state of sex education, the sky-high rates of teenage pregnancy and STI, and the shameful patchwork of inadequate sexual health services for our adolescents.

Why the cultural differences? we wondered aloud. For one thing, British educators are not stopped in their tracks, as sex educators often are here, by two uniquely American myths. We've heard the myths hundreds of times: The first is that although knowledge is a good thing, sexual knowledge might not be (the old "tell them about it and they'll go right out and do it" bugaboo). The second is that giving information, particularly contraceptive or prophylactic information, is the same thing as giving permission.

Often pronounced as self-evident truth, *without a shred of empirical proof*, these arguments are widely cited by the anti-sex-education lobby. The myths didn't seem to exist—not even a trace—in this British crowd, even though the origins can probably be traced back to the Puritans. The excruciating irony of this last point was not lost at all on my audience, who, looking very pleased with themselves, bragged, "Why do you think we had the good sense to send them over to you!"

Ironically, then, while other cultures aim so earnestly to protect their young from ignorance, we misguided Americans have decided instead to enlist it in the fight!

Moreover, we in the United States, who worry so obsessively about giving our kids mixed messages if we preach abstinence while telling them about condoms, end up giving them one of the most dangerous kind of mixed messages: "Do as we say, not as we do." We should instead take our cue from cultures that know how to give it as one message, loud and clear: "We love you and want you to be safe. The very best way to do that is to abstain in any potentially risky situation. The next best is to protect yourself and others as competently as you can. Here's how."

What other cultures understand and in fact never even seem to question is that sexual knowledge *is* good, and that it leads to only one thing: *knowing*, not doing. Talking openly about sex tacitly gives a child permission, all right, but only to do just that: to talk and to think, to reason, to understand, to clarify, to ask questions, and to come back later and talk some more. And to see us as credible and trusted sources of information. The erroneous equation of knowing with doing and information with permission is fabrication that we Americans have added out of our own projected anxieties. Not only does it cause us to "protect" our children in false ways, it also handily provides us a self-serving justification for avoiding conversations that many of us, in truth, would rather not have in the first place.

## Starting Over: Six Essential Truths

When I was a teenager, I would spend part of almost every summer break staying with my extended family in New England, where my father was born and raised. I especially liked staying with my Uncle Will and Aunt Florence. Once in a while we would go out on an excursion in my uncle's Oldsmobile; I can still conjure up the smell of the interior. We always seemed to get lost, arriving at our destination several minutes late at least. Uncle Will's excuse was always the same: "It's not my fault. You just can't get there from where we started. Obviously, you have to go somewhere else and start from there."

No matter how many times he said this, he could always get me for a second, until I remembered the joke and the absurdity of the remark. I think of Uncle Will and this story often, because, in truth, I have come to accept that sometimes in life's journey you really *can't* get there from here. Sometimes you are just so enmeshed in a set of false perceptions, beliefs, and conclusions that you absolutely are doomed to repeat the mistakes of the past unless and until you can consciously recognize and take steps to correct your original error. This is one of the reasons people enter therapy; they simply can't get past where they are unless they go back to an earlier path, reassess the conclusions they drew about their life at that particular fork in the road, and start over again from there.

If where we want to go is toward a day when all children in this culture are guaranteed a sexually healthy upbringing, with parents and schools universally engaged in supporting positive development at every step of the way, *we truly cannot get there from here*. We must go back as an entire culture and reexamine our assumptions and beliefs about how children learn and what they need to know. Even more fundamentally, we must explore how we have come to define and think about six essential concepts that are basic to fostering healthy sexual development: age appropriateness, sex, sexuality, gender, values, and family/school partnerships.

This process of reevaluation is so primary and so vital that a discussion of these six concepts constitutes the entire first section of this book. Then, in Part 2, we'll identify and practice five core skills for parenting, teaching, and nurturing children and adolescents as they grow toward sexually healthy adulthood.

Throughout the entire volume, several of my own most deeply held beliefs, both personal and professional, will be at the center of the discussion. Each day, as a parent, teacher, and parent/teacher educator, and as a friend, colleague, and confident to many young people and adults, I become more convinced of their truth and worth.

## Sexual Knowledge Is Good. Talking about Sex Is Good, and Good for Our Children

The United States is a nation that values, even reveres, knowledge; after all, the historical era in which we currently live is proudly known as the information age. So deep is our respect for knowledge and education that we consider them to be the cornerstone of many of our most cherished ideals: political freedom; justice; equality; personal, family, and social responsibility; prosperity; health; and human progress. And yet, one vast and essential area of knowledge—sexual knowledge—has traditionally been branded as inherently problematic, even potentially dangerous, and therefore something to be kept from children as long as possible. What hypocrisy. As a nation we decry illiteracy as inherently damaging to individuals and dangerous for our society, yet we proudly and actively promote the concept of sexual illiteracy for our own children.

It is way past time for us to acknowledge that we have been wrong in trying to "protect" children from sexual knowledge, and that if we are honest, it is we adults whom all along we have been trying to shield. Under the guise of false protectiveness, we have made our children's right to know subservient to our own need to avoid confronting topics that may make us feel embarrassed, uncomfortable, or ignorant. If we are embarrassed, we need to overcome it. If we are uncomfortable, we need to get through it. If we are ignorant about what is healthy and age-appropriate for children and adolescents to know, we must find out. If we are afraid of what the neighbors or family members will say if we are "too open," we need to figure out how to take the heat.

We are living in an age, very fortunately, where much guidance is available to help us do these things. Significantly, we are the first generation of parents who can truly make this statement, and that gives us unique opportunities and an irrefutable responsibility to act, and act now. Ironically, it is the HIV/AIDS epidemic that has helped more than anything else to provide these resources and supports. Although there is certainly nothing positive to be said about AIDS the disease, there have been many positive outcomes for our society as we have been forced to deal with its horrors. One is an ever-escalating resolve to confront—finally—some of the potential risks and hard realities our children face as they grow up in today's world. Another is a newfound and respectful openness in the popular news media about sexual health topics, making important information more easily accessible to the public and giving all of us, especially parents, permission and encouragement to raise our own and our children's level of sexual literacy. Much of this book is dedicated to facilitating this process.

## "Too Little Sexual Knowledge, Too Late" not "Too Much, Too Soon," Should Be Our Biggest Concern

Unbelievably, but sadly predictable, most school-based sex education programs in this country lag at least six years behind—and in many cases, eight or more years behind—the average child's normal developmental timetable for sexual learning. Americans traditionally have been so afraid of overwhelming children with information about sex that is "too much, too soon" that, in reality, what we end up providing instead is woefully "too little, too late." Both in school and at home, our children are missing out on crucial developmental steps in what should be a gradual, but steady and proactive educational process, beginning at the age of one.

Most parents and professionals working with children today themselves grew up with few role models to demonstrate what an adult looks and sounds like when he or she is conversing confidently and competently with a young person about sex. Especially when it comes to the educational needs of the youngest of our children, adults have little or no understanding at all of what information or approaches might be age-appropriate. Chapter 2 provides detailed and reassuring information about both.

### Sex Is Much Broader Than Intercourse

If the Clinton/Lewinsky scandal and Kenneth Starr investigation have taught us anything worth knowing about sexuality, it's that our cultural definitions of sex are remarkably imprecise and even detrimental. For a country as obsessed with things sexual as ours, our difficulty agreeing on a common meaning of the term is revealing in itself.

Young people need and deserve clarity from us about the range and meaning of behaviors. They also need for us to use language that is neither sexist, heterosexist, nor exploitive, and that is evocative of what we believe to be the proper context in which sex should occur. Present ways of speaking accomplish none of these goals, and in fact are counterproductive to the process of developing healthy sexual attitudes and values. In Chapter 3, we'll explore the importance and power of sexual language as a transmitter of information *and* values, and consider new ways of thinking and speaking.

## Values Education Is the Heart of Sexuality Education.
## Sexual Values Are Moral Values

For all our worry and consternation about the pop culture and "junk values" to which children are constantly exposed, adults are often tongue-tied when it comes to expressing clearly just what values we want our children to hold, and why. The much touted but worn phrase "family values," for example, has several possible and widely disparate meanings that we rarely stop to clarify, either in listening or speaking. Being clear within ourselves and with our children requires that we understand not only *what* we value, but *what kind* of value it represents and *why* we value it.

Chapter 4 prepares parents and teachers to handle discussions of sexual values confidently and articulately, first by identifying helpful ways of classifying values and values systems, and then framing persuasive messages about sexual values in ways that underscore personal, religious, and universal codes of morality.

## Sexuality Is Much Broader Than Sex

Our sexuality—how we think, feel, and act as males or females—is fundamental to who we are as human beings. And yet, in American culture it is an aspect of ourselves that few of us can even pinpoint, let alone adequately describe. So focused, even obsessed, are we as a society on the genital components of sexuality ("genitality"), that we fail to understand that the largest part of who we are as sexual people has to do with our gender, not our genitals.

To foster healthy sexuality, parents and teachers must first be able to better understand this elusive and most invisible aspect of sexual development. Issues of "genderality," meaning those aspects of identity and personality that are gender-based, must take their place alongside other more explicitly sexual concerns on the parental radar screen. Chapter 5 discusses sexuality as most fundamentally an issue of identity, not behavior, and affords a much more dynamic and broad-based understanding of our children's sexual development.

Chapter 6 continues the gender discussion and begins with the observation that our understanding of gender-related issues is narrow and often confused. Typically, we fail to adequately distinguish between four unique and nonoverlapping gender concepts: biological gender, gender roles, gender identity, and sexual orientation. As a result, we create unnecessary pressure and confusion for young people as they come to terms with their own personal, sexual, and gender development.

In today's world, children are exposed increasingly to simplistic and sensationalistic representations of sex and gender in the media. These distortions further fuel the existing cultural confusion about the components of our gender makeup. Especially for young people whose gender profile does not fit the typical or the stereotypical, grave hardships and social handicaps can result. This chapter will address how best to help young people understand and accept the gender diversity in the world around them.

## Parental and School Involvement in Sexuality Education Is a Moral Responsibility. Ignorance, Embarrassment, Discomfort, and Fear of Controversy Are Not Acceptable Excuses for Abdicating These Roles

Once sexuality education is understood as an ongoing and interactive process of growth and development—and not simply as the didactic transmission of sexual information—it becomes clear that families, schools, and for that matter, every other individual and institution in a child's life, all play a role. The question then becomes not *whether* to become involved, but *how best* to do so in ways that maximize health and growth.

The role of schools in sexuality education has been particularly misunderstood and mischaracterized. School-based programs have been perceived, at best, as providing a less-than-ideal substitute for parents who are not doing the job themselves, and, at worst, as attempting to inappropriately usurp parental rights, responsibilities, and prerogatives.

Chapter 7 delineates the responsibilities of schools and families as the most important sources of sexual education in a child's life and defines their unique but complementary roles. It also makes the case for comprehensive sexuality education, at home and in schools, as a moral imperative in today's world.

# 2

# Age Appropriateness: Too Much, Too Little, or Just Right?

A colleague in Oregon tells a story that really says it all about the vexing issue of age appropriateness. One evening at a parents' meeting, when she announced that sex education would be moved from sixth to seventh grade that year, a mother sitting in the front row immediately exclaimed, "But that's too late!" At the very same second, her horrified husband right next to her blurted out, "But that's too early!"

As the couple demonstrated so classically, there is no adult consensus—sometimes not even in the same family, let alone in the public—about exactly *when* parents and teachers should begin talking to our children about sex, *what* we should be talking about, and *how much* we should be saying.

Why not? And why does it seem so impossibly hard for us to figure this out?

## Gatekeepers and Controllers

Historically, adults have seen themselves not so much as educators, but as gatekeepers of sexual knowledge, and controllers of the sexual learning process. These roles are deeply woven into our culture. To prove it, we

19

need only notice the tightly scripted and prescriptive curriculum mandates codified and institutionalized in the majority of school districts across the United States. State departments of education, local school boards, community advisory groups, and in some cases even the federal government dictate what can, and more significantly, what *can't be* taught or discussed in our children's classrooms. And even then, most districts require that children bring written permission from home—from a parental gatekeeper—before they may participate.

Consciously or unconsciously, most parents also cling doggedly to the gatekeeper and controller roles, attempting to put a hold on discussions of sex and reproduction until they are certain the child is "ready," or that the time is absolutely "right." As any educator who works with parents can confirm, their most commonly asked questions are, "When should I begin?" and "Exactly how much should my child know, and when?" They worry—sometimes to the point of obsession—about getting the timing exactly right, and about doling out the information in just the right way and just the right doses. And, believing that they probably don't know how and when to do that correctly, they may feel terribly inadequate and anxious.

Most people would reasonably agree that there is a vast difference between educating and controlling, and yet when the topic is sexuality, we often forget this difference and treat education and control as if they are the same. The confusion is compounded by the fact that at times the gatekeeper and controller roles are absolutely necessary and appropriate in contemporary American society, with its ready access to sexual material that is too explicit, distorted, or advanced for young people. But, even when information is or might be age-appropriate, adults too readily slip into the controller rather than the educator role, just because the subject is sex. This lack of role clarification, that is, not knowing when control is appropriate and when it is not, is the major source of our continuing ignorance about what children really want and need to know. It is also the basis of our most glaring age-*in*appropriate decisions.

## Checking Out Our Assumptions

Getting clear about age appropriateness requires getting clear about how and why we have come to confuse the educator and controller roles, and coming to terms with how and why we have felt the need to control, rather than to educate. Consider the following assumptions—familiar to most of us and still very much a part our cultural heritage—that govern the gatekeeper/controller approach:

- Children are born "innocent" and ignorant of all sexual knowledge, and they should remain so unless and until the immediate adults in their lives choose to provide it.
- The universe of sexual knowledge exists within adults and the adult world, and is to be kept scrupulously away from the eyes and ears of children until they are "ready."
- Sexual knowledge is inherently and uniquely powerful. Unless it is provided to children at just the right time and in just the right way, problems, or even trauma, can and probably will ensue.
- Adults responsible for the child should give over the information, very gradually and at carefully selected ages and stages of development, until the child and the adult eventually share the same universe of knowledge.

Although many Americans may continue to accept the correctness of these assumptions philosophically, we must somehow come to agreement that at least from a practical standpoint they are clearly and hopelessly out of step with today's sex- and media-saturated society. As a simple trip to the magazine rack in the grocery store line will prove (among one month's cover stories were "Cosmo's Kama Sutra 2," "Thirty Day Climax Course: 102 Ways to Sex-You-Up," and "Fifteen Secrets of Sexy Wives"), even the youngest of children in today's world have multiple opportunities, often on a daily basis, for exposure to information about sex. Curiously, as adults we know what's out there, but both in families and in schools, we continue to think and act as if we are in total control of what our children can and will learn.

Although we may be successful at fooling ourselves, we will not fool them. Once they reach middle school age, if not before, they will have figured out our pretense. Ironically, when that happens, we run the risk that they will begin to discount us—teachers and parents—as credible sources, while we continue to delude ourselves that we are their *only* sources.

## The "Other" Facts of Life

At parenting and teacher workshops, as I listen to participants think out loud about their families and schools, I hear constant evidence of these assumptions in play. Adults everywhere worry about children being over-stimulated or confused, or about putting ideas in their heads, or overwhelming them with "too much, too soon." They wonder about the child sitting in a classroom who isn't "ready," even though her or his "more advanced" classmates might be, or what they'll do if their child tells another child down the block who doesn't know yet and an angry parent calls up. They want to know if it's all right to bring up the subject, even if their child hasn't mentioned it yet. Some worry about children at the other end of the spectrum: "But my child hasn't asked anything yet. Won't she be left naively behind her classmates?" Parents and teachers of adolescents question whether giving "all this information" will lead to experimentation or will be seen as giving "permission."

Sometimes it helps simply to reflect these same questions right back to them, substituting different subject matter: Suppose my child is overstimulated or confused by too many math facts? What if someone puts ideas in a child's head about astronomy? How about the child who hears about soccer for the first time from the kid up the block? But what if my son isn't ready yet to learn long division, and three other students in the class are? My child hasn't asked yet why we believe in God. Should I bring it up? If you teach my daughter about communism, won't she want to move to China and, in fact, think you want her to?

There are many ways, of course, that discussions with children and adolescents about sexuality are and should be different from discussions about math, astronomy, sports, and even religion, but the point is well taken. On some fundamental levels, these subjects are also the same, since they all represent in one form or another "facts of life." However, we don't question that children can and do learn about these other facts of life in ongoing and gradual ways as they grow up and go about living their lives. We accept totally that the circumstances of their learning will be both formal and informal, systematic and haphazard—in school, at home, and out in the "real world." We know that sometimes the agenda will be adult-driven, sometimes peer-driven, and sometimes curiosity-driven. We also realize that each child or adolescent will learn at his or her own unique pace and will sometimes feel overwhelmed, confused, or even overstimulated. We recognize that children's learning will usually be on a par with their peers', sometimes ahead, and sometimes behind. We may worry that a particular child is not learning or being taught a particular kind of subject matter in the best possible way, and we may take steps to correct the approach, but, generally, we believe fundamentally in the educational process: *we don't inherently fear the process or the content of the learning itself.*

Therein lies the key to how we have come to misdefine our role in the sexual learning process. In fundamental ways, we do see the teaching of sexual and reproductive "facts of life" as different from others, because *we do inherently fear the process and content of sexual learning itself.* In other words, we don't trust sexual knowledge, and our need to see ourselves primarily as controllers and gatekeepers, rather than educators, derives from precisely this fear: If the process of providing sexual information is potentially harmful and maybe even downright dangerous—indeed, if the content itself is potentially harmful or dangerous—then surely it must be dispensed in just the right amount, by just the right adult, in just the right way and time. Or else.

No wonder we pressure ourselves so much about this topic, sometimes to the point of paralysis. No wonder we hear about a new sex education program in our child's elementary school and immediately feel a vague but unmistakable feeling of anxiety and protectiveness. No wonder so many parents—and schools—fall into the convenient trap (and ultimate abdication) of deciding, "Oh, they're too young," when children are little; and later, "I'm not sure they're old enough," as they become middle schoolers; and "Oh, well, I guess it's too late, they probably know it all by now," by the time they're in high school.

## The Age-Appropriateness Demons

Adults tend to attach such huge intrinsic power to sexual knowledge, even to the mere mention of sexual words (notice how often people soften their voice and look around as they say one), that we tend to distort its potential impact way beyond what is even faintly reasonable. Our exaggerated fears can easily become psychological demons, making us second-guess ourselves at every turn. I know this not only from listening to hundreds and hundreds of parents, but also from direct experience.

By the time my older son, Josh, was five, he had pieced a little bit of this information together with a little bit of that information, as children do. He had decided that the way a woman gets pregnant is that God "plants a seed" in the mother's uterus. His father and I thought that this was a lovely notion, and we were fully content for him to hold onto it as long as he liked. Then one day he happened to mention his creation theory to a friend at work, who, before I could put my hands around her throat, practically shrieked, "How could your mother, of all people, let you think such a thing? God doesn't plant the seed, the daddy does!"

"That's just not true," Josh most emphatically informed her. "If it was, my mom would have said so!"

Oh great, I thought, as I quickly surveyed my options: (1) discredit a good friend; (2) permit my child (son of sex lady) to go through life wantonly spreading misinformation; or (3) tell an innocent child his mother is a liar.

I opted, finally, for a variation of the latter, trying to soften the effect with a casual "oh, by the way" approach on the ride home. Josh wasn't buying. He didn't understand, and didn't want any part of my explanations. All this ridiculous stuff about penises and vaginas. What did that have to do with anything?

Now I had really done it. Convinced my son had been traumatized for life, I surrendered all rational thought to the "age-inappropriate" demons sermonizing loudly in the back of my head. Racking my brain for the names of other young mothers I could call, I desperately needed reassurance that there was at least one other five-year-, three-month-, and twelve-day-old child in the universe who had heard this information and survived.

Two weeks later, when Josh asked hopefully and totally out of the blue if there was some way he could give his penis away, I almost turned myself in to the authorities. (As I found out later, he had gotten that idea from another little boy up the street.)

Trying to calm myself, I thought back to my own experience as a child. Better to be in the dark, I asked myself? My mind flashed to the only conversation my mother and I ever had about the subject of sex. It was the day of the "period film" in fifth grade, and we were walking home together from school. (In my elementary school, you not only had to bring a note from your mother in order to be allowed in to see the film, you had to bring *her*!) As we walked along, enjoying a beautiful spring day, I relaxed and gradually began to ask her questions about periods and some of the other things in the film. I started with the easy ones, like the ones I didn't really care that much about or already knew the answers to, and I was really surprised, and happy, at how well the conversation seemed to be going. Getting up my courage, I got to the one right before the one I *really* wanted to know about. Visibly shocked and uncomfortable, my mother immediately stopped dead in her tracks. "You're not old enough to know about that," she said forcefully, and that was the end of that.

The effect was devastating. Not only did I not get my question answered, but I suddenly felt very ashamed of myself, in the eyes of the person whose respect I needed the most, for even wanting to know something that was obviously so terribly inappropriate. From that moment on, whenever I had a question about sex or even inadvertently learned anything about it, or probably even just thought about it, I felt an overwhelming sense of guilt and aloneness. Never knowing when or if I had ever crossed the mysterious, invisible age-inappropriate line, for a very long time I was too afraid to ask anybody anything about sex, for fear of letting on that I had done it again.

Understanding how that experience in the fifth grade affected me was very liberating, but it also made me very sad. My mom and I had missed out on a lot of important conversations from that moment on. Looking back on how some helpful simple, straightforward information would have been, I stopped worrying about Josh and thinking I was a bad mother.

From then on, I continued to make "mistakes" with Josh and later with his younger brother, Adam. Sometimes, I would tell "too much too soon," giving a whole dissertation when a simple sentence would have sufficed. Like the time Josh asked how birth control pills work and I explained—with an in-depth lesson about ova and hormones.—

His reaction was classic, and right on track developmentally for a still very concrete-minded nine-year-old: "You mean, you kept me, little helpless Josh Roffman, trapped in your ovary for *five whole years?* How could you?" He probably would have been totally content with, "A woman takes them by mouth with a glass of water or juice, if it's handy."

Sometimes, I held back too long, profoundly underestimating their level of comprehension. After the way Josh had so over-personalized the birth-control pill saga, as Adam grew up I vowed to wait until he was at least thirty before even uttering the word *abortion* in his presence. As it ended up, I was beaten out by an eight-year-old in a car pool. The word was spoken by a reporter on the radio, and Adam's friend wondered aloud what it meant. I almost couldn't believe my ears. Adam, whom I had "protected" so diligently, matter-of-factly replied, "Sometimes when a woman becomes pregnant and can't take care of the baby, she goes to a doctor and has an operation or something so that she's not pregnant anymore." The other child said, "Oh, that's really too bad," and the conversation turned to that night's math homework.

In truth, I was only half surprised at being so off the mark. By then I had learned that my "mistakes" with each of my children were simply inevitable miscalculations, and wonderful teachable moments, especially for me.

## Understanding Our Role as Educators

Taking on the role of educator, as distinguished from the role of controller or gatekeeper, requires a new set of assumptions about sexual learning and about children as sexual learners. Contrast the following ideas with the beliefs cited earlier in the chapter:

- Children are born ignorant of sexual knowledge, but they are active learners from birth on. In the process of their normal intellectual, social, and emotional development, and as they continuously absorb information from the world around them, they begin to form and pose questions that can easily lead adults to provide age-appropriate information about sexuality. If an adult responds in a welcoming manner, these questions will continue, in a wholly predictable manner and sequence, through childhood and even well into adolescence.

- The universe of sexual knowledge is vast and growing constantly, and it is easily accessible in multiple ways in our society. Children are capable of learning sexual information in a gradual and ongoing fashion, beginning at about the age of one year, when they acquire language and begin to learn the names for their sexual body parts. Especially when children are young, it is best that they learn this information from the immediate adults in their lives, particularly parents and teachers; absent their involvement, children will learn from others.

- Sexual knowledge, like all knowledge, is powerful. Used carefully and deliberately, it is the cornerstone of safe, healthy, moral conduct.
- Sexuality is an essential part of life, and sexual knowledge is essential to a responsible life. The immediate adults in a child's life are morally responsible for passing on sexual knowledge to children and adolescents in an informed, deliberate, timely, and skillful fashion.

This set of precepts—which acknowledges the realities of today's world as well as the true nature of how children grow and develop, provides a framework for facilitating ongoing teaching and learning between adult and child. The child is no longer viewed as a passive, empty vessel—to be filled only at the discretion of others and needing protection until just the right moment by an all-knowing adult—but already a full, active partner and participant in the learning process. Children are depicted as ignorant, but not innocents, for that would imply that sexual knowledge somehow taints or lessens a child or takes away his or her childhood. And, adults are required to accept that *children are responsible for initiating and pacing their own sexual learning*; that being knowledgeable is better than being ignorant; that sexuality is fundamentally good and good to know about; that knowledge is empowerment; and that even when it comes to sexuality, empowerment is better than control.

In the United States, even at the dawn of the twenty-first century, that is a tall order indeed. Fortunately, if we are willing, help is amazingly nearby.

## Children Are Our Best Teachers

In truth, it is our children who are our best teachers and our most important allies in sorting out the thorny issue of age appropriateness. If we are willing to be their students—truly willing to commit ourselves to hearing and heeding what they have to say—they will teach us almost everything we need to know. And by listening carefully to the youngest of them, starting at about age four, we will even know why, how, and when to get the process started.

As many parents experience, it is very common for young children, sometime between the ages of four and six, to begin to inquire spontaneously about their origins. "Where do babies come from?" they ask, or even more directly, "Where did *I* come from?" Especially if they receive a positive and welcoming reaction, this will be a golden moment, because it will become the first question of many for years to come. Very gradually, but steadily and according to a remarkably predictable timetable, these children will—on their own—continue to initiate a series of increasingly pointed conversations about "the facts of life."

In many families these first questions are likely to coincide with the pregnancy or birth of a younger sibling, prompting everyone to assume, quite logically, that one event has precipitated the other. However, that is really not the case, and we should not be misled. It is vital to understand that these questions are generated *internally*, in tandem with the child's evolving cognitive abilities, *not externally*, because of some dramatic pre-cipitating event. In a way it's a lot like toilet training: It happens when children are ready, and when they are not—regardless of any creative, well-intentioned, or constant prompting they may receive from us—they're not. Likewise, when they are ready, children will ask about their origins in the total absence of pregnant women or newborns, and when they are not, Mom could be expecting triplets and it won't really matter.

Intriguingly, questions about origins often come along at about the same time developmentally as do questions about death. Observing this coincidence of timing in my own family years ago and hearing about it so often from other parents, I soon wondered whether it was indeed merely serendipity. I was also perplexed: Questions of birth and death seemed to me too abstract and advanced to fit the age. As I struggled to discover the right four-year-old connections to—and between—the concepts of birth and death, it finally struck me that I was thinking on the wrong level. A young child's interest in birth and death is not directly about those topics per se, but rather an extension of interest in two far more primitive and concrete ideas: beginnings and endings.

Children at the preschool stage are busy acquiring and trying out pow-erful new mental abilities. One of these is the emerging capacity to think about the physical world according to a profound and universal intellec-tual principle—that *virtually all things that exist in life have a clearly delin-eated beginning and ending*. Equipped with this new and important conceptual handle, they become better able to organize and "concretize" their experience and to manipulate more capably the concepts of space, time, and distance: This chair is a chair because it has a beginning here and an ending there; so does my house, and my family, and my trip to Grandma's house, and my neighborhood, and the house next door, and my preschool, and my summer vacation, and my school day, and so on. It is also their way of discovering and conceptualizing their own unique and separate identity, as distinguished from all others—especially from those special caretakers who at earlier stages were thought to exist as an extension of their own emotional and physical selves.

## The Principle of Beginnings and Endings: Where Did I Come From?

As they begin to master the principle of beginnings and endings—intuitively and unconsciously, over time and through constant life experience—children gradually gain the confidence and mental facility to explore larger and larger physical and intellectual worlds. Eventually they even formulate beginning and ending hypotheses, or hunches, as they begin to apply the principle to questions outside their own immediate experience. I envision their inquiries about origins and death as coming from one such mental leap: *If everything in my universe has a beginning and an ending, then so must I!*

So, one day, prompted by this internal hunch, they approach the nearest trusted adult and say (in a much shorter version and in their own words, of course): "You know, I've been spending a lot of time recently paying attention to and learning about the principle of beginnings and endings, and I just made an association that's really interesting to me. Since everything in my universe seems to have a clear beginning (and ending), then I just figured out that I must have had one, too. So tell me, please, what was *my* beginning? Where did *I* come from?"

Since children at this age typically have no firsthand knowledge of reproduction or sex, it is crucially important to understand that this question is truly about neither. Adults who intuit a deeper meaning ("Oh my God, she wants to know about sex!") make a hugely inappropriate conceptual leap, either because they are projecting their own anxiety onto the situation ("Oh no, I knew this question would come sooner or later, but did it have to be now?") or because they fail to understand the question within the unique developmental context in which the child is asking ("This question sounds to me like it's about sex or reproduction, so it must be!"). They may forget, or they don't stop to remind themselves, that this is a four-year-old's question, which requires and deserves to be treated on a four-year-old's level.

The key to the best response, as researcher Anne Bernstein explains in her insightful book, *The Flight of the Stork,* is to remember to take all questions at this age entirely at face value. Put as simply as possible, *what the child is asking, is exactly what the child is asking!* "Where did I come from?" means precisely that: literally where, as in *geographically* where.

How funny. The proverbial dodge, "You came from the cabbage patch," would be right on the mark, if only it were accurate!

The second most important rule of thumb is to give an answer that is short and simple, but direct and honest. Something like, "You came from a special place inside Mommy called a uterus or womb," would be just about perfect.

Adults might expect the child to ask, "What's that?" or "Where is that?" But in all likelihood, the response will simply be, "Oh." Followed maybe by, "What's for lunch?" or "Can we go to the playground now?" Curiosity momentarily satisfied, he or she will quickly be on to the next thing. At this juncture, all that was needed was a simple word or phrase, just enough information to adequately set up the "Where did I come from?" file in the child's mind. After all, new words to a young child are enormously powerful and empowering—great big, open windows, overlooking brand new stretches of knowledge. Conversely, consider that when we choose not to provide language to a child, or worse, when we make up falsehoods and fairy tales, we in effect disempower them.

Should the child go on to inquire what a uterus is like, or where it is located more precisely, those questions can be handled in the same way as questions about stomachs or eardrums or any other internal organ that a child cannot see but might need or want to know about. Sooner or later, his or her curiosity will be satisfied, and the child will be off, intellectually or physically, to explore something new.

## The Concept of Before, Now, and Later: How Did I Get Out of There?

This may be the end of it for quite a long time, even as much as a year or so. By then, the child will still be working on the same question of origins, but coming at it from a different direction. This is because she or he will have moved on intellectually, from musing about beginnings, middles, and endings, to a near obsession with the related but more abstract concept of temporal sequence. (Have you ever sat and observed a five-year-old intently immersed for the first time in the maddening process of trying to decipher a clock?) As concepts like yesterday, today, and tomorrow, and before versus now versus later, become increasingly operational, an important connection is eventually made.

I think it happens something like this. One day, the child is hopping and skipping and jumping around through life, discovering the before-now-later concept in some new form or another, when she or he is somehow reminded of the previous conversation about geography.

I picture that at this moment, she or he comes to a screeching halt, with a sudden realization: "Wow! Last year about this time they told me I used to be inside Mommy, in that special place called a uterus. I just noticed something! I'm out here!"

So, absolutely intrigued, the child makes a beeline for the same or another nearby trusted adult and asks, "Hey—you didn't tell me! How the heck did I get out of there?" In the child's mind, the whole where-did-I-come-from issue has just made the quick, logical transition from a burning question of geography, to the very practical matter of . . . you guessed it, transportation! (Come to think of it, the old-fashioned stork concept actually fits quite nicely here, too.)

Therein lies the clue to our best response. First of all, we're in great shape because the two of us now have a history about this topic, ever since the child's mind first opened up the where-did-I-come-from file.

"Remember last year (or week, or month, or the last time we talked), we said that you came from that special place inside Mommy's body called a uterus? Well, right next to it is another special place. It's called a vagina. On one end the vagina is connected to the uterus, and on the other end it has an opening just near the outside of Mommy's body, right between her legs. When you were ready to be born, Mommy pushed and pushed really hard, and you came out through the opening."

This is liable to sound so utterly amazing that the child will probably say, "That's neat!" rather than, "Oh," before asking what's for lunch.

## The Concept of Causation: How Did I Get in There in the First Place?

Next, but usually not until a year or so later, commonly at about age six, comes what for most parents is the biggie: "But, Mom or Dad, there's something I still don't understand. Exactly how did I get *in there* in the first place?"

As scary, dreaded even, as it may be, never fear: This question, too, represents just another sequential and exquisitely normal piece of logic in the child's thinking. Actually, it signals an event of great developmental significance, a veritable milestone, because it is a sign that the child has advanced to a much more complex level of thought.

Able now to reason with a brand new intellectual handle—the concept of causation—he or she can pose a far more sophisticated question about the concept of origins than any of those asked before: "Tell me. What is it that brought me into being? What *caused* me?"

I still find this question breathtakingly profound for a six-year-old, and yet, its level of sophistication should not really surprise us. It is precisely at this age that we place children in "real" school, not "pre"-school, where we hold them to a wholly different set of expectations. Isn't that because we know that they are now able to grasp the concept of cause and effect and, therefore, accountability?

"Well, remember last year," we could begin, "when we said there was a special opening between the mother's legs where the baby comes out? Well, like all other body openings, things can come out, but they can also go in! The father has a very important part in making a baby, too. When he and the woman make a baby, his penis has an erection. (Won't it be helpful at this point if our conversational history has also included an explanation of erections? If not, we simply take a sidetrack for a moment.) It becomes just the right size and shape to fit into the mother's opening to her vagina." By now, we'll probably reach for—and won't it also be useful if we've bought or borrowed a book in anticipation and have it handy—or draw a picture, as we gradually add the concepts of egg and sperm, and how and where they meet, into the story.

## Rediscovering Our Common Sense

At my workshops, I love to look at the faces of parents and teachers, as together we sort through this particular sequence of questions and answers. Many have been struggling so hard over the years, and now they become, suddenly, so visibly relieved. "Why, it's all so logical," they say, in a burst of newly rediscovered common sense. "Why couldn't *we* have figured this out?"

First of all, I remind them, it's a matter of background music. The words are likely to stick in our throat, even if we can come up with them, because of all those uncomfortable and inhibiting melodies left over from our own childhood. I remember one young man in a class who said it best, just as we were working our way through the explanation. He threw his hands up in the air, in total exasperation, and hollered, "I am a grown adult. I am a teacher! I know where babies come from! Why is this so hard to say?"

But it is also, plain and simple, a matter of near total inexperience. When have we ever heard this sequence explained? Who, as we were growing up, nurtured our questions? Who modeled for us the kinds of things we need to say and do, as parents or teachers, to be a sex educator?

Something else commonly gets in our way: a need to add information and concepts to our explanations that the child is not really asking about. Since these extras are usually purely adult concepts, we often get hopelessly stuck trying to figure out how to explain them on the (nonexistent) child's level.

We often feel compelled in these moments, for example, to throw in some high-sounding pronouncements about love, marriage, maturity, and feelings of intimacy, which for the child, at the moment, are not only too advanced, but also totally irrelevant. It's a good example of how the "knowing leads to doing" myth—we're talking about a six-year-old here!—can cause us to make so many age-inappropriate decisions. The child, after all, is asking on the level of geography or transportation or causation and will not necessarily make the connections we are hoping for.

A young father shared an incident that taught him this lesson well. He had recently explained the concept of intercourse to his seven-year-old daughter, making it very clear that people never, ever do this unless they are married. The next evening, his wife mentioned at the dinner table that the couple next door was getting a divorce. When the little girl asked what the word *divorce* meant, her parents explained that they would no longer be married.

"Oh," was her only comment, "I guess that means Mr. Lane won't be putting his penis in Mrs. Lane's vagina anymore!"

There is nothing wrong at all with introducing some of these ideas in passing as we go along, but there is no real need, and certainly no great rush, to tell the whole story all at once. If we are doing a good job of simply tuning into the child's current level of thought, especially early on, there will be plenty of time and opportunities later—when the child is ready for and naturally interested in more adult concepts—to elaborate.

It is only fair to point out the opposite tendency, which is to leave out of our explanations altogether, certain relevant but select pieces of information. Like the little matter of the father's role in all of this or that people have intercourse for reasons other than to have babies. There's certainly no need to rush into sharing these concepts, but when we happen to have a logical opening or the timing seems right, it's a good idea to mention them. Despite saving us some momentary throat clearing, these misleading omissions can cause untold confusion for children later on, and the need for tricky backpedaling for us. It was one such omission, remember, that had gotten me in so deep with the "God plants the seed" incident.

I too learned my lesson well. When Adam, at about age four, asked me whether I had known him first, or Daddy, I took a deep breath and answered that it had to have been Daddy, because daddies and mommies make their children, together. This handy idea happily became our very first piece of conversational history about his origins and made things go a whole lot easier later on.

## Dealing with Special Circumstances

After I've given a talk to parents of young children, almost invariably at least one parent—usually a mother—will come up to speak with me personally about the fact that her child or children are adopted. Imparting the "facts of life," which is challenging for so many parents, is at least doubly so for many adoptive families. Often, the topic is fraught with symbolic meaning and all tied up with the complex history and emotions connected to the couple's fertility problems and their adoption decision. For children, too, the issue of adoption eventually raises sensitive and complex questions that go far beyond the basics of reproduction.

It is very important for couples to talk these issues and feelings through, and ideally they will want to do so before they enter into these conversations with their children. With luck, they will realize that initial questions about origins from their children, too, can be answered in the same matter-of-fact way that I have been describing all along. Regardless of their present situation, their children were conceived and born in the same way as almost all other children in the world. That they now have adoptive parents, as well as birth parents, is an additional piece of information to be added to the story. Anne Bernstein's *Flight of the Stork* is an excellent source of guidance for talking with children about the issue of adoption, from the preschool through the adolescent years.

Of course, many children in today's world were *not* conceived or born in the traditional way, but the same principles still apply. Children delivered by cesarean section, for example, can learn that most babies are born through their mother's vagina, and that some are born through an opening that the doctor creates through the mother's abdominal wall. (Please take care not to say "stomach"; that sets up incredibly confusing ideas and images for young children).

For children who have been conceived in one of the various ways that require medical intervention, parents will need to make their own decisions about the depth of information they wish to provide and when they think it best to provide it. They can always begin, though, with the same basic steps we have described, with maybe a slight addition. When the child asks how babies are made, the parent can say, "Well, here's how it happens almost all the time." At the end of the explanation the parent can add, "Sometimes parents have trouble making babies this way, and a doctor has to help a sperm and egg come together. It's pretty complicated, but we can talk about that later sometime if you'd like." That prepares the child for the concept of alternate methods of conception and opens the door to further conversation, but doesn't necessarily require the parent to give details to the child about his or her particular conception (or gestation, in the case of surrogate parenting). That decision can then be made at a much later time.

## Some Final Pointers

The sequence of four- to five- to six-year-old questions demonstrates several reassuring points. First, we need not fear the questions, but anticipate and treasure them for what they truly are: wholly logical and predictable extensions of the kinds of normal, developmentally based questions that young children are asking about the world in general and only incidentally about sex and reproduction. Therefore, if we simply follow their lead, it will be impossible for us to go too far wrong. And we certainly don't need to worry about putting ideas in children's head. The ideas and questions are theirs—we're only providing the details and helping them connect the dots, so to speak.

## Positive Framing

What's more, in today's world, where information about sex—much of it scary and negative—is so readily accessible, these positive early exchanges set a very useful and timely stage for further conversation in the not-too-distant future. By the time children are eight, for example, it's not unusual for them to begin asking pointed questions about sexual topics—like AIDS and rape—that are far more complex and serious. At about this age, again for developmental reasons that are wholly logical and predictable, they naturally and effortlessly will begin paying a great deal more attention to the world beyond their immediate lives, in a myriad of ways.

As their intellectual radar screen adjusts its scope across a new and more sweeping horizon, a much broader universe of factual, social, and emotional data will be suddenly available to them. Snippets of conversations, advertisements, and news stories on radio or TV that would have sailed right over their heads a few months or even weeks before will now catch their ear and stimulate their curiosity, especially if they sense an edge of importance or emotional intensity about them.

When these questions surface, if we have not talked with children earlier about sex in any kind of positive or detailed context, we may find ourselves in a terribly difficult jam. Topics like rape and AIDS, of course, are not where we would choose to start the educational process. They will seem way too complex for beginning conversations—like opening a textbook in the middle of chapter 12—and overwhelmingly negative. To avoid leaving children frightened and confused, we'll need to quickly cover large territories of uncharted ground, to try to create a larger and more positive frame in which to fit these very scary and negative concepts. Daunted by this lack of context, many adults will be tempted to put the question off indefinitely, assuming the topic is beyond the child's intellectual or emotional reach.

How much easier it will be if we've already helped them understand sexual intercourse in the most joyous context possible—as the way they came into our lives! Without pushing them at all, but simply by following their own normal timetables and proclivities, we will have provided just the right kind of unequivocally positive and solidly factual base. Later, we'll be able to explain these new facts without having to backpedal first to cover missed ground, and we'll be able to say something like: "Do you remember when we said that sexual intercourse is a wonderful part of nature (or love, or a couple's married life, or God's design, or however we else we have framed it for the child)? Well, sometimes it can also be a problem. Let me explain what can happen." There will be more about broaching negative and potentially frightening concepts with children and adolescents in Chapter 10, but this kind of positive framing is the first and most important step.

## But What If . . .

Many times, even when they agree in principle with the idea of being open with young children about the facts of reproduction, adults worry that information may get too far beyond their immediate control: What if my son tells something to the little boy up the street, before his parents want him to know? Suppose my child asks a question in front of her younger sister? I understand that some children in my daughter's class might be ready for this information, but what if she isn't? Then what do I do?

Let's deal with the last question first. The difference between two often-confused concepts, age appropriateness and stage appropriateness, is crucial. Here's the distinction: If a child at a particular age has not yet thought of a given question or idea, then it may not be a perfectly age-appropriate topic for him or her at that instant. However, if other children *near* the child's age are thinking about or verbalizing that same question or idea, then it is a perfectly stage-appropriate topic for everyone in that age group, including those who have not yet thought of it. In other words, there is absolutely no danger—there's that "age-appropriate demon" again—in children of the same stage learning from and about each other, especially in the presence of a knowledgeable, skilled, and caring adult.

Everyone has heard jokes (or horror stories) about the little child who goes around to all the customers in the supermarket—or all the guests seated around the living room—pointing out rather loudly and proudly just which ones have a penis and which ones have a vagina. (Actually, no great harm is done, since everyone present pretty much knew who had what already). In truth, fortunately, at about the same time that children are ready to learn the details of intercourse and reproduction, they are at an age when they can also firmly grasp the concept of privacy. They can understand that this is very special and important information, so special that other parents like to be the ones to tell their own children about it. "So," parents can say, "let's keep this information in our own family for now."

It's important to remember, too, that children are much less likely to willfully go around spreading information if they have learned it in a context that is positive, respectful, and open. When children learn from each other—amid whispers and jokes that make them feel naughty and bold—they are much more likely to want to show off what they know.

We also have to stop and look at why we are so concerned about this issue in the first place. If we take it out of the context of sex, would we still mind children passing on interesting new information they have just learned about a pretty neat, in fact downright fascinating and important, subject? Or, perhaps, is it we who think that there might be something naughty about children having this information at an early age? And if we don't, instead of trying to shield other children in the neighborhood or school yard from ours, shouldn't we be trying to help their parents understand that this is age-appropriate information for *all* children?

Think about the numbers of children who constantly pass on information—more likely misinformation—about sex in an atmosphere of silliness, disrespect, and even intimidation. (For example, when my sister-in-law was in the fourth grade, she paid a bully twenty-five cents a week so that he wouldn't tell her mother she knew what sex was; this was right after he had taken it upon himself to explain it to her.) Why wouldn't we want the respectful, knowledgeable ones to get in on the act?

As for siblings overhearing conversations with older brothers and sisters, parents can simply relax; most of the time it's not a problem or an issue at all. If the facts or ideas being discussed are way beyond the understanding of the younger child, they will merely whiz right by. And if not, the child will simply take away whatever information seems interesting or appealing at the moment. The child might even ask a question or two at his or her level of comprehension, enjoying the opportunity to be included in such a serious and grown-up conversation. Most importantly, what the child will also take away is the pleasant and comfortable hum of the background music that this kind of warm and open conversation creates in a family's life together. He or she will learn that this is a good, safe topic to bring up, no matter what or when.

On occasion, an older sibling might raise a topic or an issue that is really scary or intense—for example, a news story about child sexual abuse or a sexual rumor about someone known to the family. Such a topic might make the parent nervous, and rightfully so, in the presence of a younger sibling. The older child in these circumstances needs the parent's undivided attention, without the distraction of having to simultaneously translate or diffuse the issue on a level appropriate for the younger child. It's really good at these times if the parent and older child have worked on a signal they can use to head off conversations that probably are best conducted out of earshot of younger kids. In fact, these are situations that the older child can be helped to feel really good about. "You're really growing up," the parent can say. "There will be times when we should talk, just the two of us."

## Children Who Don't Ask or Won't Talk

Often I hear from parents whose concerns are just the opposite. Although they're ready and willing—anxious even—to have conversations with their son or daughter about anything and everything, they're frustrated because their children are just not forthcoming. Either they don't spontaneously ask questions at all, or they won't take the bait when adults attempt to bring up the subject or try to capitalize on what seems like the perfect teachable moment.

First, all children are different, of course. They have their own unique temperament and personality, and they mature intellectually, socially, and emotionally at their own individual pace. There are no hard and fast rules about when—or if—they will raise certain ideas or questions. The four- to five- to six-year-old question sequence, for example, is a developmental pattern that is observed frequently, but by no means universally. Some girls and boys ask these questions earlier, some later, some never—and all of these children are normal. As the child continues to grow and develop, and if parents continue to model an open and inviting attitude toward sexual topics, sooner or later questions and conversation will come.

Moreover, as later chapters will discuss, there are occasions in children's development when they normally need and want more emotional distance and privacy in their relationships with adults, especially during periods when they are in the throes of rapid body changes or intense adolescent separation issues. As we will learn in Chapter 7, these are times when a sensitive but less personalized school-based program can become an important and more comfortable setting for providing timely information and support. And it is not uncommon for the very same child who is so quiet about these issues at home to be right in the thick of the conversation in the classroom! At the very least, she or he will continue to be listening and learning.

Even in the most extreme cases—when nothing at all seems to work—parents still have two effective alternatives that almost always will succeed, even with the most reluctant adolescent. The first is to make sure to talk about topics related to sexuality (exactly what the topics are doesn't truly matter) when the child is within earshot. He or she will still be getting the most important message of all: these are important topics to think, learn, and talk about. Moreover, sooner or later, something will likely pique his or her interest.

The second is for the parent to recognize honestly where the need for conversation is coming from. Truthfully, what we all want is *for our children to want to talk to us,* so that we can feel like good parents. Sometimes try as we might—we buy books, we look for teachable moments, we try to seem as open and interested as we possibly can—our children just don't take the bait. Eventually what almost always does work is for us to take responsibility for *our own* need to talk, so we say something like this: "You know, I've been trying all kinds of things to get you to want to talk to me about sexuality. Clearly, they haven't been working. So I'm just going to say it straight out. *You* may not want or need to talk to me, but *I* really need and want to talk to you. There are important things I need to make sure you know, or have thought about, in order to feel like I'm doing my job as a responsible parent. So, you tell me when—time and place—but we will need to talk, or at least you'll need to listen." Most often, children and adolescents are at least ambivalent about talking with us, and if they can save face by saying "OK, I don't really need or want to but I'll do it for you," it can provide just the permission they need to become engaged.

### Never Too Young, Too Old, or Too Late

Just as children and adolescents are never too young to ask and receive an answer about sex or reproduction, they are also never too old for dialogue with adults about sexuality. As discussed in Chapter 5, our sexuality, understood in its broadest sense, is a core component of our lives from birth to death. Therefore, at virtually every stage of child and adolescent development, there are topics and issues that are important for parents and their children to recognize and address.

In my work as a parent educator, I'm often sad to note that as adults become better informed about the reality of children's and adolescent's sexual education needs, they also feel guilty, sometimes intensely so, about the many important opportunities they now realize they may have missed as their children were growing up. Although undoubtedly I have been making a strong pitch for early and continual communication with children around these issues as an ideal approach, I don't want to overstate the point. Millions of parents may have rarely—perhaps even never—spoken directly to their children about explicitly sexual topics, but nonetheless have contributed positively in countless ways to their children's healthy sexual development. All good parents, both by example and by direct instruction, teach about the values of love, affection, closeness, integrity, responsibility, and commitment. There are no more important cornerstones of a healthy sexual life.

## A History Called "No History"

It's also important to remember that it is never too late to start the verbal part of the communication process. In earlier examples, I've often used the phrase, "Well, remember last time we spoke . . ." as a good way to preface a response to a child's question or to begin an explanation of a new and more complex idea. Not only does this opening reinforce earlier learning, it provides a logical and comfortable context for sharing the next piece of information.

All parents and children share a long and rich history about everything that touches their lives in a meaningful way. Even in families in which sexuality has not been openly discussed, parents and children eventually at least come to share the same awareness that something important has been omitted from their direct experience together. In other words, the history they share is that they share no history!

This shared history of "no history" can become the very opening that parents need to create a logical and comfortable context for an opening discussion. Even if their children are as old as high school age, a parent can always begin by saying, "You know, there is something we've never really talked about, and although it's uncomfortable for me to bring it up after all this time, and probably for you, too, I've come to realize how important it is for us to talk."

Although conversations with my own parents about sex and reproduction were brief and only occasional, I do recall one very special period in my mid-twenties, when my mother and I were able to broach this long-standing void in our relationship. At the time, I was very pregnant with my first baby, and quite obviously, neither of us could pretend any longer that at least one of us wasn't a sexual person! My ever-growing belly gradually gave us permission to begin talking about things we had never even come close to discussing earlier at any other time in our life together. I remember it as a healing and touching encounter for us both; many of my women friends have described similar experiences.

## Parenting Is Almost Always a Do-Over

One final reminder: Over the years, I have become alarmed by what I see as an ever-escalating cycle of self-imposed and culturally imposed pressure on today's parents. They—and everyone else, it seems—expect nothing short of perfection in carrying out their parental jobs and roles. This superparent complex is to a degree normal and expected, I suppose, within the context of our increasingly tense, intense, and complex way of life. But it's also an expression of the cultural "guilting" (a handy word I learned from my students) of today's parents, who must bear the weight of a half-century's emphasis by the social sciences on the almighty power of psycho-social influences on a child's development. No wonder they feel as if they have to do everything right all the time.

Whenever I look out on a crowd of parents who have come to hear a presentation, I'm always tempted to say something like this: "Hey, listen. I'm really glad you came tonight, but the truth is I know already that you're good parents, simply because you're here. After all, of all the possible things you could be doing with your life right now, you've chosen to come to a parenting lecture! Anyway, I'm sure you're tired from a very long day already, taking care of all kinds of important matters, and since nobody's expecting you at home for a least a couple of hours, why don't you all just leave now and go do something fun, just for yourselves! I promise not to tell."

Of course, I always do give a presentation, but sometimes I say this anyway, just to make the point. Even so, there are always parents who come up at the end to ask nervously about a particular thing they've said or done in their parenting, just to make sure they haven't blown it entirely or ruined their child forever. Relax, I try to tell them, you've done just fine, and even if you didn't, there's always tomorrow. The thing about parenting is that your children are always still there in the morning, for an instant do-over. You can always go back and say, "You know, I really don't like the way I handled this or that. Can we try it again?" They'll love and appreciate you even more, for your honesty and willingness to make yourself so vulnerable. And you'll help take the pressure off of everyone to have to be perfect all the time.

## Many More Questions to Come

This chapter has covered a portion of the kind of information that is appropriate at different ages and stages of a child's development. Chapters 9 and 10 will provide even more detail, but the principle will be the same: There is a logical and predictable sequence of concerns and questions that children pose, beginning as young as age four and continuing all the way through the end of their high school years.

We'll also consider another handy and reassuring piece of developmental wisdom: There are only eight basic types of questions about sexuality that children or adolescents will ever put before us. Once we've learned how to correctly interpret a particular question or concern, and after we've thought through some helpful ways to respond in each of the question categories, we'll hopefully feel prepared for almost anything they might toss our way. How's that for incentive to keep on reading!

# 3

# Sex: What Is Sex, Really?

The year 1998 will be remembered as a watershed year in the evolution of American sexual attitudes, but maybe not for the reasons the polls and pundits have predicted. In the midst of being very wrong about numerous other things, it seems as if Bill Clinton got it exactly right when he asserted before the nation, and before a federal grand jury, that Americans think of "real sex" as vaginal intercourse. In the process, he may have taught us as much about our sexuality as his own.

If you doubt me, try this simple quiz: Your son or daughter asks you if it's OK to have sex before marriage. Do you say (a) yes, (b) no, or (c) maybe? Or do you (d) refuse to answer and say instead, "Well, that depends. There are all kinds of sexual behavior that two people can engage in, from kissing to touching body parts to having intercourse in its various forms. What kind of sex are you asking about?"

Tell the truth. Did you hear the word *sex* and think "vaginal intercourse" so automatically that you didn't even realize it? Or did you immediately insist on clarification, knowing and carefully acknowledging to your child that sex and sexual intercourse are not one and the same?

See what I mean?

It's certainly fair to ask why these seemingly tedious distinctions are important or relevant, apart from President Clinton, his troubles, and his legal strategies. Americans have yet to face the irony that this whole "what is sex?" question isn't the no-brainer we make it out to be. Truth be told, whenever Americans speak, write, or hear the word *sex*—unless used as a synonym for gender—it almost always means sexual intercourse. Prove it to yourself again. Pick up any magazine or newspaper written today, look for the word *sex,* and check out its intended meaning.

No doubt the sex-equals-intercourse paradigm evolved partially as a convenient shorthand for the sexually embarrassed. But there is more to it. The equation cuts to the heart of deep-rooted cultural beliefs, making it difficult to think of sexual behavior other than intercourse as being truly sexual. (And it's not just President Clinton and his lawyers who sound nutty about this.)

I'm thinking of a sixteen-year-old student in one of my sexual health courses, for example, who raised her hand and asked, "Well, suppose there is a girl and a guy. They're not having sex, but he ejaculates near her vagina. Could she get pregnant?"

"Huh?" I replied. "An erect penis is ejaculating near the vagina, but there is no real sex going on?"

"No, not *actual* sex," she said. "They're just fooling around. You know, just making out."

"Oh, I understand. You're not worried about them having an actual baby in nine months, just a make-out or a pretend baby? And taking care of it will really just be fooling around, not real work?"

"Well, yeah. But I still don't think what they're doing is sex. You could-n't *really* consider it sex."

The class nodded its agreement.

"OK, so what is it?" I inquired. "Roller skating?"

The class smirked and rolled their eyes at me. They did laugh, though—loudly—and I knew I was starting to get through.

"No, no," I insisted. "I'm really serious. You say what they're doing is not sex, and granted it certainly isn't roller skating, so what is it? Into ex-actly what specific category of human behavior does it fall?"

The class was suddenly at a loss. Why wouldn't they be? If all of their lives they had assumed that the word *meal,* for example, was totally equiv-alent to the word *breakfast* and that breakfast food was, therefore, the only real food, how comfortable would they be with the concept of lunch or dinner? Of eating pizza, steak, or grilled cheese? Might they think of those experiences, too, as minor pastimes of some meaningless, frivolous, or less real nature, for which one need not feel accountable or worried or guilty? No real calories or consequences here, nothing really important to consider at all.

## The Power of Sexual Language

Language is powerful, not only because it communicates *what* we think, but because it actively shapes *how* we think. Conversely, a change in language can prompt changes in how we think and act. As long as we unconsciously continue to use language in a way that relegates noncoital sexual activity to the realm of the unreal, we reinforce a whole host of inadvertent and problematic assumptions that never get questioned, critiqued, or remedied.

If certain kinds of sexual behavior are unreal, then does that imply that we can participate in them without having to take any kind of real personal responsibility? Can we conclude that those other behaviors don't count? That they exist in some kind of ethical free zone where questions of morality simply don't apply?

Listen to kids like my eleventh-grade students talk about noncoital sex, and you'll hear old, familiar terms that play this very assumption right back to us—that noncoital sex is just fooling around, making out, or only going to first, second, or third. It only counts as real sex when you have vaginal intercourse, or go "all the way."

Listen even to some twenty-five-year-olds. Monica Lewinsky, in her first public interview with Barbara Walters, in front of a TV audience of 70 million Americans, maintained that she and the president had not had actually had sex, since they'd only "messed around"—this after the disclosure of that very nonsexual behavior had tied the entire country in knots for an entire year, brought the highest levels of federal government to a standstill for months, and nearly brought down the most powerful man in the world. What a mess, indeed.

And where does the sex-equals-vaginal-intercourse-only way of thinking leave gay teens and adults? Is it just another way that society invalidates their very existence and legitimacy? Where, too, does it leave prevention messages about sexually transmitted infections (STIs), which depend on an understanding that very real consequences can result from very real kinds of noncoital sex?

# A Heritage of Denial

We can only guess at the origin of this narrow and arguably delusional way of thinking that persists in our thought and speech—even as we deny its existence. Of course there was a full sexual affair between Clinton and Lewinsky! Of course they had sex! Anyone who says they didn't is a fool or a liar, the American public says. Yet, as I have often wondered, what if we administered the multiple-choice quiz that began this chapter to the House impeachment managers or even to Kenneth Starr himself? What's the chance that even they would choose "d" (the option that implied that sex and intercourse are not equivalent)?

How did we become caught up in this cultural conspiracy of denial and hypocrisy? Since its roots are so deep-seated, its origins must be very old. The denial must be about something in ourselves we can't quite face.

United States cultural heritage is bound up in puritanical and other fundamentalist interpretations of sexual morality that date back to Christian theology and practice from several hundred years ago, during which the only legitimate form of sexual activity was penile-vaginal intercourse in marriage for the purpose of procreation. Any other expression of sex—masturbation, mutual masturbation, oral sex, anal sex, intercourse with contraception, homosexuality, etc.—was explicitly and strictly forbidden and hence was considered *illegitimate* (as in *unsanctified* or *unsanctioned*). Sex simply was not supposed to exist in people's lives, except in this very narrow and prescribed fashion. Therefore, in the eyes of the Church, which was then the sole and ultimate authority concerning sexual morality, sex most certainly did equal vaginal intercourse—or it better had.

Most people in the United States, even practicing Christians, no longer look to medieval Church teachings for sole or ultimate guidance about sexual behavior standards, yet obviously, and quite remarkably, the power of these earlier religious definitions and sanctions remains. The ideas persist, however, in an ironic and much mangled form: in late twentieth-century America, noncoital sexual behavior continues to be seen as illegitimate, but, curiously, not in the original sense of "unsanctioned" or "unsanctified." It is illegitimate not because it is *forbidden*, but illegitimate in the sense of its not being *real*. In other words, unless it's vaginal intercourse, it's not the genuine, or legitimate, article.

How did official sexual status, not just official moral status, become the province of vaginal intercourse only? One plausible explanation is that this convenient little linguistic shell game evolved gradually over scores if not hundreds of years, as an accommodation to the sexually frustrated and/or a comfort to the sexually guilty.

According to original religious teachings, you committed a sin if you had nonmarital coital relations, or if you had noncoital relations, whether marital or not. This sweeping combination of rules pretty much confined everyone to a life of totally delayed sexual gratification until marriage. In previous eras, marked by later pubertal age and considerably earlier marital age, the realities of biology and society meshed easily, neatly minimizing the time gap between full sexual and social maturity. Moreover, close adult supervision, particularly concerning unmarried girls whose sexual inexperience was not only a religious duty but an economic necessity (in terms of bride price or upward mobility as a desirable marital partner), assured a modicum of sexual restraint. No doubt people found ways to break the rules anyway, but at least the rules were clear and serious attempts were made at enforcement.

As American society gradually became more urban and diverse and less dependent on religious institutions as monolithic sources of authority, strict traditional views of sexual morality began to give way (although, arguably, they are, still in many ways the officially sanctioned view of contemporary American society). At the same time, the combination of better nutrition and health care, thought to be the cause of sharply lowered average pubertal age, and the expanded educational necessities of an increasingly factory- and technology-based economy, eventually gave rise to the thoroughly modern concept of a greatly protracted period of adolescence.

Teenagers and young adults ultimately found themselves trapped in a two-sided time warp. With sexual maturity coming much earlier chronologically than full adult status, more than a decade of sexual abstinence would be required to live a moral sexual life according to strict traditional religious standards. Moreover, no direct help for this dramatic and unprecedented predicament was being offered by families, schools, or religious institutions, all of which until quite recently have remained silent on sexual mores, except of course to say, "Don't do it (meaning sexual intercourse) until you're married." Through decades of unparalleled social change, then, these "predults," as I like to call them, were left almost entirely on their own to try and figure out just how to successfully apply fifteenth-century sexual standards to a twentieth-century life.

For many, I think, "making out" or "fooling around" must have eventually become the unspoken compromise—a way of expressing one's sexual needs, at least to a degree, without breaking the rules too much and without exposing oneself potentially to too much guilt, too much physical risk, or too much social, parental, or divine condemnation. By that time the original dictum—no noncoital sex at all, marital or not—had been lost to the passing centuries, probably because the offending behaviors were too embarrassing or unseemly for adults to describe, or proscribe, with any kind of sufficient detail. So behavior once forbidden because it wasn't *right* sex was accepted because it wasn't *real* sex.

## Language as a Conveyor of Culture

As even these cursory history lessons confirm, the modern view of sex is actually a complex hybrid, the product of many centuries of gradual evolution and adaptation, ongoing even at this moment. Layers and layers of our heritage remain with us in composite form, as we build new attitudes on top of old paradigms. History moves through our lives as a conveyor belt of culture, bringing the past into our present, and an amalgam of both into the next generation's future. And it is language—the most immediate and accessible component of culture—that forges that path.

It was my older son who first put me onto the concept of language as culture's primary conveyor of sexual attitudes. A third-grader at the time, he came home one afternoon and asked me straight-away to explain the concept of bases, which he'd heard spoken earlier by a classmate on the school playground. He knew it had something to do with sex because of the snickering that accompanied its mention, and with the game of baseball.

How cute, I thought. I immediately recalled overhearing the exact same expression bandied about by the boys on my own third-grade playground. For an instant I felt totally transported in time, as an image of my younger self flashed in my mind. Suddenly there I was, a little girl perched at the edge of a hopscotch patch, one foot raised, worn rubber heel in hand, and looking every bit as confused as Josh did. As we talked, I was amused and even touched by the whole exchange, as adults commonly are whenever they unexpectedly recover an endearing or forgotten piece of their own childhood.

Most of all, it astounded me that third-graders still spoke to one another in this way, and I decided to check out the lingo with my most important consultants on such issues, my current seventh-grade class. The conversation the next day was so revealing that I've repeated it with every class since. Remarkably, it almost always looks, feels, and sounds pretty much the same.

At first the students are visibly aghast that an adult is privy to such language. (Each new batch of kids apparently believes that it has spontaneously invented the game out of its own clever resourcefulness.) I usually have to coax them to give me details—as if they were being asked to turn over some heavily guarded kid secret to the enemy. And they are relieved to learn that they haven't divulged anything I hadn't already known about for quite some time—since the first year of Dwight David Eisenhower's second term in the White House, to be exact.

However, they get quickly caught up in the excitement and novelty of examining the metaphor. The batter, they deduce, is the boy, and sex, they reason, well, that must be the baseball. The game begins when the girl throws him a curveball, a slow ball, or a fastball, depending on her strategy. He then tries to hit it as hard as he can and to run over as many of her bases as possible. The exact definitions of *bases* vary somewhat from school to school, grade to grade, and even kid to kid, but generally, her mouth, then her breasts, and then her genitals represent first, second, and third base. He is expected to do this fast and often, with his ultimate goal being to score as many times as he can, which he does by touching and going all the way around the bases and quickly sliding into home plate. (The class predictably shrieks, "Oh God, her vagina?!" at this moment.)

Her ultimate goal is to allow him to get to, and keep him at, a safe base, the strategy being to let him go just far enough around the bases so that she will not be called a baby, a tease, or frigid, but not to let him go so far that she might be called a whore, a nympho, or a slut. (It is usually at this point in the conversation that I shake my head and ask myself, "Sexual revolution? What sexual revolution?")

Once facile with the comparisons, students—both middle and high school—are captivated by how seamlessly baseball and sex terms can coincide. (By high school, kids have usually given up this way of speaking about sex, though they certainly remember talking this way when they were younger.) They often take turns challenging each other, playfully tossing out other common baseball terms to see how easily they can be ascribed a sexual meaning. The results are uncanny, the translations nearly effortless.

Glove—that's easy, a condom; catcher's mitt—how about a diaphragm, a sponge, or some contraceptive foam? Walk—what he does if she gets pregnant; or balk—when she says no at the last minute. As for strategy, if she doesn't really want to go to first, he could try to talk her into it anyway with a base on balls; or, she could declare a ground-rule double and tell him in advance she is only going to second and no further. (Of course, he could go for a stolen base, by trying to touch third anyway.) At any time in the game, there could be a sacrifice (if she gives up her virginity so that he will still date her), a rain-out (if she goes home to wash her hair), or even a pop fly (if he ejaculates early). Worse yet, he might be sent to a cold shower (should he be thrown out of the game by her parents, who come home early) or might get himself benched (should he happen to turn up with a positive STI test). Unfortunately, the best scenario she can hope for is a shut out (if she can keep him from scoring for the game's duration); at worst, he might turn out to be a real slugger (rapist), or she might even get killed by a grand slam (gang rape), while the rest of the players stand on the sideline and cheer.

The conversation up to this point is usually light and humorous and even a bit zany, as the group discovers how close are our cultural definitions of sexual relations and competitive sports. The implications of terms like *slugger* and *grand slam*, however, begin to upset everyone, and the group stops laughing. The students begin to question just how this terrible system got started in the first place, some of them appalled that any of us ever used such language so easily and insensitively. The more we share our thoughts, the more we are dumbfounded to discover how many of society's most destructive sexual attitudes, beliefs, and values are so neatly tied together in this one metaphorical package: the sexual double standard, the terrible performance pressures felt by so many men and boys, the stereotypes of women as sexual objects and men as sexual predators, the sexual no-win situations so often created for women and girls, boys and men.

We conclude together that sexual behavior should neither be thought of nor be spoken about as competitive sport, in which someone inevitably wins and someone else inevitably loses, or even worse, as an exploitative game in which the most personal and intimate parts of our anatomy and person are reduced to the four corners of a baseball diamond! Moreover, men and women, or boys and girls, are not opposing teams, with one eternally on the offense (how pressured and exhausting) and the other on the defense (how anxiety- and blame-provoking). The real questions to focus on are not "How far should I go?" or "How far can I get?" Rather, they are "How close should I be with this person?" "Why?" "With what risks?" and "Can I handle them?" This proves to be the turning point; the students have begun to unravel and unlearn the powerful lessons culled unconsciously on elementary school playgrounds long ago.

Sooner or later, someone usually interrupts to complain emphatically about how stereotypical all this is and to explain how well the metaphor has changed with the times. The older and more sexist interpretations no longer fit, since females now use these terms as easily as males do and because the bases are just as likely to be on his body as on hers. (I hear reports, too, of elementary students even younger than third grade making up sexual softball bases—as in holding hands to kissing—and that on the other end of the spectrum middle school kids are now making up new variations on the theme, like "sloppy second" and "sloppy third" as euphemisms for fellatio and cunnilingus). However, these newer versions hardly portend either a positive development or a fundamental change. As long as baseball language is still in common use, even if in a supposedly more egalitarian fashion (and until the word *slut* becomes unisex or disappears entirely I'll remain dubious), it means that sex is still being portrayed as sport and still being understood in terms of distance and accomplishment, rather than closeness and intimacy.

## How the Game Endures

The near universality of this seemingly innocent, superficially cute, American-as-apple-pie metaphor is astonishing. I hear it virtually everywhere I travel and work. The metaphor's brilliant packaging—familiar, appealing, deceptively simple—makes it efficient and powerful as an insidious conveyor of all that is unhealthy, wrong, and wrong-headed about American sexual attitudes. For our children it's a bona fide rite of passage and a particularly toxic form of cultural secondhand smoke.

To explain the metaphor's enduring value, we must consider its function. Middle to late elementary students are at the developmental stage at which they can now conceptualize the notion of society in terms beyond the confines of their own immediate social world. Figuring out how this larger universe works—which essentially means coming to understand its central values, goals, rules, and procedures—is one of the major developmental challenges, or psycho-social tasks, of the age. This capacity will prepare and enable them to navigate adolescence, during which stage they will be expected to manage larger and larger chunks of their physical, intellectual, social, and emotional lives.

As many a savvy fifth-, fourth-, and even third-grader can already tell you, like it or not, sex is one the linchpins of American culture. For many children at this age, random but constant exposure to sexual content and innuendo through media, advertising, friends, peers, and adults abruptly coalesces into new interest in sex. Given the developmental imperative of the stage, a child's figuring out of how society works sexually, that is, his or her understanding of its sexual values, goals, rules, and procedures, suddenly becomes a pressing priority.

Children at this stage, however, are also experienced and judicious enough to know that although American society considers sex crucially important, it also considers sex private, mysterious, naughty, and even secretive and that most adults mean to keep it that way. Children inevitably face a thorny dilemma: how to figure out the rules of sex when they can't go to their parents or teachers (up until now their accustomed and ready source of straight information about things they don't understand) and when the only other available resources are classmates who obviously don't know any more than they do.

Enter the older kid, someone who can teach some tiny morsel, some precious new sexual tidbit that children can make their own and bring to the ongoing banter back at school. In Josh's case, I was merely an older kid substitute; if he'd had an older brother, I doubt I would have been tapped. I did, however, do my part to support the information mill back at the playground. Knowing how ignorant Americans are about male anatomy, I sent him into the huddle with a few choice words of my own—vas deferens, prostate gland, and seminal vesicles. All those syllables! He was king of the jungle gym for at least a week.

Inevitably, through the older-kid network, the torch will be passed and sexual baseball will enter the deliberations. And what a find it will be: the rules, at last! Society's sexual values, goals, procedures, expectations, rewards, and punishments, all tied up in one neat, familiar, all-instructions-included package. And for an added perk, you don't even have to say any of those yucky, embarrassing words to play! The kids are set; they won't even have to think about going to an adult for advice again. And they're stuck with whatever lessons the metaphor will continue to teach them about sex and about how they are supposed to relate to each other.

## Reinventing Sex

Apart from its sexist and dehumanizing underpinnings and the communication wedge between children and adults that it so effectively cements, the baseball metaphor also helps set up the sex-equals-intercourse problem. The notion that sexual behavior is, and ought to be, a goal-directed enterprise, with penis-vagina intercourse the ultimate and only legitimate goal, is one of its basic tenets. All the rest—first base, second base, third base, and everything in between—are only less real substitutes, for which, regrettably, one must settle some of the time. At best, the bases are just a prelude or warm-up to the real thing (the kid equivalent to the silly adult concept of foreplay). In fact, these substitutes don't really count at all, since as everyone knows, you only score if you make it all the way to home. Aren't we back to where we started at the beginning of the chapter?

Once clued in to the metaphor's cultural significance and potentially destructive power, parents and teachers can certainly learn how to listen for it and actively challenge its use in children's and adolescents' vernacular. If we catch it early enough, we may even preempt it entirely. The older the children, however, the less influence we are likely to wield. Interlocking habits of speaking, judging, and behaving will have become consolidated over time, and change will require an intricate process of both *un*learning and *re*learning. We may even find that adolescent children vigorously oppose giving up ways of talking and relating that have long since become an integral component of their peer group dynamic. Even if adolescents can rationally see the point, they may resist and resent intensely what they view as adult interference in their own personal culture.

The best strategy of all is for adults to talk openly with their children about the meaning of sex *long before* someone else even gets the chance and long before they risk being discounted as a trusted and reliable resource. But what should we say, and how should we say it?

Such poor sexual terminology exists, in part, because of the difficulty in using mere words to explain qualitatively unique experiences. (I do recall, though, when a certain eighth-grade student years ago made an excellent stab at explanation by describing sexual feelings as "that funny twitch in your privates.") Another barrier is the enormous complexity and diversity of sexual expression, especially apparent once one has given up on the sex-is-the-same-as-intercourse equation. In fact, I remember many people who, in the midst of the Clinton debacle, eventually threw their hands up in utter frustration, deciding that it was just too hard to say what sex really is, and concluded, therefore, that it simply couldn't be defined at all.

So, what exactly *is* sex? Is there a definition that we can all agree on and that is broad enough to include all those clearly sexual behaviors (e.g., masturbation, hugging, holding, passionate or deep kissing, touching of breasts or genitals, gay sex, straight sex, vaginal intercourse, oral sex, anal sex), yet narrow enough to exclude those behaviors that clearly are not sexual (affectionate touching, holding, or kissing; gynecological exams, etc.)?

Asked another way, what exactly distinguishes a sexual act, any sexual act, from all other acts? The answer—quite simple and obvious, but only once you've realized it—*lies in the distinctive nature of the physical feelings that the behavior provokes.* It is these unique and unmistakable bodily responses that are common to all sexual behaviors and absent in all nonsexual ones, even though they may involve similar kinds of touching or contact.

Sexual or erotic feelings are hard to describe exactly, but not impossible to explain in more general terms. They can be understood as warm, pleasurable, tingly, excited feelings that occur primarily in the genitals, but often in other parts of the body as well. (Orgasm happens when these feelings gradually build in intensity, until they finally peak in a brief, but exquisitely pleasurable and exciting sensation, after which they quickly subside.) From this explanation, the definition of sex follows easily and naturally: *Sexual behavior is any behavior, involving willful physical contact or the sharing of body parts, that arouses or is intended to arouse erotic or sexual feelings.*

This reconceptualization of the word *sex* certainly incorporates the act of sexual intercourse, but it does not reduce the experience of "having sex" to this one behavior alone. Instead, it exemplifies the unique experience of *being sexual* with another human being, regardless of the specific body parts or even the gender of the people involved (although the definition is broad enough to include masturbation). It clearly distinguishes sexual behavior from other forms of intimate physical behavior that involve body contact but have different meanings and purposes. Moreover, it advances the notion that sexual behavior is most fundamentally about the concept of closeness, not distance, either around a baseball diamond or in a status race with one's peers.

To be honest, my middle school and high school students are not entirely comfortable with the notion that if you are passionately kissing or touching your boyfriend or girlfriend you are *having sex*, but they do readily get the point. They learn fairly quickly, with gentle but consistent reminders from me when necessary, to use the term *sexual intercourse,* not the word *sex,* when that is what they mean. They know that I will always do the same, and that when they or I use the word *sex,* we are referring to the broadest possible range of sexual experiences.

The high school students whom I teach are often the same ones I have taught in the sixth or seventh grade. Although some remember the earlier conversations—it's clear from the way they talk and think about sexual behaviors—many have reverted to earlier ways of thinking because that is what is constantly reinforced in the surrounding culture. They quickly catch on again, however, once reminded of the illogic of the sex-equals-intercourse equation, and pick up where the conversation left off years ago.

Some students clearly never forget. One girl in particular comes to mind. Having gone to school in Baltimore during her middle school years, she left for a New England boarding school in the ninth grade. I came across her again quite by accident when she was a junior, after a session at a regional workshop for independent school students and teachers on sexual decision making held at her school. The session was really good—quite creative and engaging—but the presenter kept using the word *sex* whenever she meant sexual intercourse. By the end I was feeling very frustrated. Walking out, I spotted my former student, who immediately grabbed me (which surprised me because we hadn't been particularly close) and said she couldn't believe I was there. "I've just been thinking to myself over and over," she said, "why doesn't this woman know the difference between sex and intercourse? It's been driving me nuts!"

Even small children can be taught this way of thinking about sex, and how much easier it would be if this were a concept they didn't have to keep relearning later on. Children as young as five or six frequently ask questions about birth and conception, and adults can be careful to use the phrase *sexual intercourse,* not the word *sex,* in explaining the process of fertilization. (As discussed in Chapter 2, children's questions at this stage are not really about sexual behavior anyway, but about the mechanics of their origin.) Later on, parents can introduce the word *sex* whenever the time seems right to describe the more sophisticated and more adult concept of sexual relating. Sex, they can explain, is a very special, private, and pleasurable way that grown-up couples like moms and dads (or moms and moms, or dads and dads) hold, kiss, and touch one another and that makes them feel very close and loving. The specific details and options can be filled in gradually as the conversation continues to evolve.

With middle and high school students, my own approach is to offer the concept of an *intimacy continuum,* an imaginary line of behavior that involves increasingly close physical contact. The behaviors at the lowest end of the continuum—like hand holding, kissing, and hugging—involve embracing, connecting, or touching body parts considered "public" (e.g., the hands, lips, and shoulders). Behaviors at the other end of the intimacy continuum—such as sexual intercourse in its various forms—involve connections between what are considered the most private and personal parts of our bodies. In the middle are behaviors that involve increasingly intimate contact, such as touching the breasts or genitals, first through clothing, then skin to skin.

In given situations, a couple's or an individual's comfort level with these different kinds of touch—both when receiving and when giving—will vary. To identify the point past which further intimacy becomes uncomfortable, we need only tune in to the same internal cues and feelings that tell us when we are being asked to share more of ourselves emotionally or socially than we are ready to share. Indeed, the parallel concept of an emotional intimacy continuum, along which lie personal and private parts of our emotional selves, is also empowering. It allows us to explore not only the dynamic connections between emotional and sexual intimacy, but also the meaning of emotional sharing and intimacy in all human relationships.

Of course, as behavior moves further along the continuum, questions of intimacy (how much physical closeness do I now feel comfortable sharing with this person?) are not the only ones to consider. Other considerations and questions also become paramount:

- Integrity: Do I think that this kind of intimacy with this person at this time is morally right or wrong?

- Safety: What are the physical risks, and are we adequately protected?
- Maturity: Am I emotionally, intellectually, and socially ready for this experience?
- Mutuality: What are the needs, desires, and expectations of the other person involved, and how do they relate to mine?

## Changing the Way We Think and Act by Changing the Way We Speak

Consider the possibilities once language, thought, and eventually behavior are liberated from the sex-equals-intercourse paradigm. Sex would become characterized not as a single act, but as a wide, open-ended, and fluid range of physical intimacies. According to most sex therapists and counselors, that would be a very healthy change. As they have warned us for years, the highly scripted and goal-oriented approach typical of adult American sex—i.e., foreplay followed by intercourse followed by orgasm—easily becomes a prescription for boredom, diminished intimacy, and even sexual dysfunction for many couples. Also, the destructive notion of the intrinsic legitimacy or superiority of one kind of sexual experience over another (e.g., the lingering debate over vaginal versus clitoral orgasm) would simply become irrelevant. The heterosexist assumption inherent in the belief that vaginal intercourse is the sole equivalent to sex would likewise disappear, as would cultural confusion about the behaviors that constitute gay sex. The factually correct answer to the question (wondered about almost universally by middle school kids, in my experience), "but how can homosexual people *possibly* have sex?" would become very clear: Gay people have sex in the same ways that straight people do, except for penis-vagina intercourse, which is physically impossible.

HIV/AIDS educators have urged from the very inception of the crisis that the language used to explain transmission be as precise as possible. Even so, nearly twenty years into the epidemic, it is almost universally said that HIV and other STIs are acquired from sex. Not only does this way of speaking reinforce the sex-equals-intercourse, intercourse-equals-sex mode of thinking, it also implies, very misleadingly, that *all* sex is implicated in HIV transmission. It is also inherently antisexual in tone; in this manner of speaking, the diseases are linguistically blamed on sex. (In a parallel context, for example, we do not refer to colds or tuberculosis as BTIs, or breathing transmitted infections!) The much more precise, accurate, and sex-positive statement would be to say that these diseases are caused by germs transmitted through certain kinds of sexual contact— namely, vaginal, oral, and anal intercourse. Admittedly, the verbiage is more cumbersome than *you get it from sex,* but the language is crystal clear, and its context is antidisease, not antisexual. It connotes as well that there are many other potential sexual options that people can say yes to, even when they have decided that it is wise to say no to a higher-risk variety.

The most important benefactors of this conceptual and linguistic shift would be our children, because parents and teachers would become equipped with the language and concepts needed to give the children truly helpful information and guidance. All types of sexual behavior between people, we could explain, are to be considered real, meaningful, and significant. All involve real feelings, real decisions, and real accountability. Although some sexual behaviors may be more powerful than others and require much more maturity, commitment, and thoughtful consideration, all involve unique and special powers—physically, socially, and emotionally. Therefore, there are no ethically free spaces when it comes to being sexually active, whether that activity happens to include sexual intercourse or not.

Later, when your son or daughter happens to ask you something like, "Is it OK to have sex before you are married?" or "How do you know when you're ready for sex?" you'll know exactly what to say: "Well, it depends. That's a complicated question. What kind of sex? At what age? With whom? And under what circumstances?" What previously might have been a single question or a single conversation instantly becomes transformed into dozens of other potential questions and discussions. Whereas the static understanding of sex as intercourse collapses and stymies conversations with our children (and our partners and others), the dynamic notion of sex as intimacy amplifies and enriches them. Once the word *sex* becomes open-ended, so do all the concepts attached to it.

## Changing the Sexual Paradigm

The remarkable tenacity of the sexual baseball metaphor in a culture that supposedly fought for and won a sexual revolution more than a generation ago conclusively proves that it has yet to happen. As long as the youngest and most impressionable of our children still gather on playgrounds to talk with one another about sexual scoring and bases—rather than with parents and teachers, in homes and classrooms, about the real meaning of sexuality and intimacy—it will mean that the most immediate and trusted adults in their lives have chosen to remain woefully out of touch with their real developmental needs. The paradigms will change when we adults decide to reinvent them. By changing how we think and talk, we will eventually change how our children act and relate. And that will be the real revolution.

**4**

# Values: Becoming Your Child's Cultural Interpreter

I wish you could be a fly on the wall in my classroom, especially on the first day of class. The students are so nervous, particularly the younger ones. They fidget and wriggle like a veritable sea of worms, and there is such tension in the air that they are induced to laugh and giggle at the slightest provocation. An eruption of sideways glances darts periodically across the room, as the students nimbly canvass the group to calculate how many others are as uncomfortable as they are. Toss them any bit of rope at all, and they will blithely spend the entire period cracking silly jokes, making fun of each other, dropping books, even falling off chairs—anything to distract themselves and divert attention from what the class is really supposed to be talking about.

The students are nervous because they are afraid of a lot of things: Do they know as much—or as little—as the other kids? Will they say something that will make them look stupid or foolish? Will the other kids laugh at them or put them down? What will I "make" them say or do? How long will it be before they are really grossed out or embarrassed? (Will there be homework?)

Thankfully, most of their fears—as well as their zany, symptomatic behaviors—are quelled fairly quickly and easily. Immediately, we set clear ground rules about how we will treat one another, and prove to everyone right away that we will stick to them, no matter what: no put-downs; no personal questions, unless you are prepared to answer the same question for yourself; no putting people on the spot; no quoting people outside class without their permission; no laughing or jokes about subjects that are fundamentally serious, especially at the expense of other people. (Parents at home are also relieved to know that we won't allow anyone to talk about people who are *not* in our class either, without their knowledge or permission.) Just a few instances of letting people know firmly that disruptive or disrespectful behavior will simply not be allowed, and we'll be off to a great start.

## "Nobody Ever Talks About It"

The embarrassment issue is tougher, sometimes a lot tougher. Embarrassment about sex is not like "natural" embarrassment—that awful feeling we get when we think we've done something really stupid in front of a bunch of other people, and wish we could disappear immediately and forever under the floor boards. (Instead, of course, nature plays the cruelest trick of all on us and makes our face turn bright red so we can't possibly be missed!)

Sex is different. People *learn* to be embarrassed and uncomfortable about sex. I'm not talking about the modesty most of us experience about our bodies, or the discomfort we might feel if we were to share something about our personal sex lives with others. Those kinds of feelings arise naturally whenever we are asked to reveal ourselves in a way that is intensely personal and private. I'm referring here to an entirely different dynamic— where the mere mention of sexual words, or even just the prospect of their being mentioned, automatically evokes feelings of discomfort and embarrassment, simply because we have learned to associate those words with those feelings.

Children, of course, bring these learned associations into the classroom and, sometimes to our astonishment, into our conversations at home. Even if we have worked hard as parents to be models of comfort and openness, in fundamental ways the culture still projects the idea all around us that talking directly and honestly about sex is somehow naughty, bad, wrong, or at very least inappropriate. I know this is so because my students tell me: Whenever I ask why they think we are having so much trouble as a class, and as a culture, dealing with this topic, they say, "Because nobody ever talks about it!"

## We Are Not Getting Through

Now I don't know about you, but personally I find that an absolutely stunning statement, and I am quick to tell them so. "Look around," I prompt them. "When and where and how often do you see or hear references to sex or sexual topics? If you went home right now and turned on the TV, how long would it take before you saw or heard one? Before you heard two? Ten? Twenty? How about in the music, magazines, movies, newspapers, or advertisements you see or hear all the time? How about when you're with siblings or friends in your neighborhood, or at religious school, or on the bus, or here in the hallway? Indeed, how many remarks about sex have you heard so far, just today?"

The unconscious disconnect they have been experiencing suddenly becomes starkly conscious, and the students are left wondering: "How could we have thought this to be so?" Clearly, up until now at least, the baseline cultural "we can't talk about this" message has been—incredulously—more powerful than the force of those thousands and thousands of media messages combined!

This paradox—which I experience, remarkably, among even my older students—is an ominous good news/bad news scenario for parents and teachers. On the one hand, it tells us that despite it all, there is a level of disbelief for our kids about what they see and hear over the media. In their conscious mind, it is still we who are the real modelers and conveyors of culture. When they say, "nobody ever talks about it," it is clearly we, the immediate adults in their everyday life, whom they mean.

On the other hand, they are telling us something ominous and disquieting as well: Although they are still paying a great deal of attention to us, we are neither coming through for them nor getting through to them in ways that are obvious, present, and lasting enough. And that although they are not consciously aware of it, perhaps precisely because they are not consciously aware of it, the media are more than likely filling the vacuum.

## "Sex Should Be . . . "

This double disconnect between the perception and reality of media influence, and most importantly between "real" adults and the children in their lives, is never more apparent to me than when I talk with students about sexual values. Ask any group of kids from middle school on up to work together on finishing the following sentence: "Sex (meaning the broad range of sexual intimacy) should be . . . " What kind of answers do you think you would hear?

I'll bet you would be very surprised. Sex, they say—and I believe they are being totally honest, not politically correct, when they say so—should be loving, caring, honest, mutual, fun, pleasurable, protected, responsible, self-aware, freely chosen, private, and meaningful. Many add the word marital, especially when the behavior includes intercourse. Most will insist that in a serious sexual relationship (one involving advancing intimacy), the context should always be an ongoing and trusting relationship, and that although the fun and pleasurable parts are important, it's the two people caring for and about each other that is essential. I'm always amazed at their ability to abstract these core values from the huge and conflicting array of messages they receive from culture about appropriate and inappropriate sexual behavior. They manage this even when parents and other adults in their immediate lives have not (yet or ever) spoken directly to them about their personal, religious, or family's beliefs.

The most frustrating and revealing part of the conversation comes later, though, when I ask the class to make a second list: "Teenage sexual relationships commonly are . . . " Almost always, what the students describe contradicts the previous list entirely! Teenage sexual relationships, or "hook-ups," as they call them, are typically short-lived, pressured, and at times even coercive. They happen frequently between people who have just met or don't know one another well. They occur commonly under the influence of alcohol or other drugs and in semipublic places, such as at parties, and they are often discussed in great detail with peers afterward. The participants tend to be inconsistently protected when pregnancy or disease is at stake, and the hook-ups are usually not as pleasurable for girls as for boys and are often performed more at the boy's insistence. Although they readily point out many exceptions—couples who care deeply for one another and whose relationships embody most of the positive values on the previous list—the students find situations to the contrary much more the norm.

## Closing the Gap

What we have created in American culture is a dangerous and untenable combination: Take a sexually moralistic but deeply conflicted society that constantly broadcasts a "do as I say, not as I do" brand of morality. Combine it with a potent, omnipresent, and amoral, if not downright immoral, entertainment media that glorifies recreational sex as the penultimate life pursuit. Sprinkle in a well-meaning, idealistic but tongue-tied post-sixties generation of parents and educators who can't sift through all the confusion themselves let alone explain it adequately to their children. Is it any wonder that we are seeing a generation of young people who might be able to define "right" sexual behavior, but can't practice it?

## What's Wrong with This Picture?

A colleague recently described a debate in the faculty room at her school about the kind of dancing many youngsters do these days at middle and high school mixers—what the kids call freak dancing. The conversation sheds a great deal of light on this very question.

Freak dancing, or freaking, involves boys and girls moving their bodies in very sexual ways, often grinding their pelvises very close to or actually in direct contact with one another, often to the point of sexual arousal. Sometimes other kids will draw a tight circle around the dancers, so that the moves occur out of sight of adult chaperones. Other times, kids tell me, the dancing happens in plain view of adults, who mostly watch with a great deal of obvious discomfort but usually say and do nothing about it.

I often try to imagine what it must be like to see this bumping and grinding for the first time as naive, unsuspecting sixth- or seventh-graders. My thought is that they must be pretty shocked and embarrassed at first, but then they look around and see everyone seemingly enjoying themselves, without any kind of adult disapproval or interference. They eventually decide that it must just be the way things are supposed to be—that it's perfectly OK and simply the norm for kids their age. Before you know it, they may be joining in or watching from the sidelines, just like everyone else.

In fact, I remember the first time I asked a group of high school kids about freak dancing, and they looked at me like I had three heads. When I explained what I was talking about, they just said, "Oh, why didn't you say so? We just call that 'dancing.'"

The debate in the faculty room was whether this was a case of kids just having harmless fun, or whether it was truly something to be concerned about. Most couldn't find anything too serious to worry about, and many agreed with a teacher who said, "Well, at least they're not someplace else, unsupervised and having sex!" Those who were bothered by her view couldn't put their finger on exactly why—my friend being one of them— and she told me she'd felt strangely out of touch and even uncharacteristically prudish, compared to her colleagues. It had been very unsettling.

I believe that "having sex" is exactly what these kids are doing, and I discuss (argue, actually) this issue with students and some adults all the time. True, there is certainly no intercourse going on—usually not even any kissing or "petting"—but there certainly is *something* very sexual going on: Bodies are touching, bumping, and rubbing against one another, with the result that many of the "dancers" experience intense sexual feelings, as both boys and girls have acknowledged to me. And yet, they will tell me, adamantly, that there is absolutely nothing sexual going on. It's just dancing. And they really mean it!

Their insistence relates in large measure to the way we define *real* sex in this culture as sexual intercourse (see Chapter 3). But it's also clear that in their eyes, freak dancing is simply a more modern, albeit much escalated, version of old-fashioned party games—spin the bottle and the like— which for generations have allowed sexual "beginners" to try out kissing and touching one another for the first time. The purpose of the game format was to provide such opportunities within the safety net of a relatively low-risk group social setting. The games were low risk because not much more than kissing (and maybe "light petting") typically went on, and because it was the rules of the game that determined who is supposed to do what with whom and where and for how long. No one ever had to make individual decisions or risk making either personal advances or disappointing rebuffs.

Besides, somebody's mom or dad was always on a nearby floor or in a next-door room. Presumably they were entirely clueless about what was going on, but you just never knew when they might come in, put an end to it all, call everyone's parents, and promptly send you home.

The stakes in this overtly sexualized dancing, especially for middle schoolers, are ever so much higher. That's scary in itself, since kissing games emerged spontaneously, probably instinctively, by kids as a means of *reducing* social risks. Freak dancing, on the other hand, has the net effect of *increasing* social risks, about which younger teens, especially, have little or no understanding. First of all, the sexual experimentation in this new "game" is much more intense and advanced than previously, since it starts out directly on a genital level. That would be the equivalent of starting a first driving lesson on the interstate highway. Also, the kids involved don't necessarily even know each other. Since anyone is pretty much free to come up to anyone else on the dance floor and try to engage them in the moves, a disturbing norm—the notion of presumed sexual availability—is in the air. By virtue of being in this relatively large, gyrating, heterogeneous, and often anonymous group, rather than in somebody's smallish, rec-room gathering of kids who are known, invited, and pretty much in the same social group, no one, especially the very reluctant ones, really has many comfortable choices.

Even if they decide to stand on the sidelines to avoid the pressures, they're still feeling left out and different. Sometimes, kids have told me, whether they are standing outside the action or not, they can still be caught totally by surprise by other kids coming up from behind, thrusting their genitals and poking them in the rear. In an age when we are struggling in so many other venues to teach young people that they have a right to grow up free from sexually harassing remarks or behavior and that no one has the right to touch anyone in a sexual way without her or his explicit invitation or permission, what a mixed message this situation presents.

The most troublesome part is the tacit sanction projected by adults on the sideline. Why don't they know enough to stand up and say, "There's something wrong with this picture!"

It's complicated. Simple embarrassment is certainly an issue for many of these adults, either because of the sexual nature of the situation or their desire not to embarrass themselves or their children publicly by stepping in. Sometimes parents and other chaperones may really want to speak up, but since no one else is saying or doing anything—and they're not sure exactly why they're uncomfortable in the first place—they decide to just ignore it too. Others stay out of it because they don't want to be seen as uncool or old-fashioned by other parents or their own kids, and comfort themselves with the notion that nothing is really happening, anyway. But the major reason, I think, is that most adults simply do not fully appreciate what really is happening.

They don't understand, primarily because they're focusing on the behavior in front of them, instead of the context in which the behavior is occurring. But it's the context that makes the behavior a problem. What adults need to ask themselves is this: What exactly is this particular context teaching these kids about sex, and is that what we want them to learn?

Regardless of our disagreements about right and wrong sexual values, I am certain that most if not all adults would want their children to understand several of the same basic moral principles concerning sexual behavior: It should be meaningful, it should occur in the context of a caring relationship, it should be freely chosen, it should be responsible, and it should be private. As I said earlier, even our children know and accept many of these principles by the time they are pre- or early adolescents. Then, why would we stand by and allow them, as eleven- to fourteen-year-olds or even as high school students, to participate in what is basically a sexual experience, in a public setting, between anonymous strangers or people who have no meaningful relationship, and in which there is usually enormous social pressure and possibly even exploitation?

This is precisely the gap between values and behavior we have been addressing all along in this chapter. It is hugely problematic in our children's lives, and a clear set-up for moral confusion, lack of awareness and responsibility, and a depersonalized view of sex. Closing this disconnect—between abstract sexual ideals and operational sexual norms—is perhaps *the* primary challenge for parents and educators struggling to raise sexually healthy children in today's world.

## Providing a Consistent Moral Compass

Clearly we are managing to convey humanistic and humane values about sex to an extent—not a small feat given a powerful and youth-oriented media culture working constantly at cross purposes. Nevertheless, we're not making it stick well enough to carry many young people through the pressures and stresses of adolescence with a consistent moral compass.

Because abstract thinking skills are just beginning to develop, a young person's ability to apply ethical and moral concepts to personal decisions and dilemmas is fledgling at best—even about much less confusing issues—well into the high school years. Moreover, in our increasingly open and pluralistic society, where competing messages abound and where young people are mobile, unsheltered, and relatively unsupervised, adults cannot expect good decision making to happen all by itself. Add the insecurities of adolescence, the pressures and uncertainties of teenage romance, an insistent sex drive, and the unrelenting demands of a powerful and watchful peer group, and we would be fools to think that we can continue to remain outside the periphery of our children's sexual and social lives.

If we wish to provide the right kind of moral compass, one that our children can carry with them and find useful virtually wherever they go, we must do our own homework. We will need first to discover precisely where we want the compass to point them and why. And to do that, we must start by reeducating ourselves with a three-step and fairly intensive primer on values and the valuing process.

## Step One: What *Are* Values?

For all our worry and consternation about the pop-culture values to which children are constantly exposed, adults are amazingly inarticulate about what to replace them with. The clearest example that comes to mind involves the national debate over the much-touted concept of family values. This phrase means entirely different things to different people, and yet people engage in whole conversations about it as if they all share a common meaning. To some, for example, the term *family values* means simply that it is important for families to have consistent values and communicate them clearly, whereas to others it implies that we must all respect every individual family's values. It can also mean that we need to value families, that families need to have more or better values, or that all families should share the same values. To many people, *family values* is shorthand for "traditional family values," and although this meaning is a rallying call for some, it's an offensive sexist, heterosexist, or even racist epithet to others.

The debate and confusion over what this nebulous phrase actually means turned quite ugly at some point during the 1992 Republican National Convention. A frustrated broadcaster finally turned to the highly regarded and family-oriented First Lady, Barbara Bush, for her take on its definition. "Well, it's really pretty simple," she replied. "Family values refers to whatever it is that *your* family values." I doubt anyone took offense at her answer, which was a welcome respite, but I also doubt that it helped clarify what all the fuss is about.

I recently sat in on a conversation among parents of preteens on the topic of premarital intercourse. One of the parents posed a question to the group: What would you tell your ten-year-old if she asked you if it was OK for people to have intercourse if they were not married? After several minutes of discussion, the group gave up; they couldn't even reach agreement on what *they* thought about the issue, let alone how they might go about explaining it to their children. The more they talked, the more confused they became about exactly what they believed and why they believed it.

The truth of the matter is, these issues are confusing and incredibly complex. But, questions and dilemmas regarding important human values should be difficult, unless we're willing to settle for empty catch phrases and simplistic solutions. As I've observed over the years, however, the difficulty is probably just as much a function of our lack of formal training in the discipline of values education as the complexity of the issues themselves. Developing clear values requires that we come to understand not only what we value and why we value it, but also what kind of value it represents in our lives.

## Instrumental Values

Part of our difficulty in thinking clearly about values derives from the peculiarities of language. Indeed, the word *value* itself may be used in three different ways: as a verb ("I value my children"); as a noun ("Exercise is a value I hold"); and as an abstract concept or ideal (such as honesty, justice, and beauty).

In everyday conversation, the concept of values is most often used in reference to specific objects, people, activities, experiences, or ideas that are important or have worth to a particular individual. Because these serve as practical guides to our actions, they are sometimes referred to as instrumental values.

Instrumental values may be mundane and relatively insignificant in the big scheme of things (I love coffee ice cream, my husband would pass on it any day for chocolate) or life determining (you may elect to become a parent, someone else may deliberately choose not to). Big or small, instrumental values are expressed moment-to-moment through what we choose to say and, most significantly, what we choose to do. Moreover, they are uniquely our own, unlike anyone else's in the entire world. My particular set of instrumental values may lead me to invest time and money, for example, in graduate classes, synagogue work, or gardening, whereas yours might direct you to politics, the Hunger Project, or ham radios.

These kinds of values or choices are not necessarily right or wrong in any ethical sense (although we may have moral concerns that cause us to make them); they are simply expressions of our inner self. In fact, every time we make a choice of any kind, we are in effect making a very personal and practical statement about ourselves and our own unique constellation and prioritization of instrumental values. At the end of the day, it is our instrumental values that tell us who we are.

## Abstract Values

The second common usage of the word *values* is less practical and much more abstract. It refers to principles, standards, ideals, or qualities that exist in thought, but not necessarily in action or reality. These precepts—for example, beauty, excellence, chastity, or human dignity—may be characterized as "pure" values; unlike the earlier examples of ice cream, gardening, and ham radios, they are seen as values in and of themselves, not merely as objects of valuing.

Individuals, groups of individuals, or whole societies may perceive abstract values as intrinsically positive or negative, or intrinsically right or wrong. Examples might be freedom, truth, equality, justice, charity, or democracy; these principles may be highly prized by some people or groups, whereas their opposites, in fact, might be valued by others. Thus, though they are values in the abstract sense of the word, they may or not be valued in the practical or instrumental sense.

People are often very sloppy conversationally in distinguishing between instrumental and abstract values. They make silly statements like, "she has no values," when they really mean "she does not live by the abstract or instrumental values that I respect." Everyone, of course, "has values"—at least in the instrumental sense—by virtue of the fact that everyone makes decisions. Or, we might hear someone remark, "This is a free country, where all values are relative, and everyone should be allowed to do his or her own thing without judgment from others." For a society to provide for instrumental freedom of choice or to function effectively in any way at all, there must be some base of shared, abstract values. In the very example of "This is a free country," the notion of freedom of choice is itself an implied, shared, abstract value.

Debates and disagreements over controversial sexual issues and behaviors are often unnecessarily frustrating and unproductive—to the point of impasse—by the confusion of instrumental and abstract values. The ongoing nationwide struggle over control of school-based sex education curricula is a perfect example. There are basically two camps in the debate, proponents of the abstinence-only approach, who hope to eliminate in the classroom any discussion of contraception or "safer sex," and those who advocate a more "comprehensive" approach, which includes discussion of abstinence *and* alternate methods of pregnancy prevention and disease prevention.

It is obvious to anyone who follows this controversy that neither side can really "hear" the other; the hostility and mutual disrespect between them are palpable, and achieving any kind of common ground seems utterly impossible. In truth, finding common ground probably is impossible, since the impasse is caused primarily not by disagreement over strategy, but underlying philosophy. Each side is arguing from an entirely different values perspective, or plane: One champions the abstract value of chastity, whereas the other advocates the very practical, instrumental value of physical safety.

Both sides are right. An absolute insistence on chastity precludes any mention of alternatives other than abstinence; attainment of physical safety in the reality of today's world requires it. The problem—determining the proper role of public schooling in regard to religion, morality, and public safety—is not theirs to solve, but the work of society at large. More on this in Chapter 7.

## Helping Children to Think Abstractly

As the previous paragraphs demonstrate, differentiating abstract and instrumental values is difficult, even for adults. It's even more challenging for early and middle adolescents.

Children at the brink of early adolescence are usually very sure and clearheaded about what they are supposed to do and not do sexually—and otherwise. Just ask them: They will tell you without hesitation that drugs are evil, alcohol is not for kids, smoking is stupid, and sex is for when you are much older. Although some youngsters may find these behaviors vaguely alluring, because of their appeal as forbidden fruit or supposed proof of grown-up status, most have great difficulty understanding why anyone would take those kinds of risks with life and health. They are genuinely convinced that they can and will avoid these behaviors as they grow up.

One of the reasons that preadolescents view sex and drug use so negatively is because their conceptual understanding of risk-taking behavior of all kinds is severely limited. Their only available mode of thinking is concretely black and white. Therefore, in their mind, any behavior that is potentially bad will be bad: Since drugs can ruin your life, they *will* ruin your life; since pregnancy can result from intercourse, it *will* result from intercourse. Although this kind of reasoning may sound reassuring to adult ears, the deceptive "wisdom" of preadolescents is often, at best, a matter of drawing good conclusions based on bad—as in simplistic—logic.

## Good Decisions, Based on Good Logic

With the emergence of adolescence comes the gradual shift to abstract thought. One of the hallmarks of abstract thought is the ability to think in much more sophisticated terms about the future, especially about the potential effects of present actions on future consequences. In other words, with abstract thought comes the ability to make good decisions based on good logic.

Ironically, this transition to abstract thought can work against young people, especially when they make health-related decisions. Adolescents will eventually figure out that their previous way of thinking was simplistic and inaccurate: If people have intercourse (or use drugs, smoke cigarettes, etc.), it is correct to say that they *might* get pregnant (or become addicted), not that they *will*. If they also understand that pregnancy can be prevented, and if they have not been taught systematically to consider other more abstract social, emotional, and moral concerns, they may be left with a morally empty basket of "why nots" when a decision about intercourse presents itself. Said another way, unless adults take an active role in helping them to embrace and apply abstract values to complex decision-making situations, adolescents are much more likely to end up making bad decisions, precisely because they are capable of good—but incomplete—logic.

# Step Two: Two Types of Moral Yardsticks

Discussions about sexual values are further complicated by our culture's tendency to apply two very different kinds of moral yardsticks to issues of sexuality. Moreover, we rarely distinguish between the two in an explicit way.

One dominant way of thinking about the morality of a sexual act is based around consideration of the *context* in which the behavior occurs. In this approach, called a *situational* approach, the morality of an act is determined not by evaluating the particular behavior itself, but by evaluating the circumstances in which it occurs. These circumstances can include the reasons behind the act, the nature and quality of the relationship between the people involved, and/or the extent to which they responsibly anticipate and attend to the potential physical, emotional, and social consequences of their choices.

In the other view of right and wrong sexual behavior, the unique set of circumstances in which an act occurs is seen as irrelevant to its intrinsic morality; *the behavior itself*, regardless of individual circumstance, is paramount. The approach is called *categorical* because the morality of an act is determined by strict, prespecified circumstances. Therefore, if an act fits those circumstances, it is considered moral (or, at least, potentially moral), and if not, it is considered immoral—regardless of any intervening contextual considerations, such as motivation, quality of relationship, and attention to consequences.

Someone who uses a situational yardstick to reason about the morality of a particular sexual act may draw a very different conclusion, using very different logic, from someone who employs a categorical approach. For example, using the contextual approach, nonmarital sexual intercourse might be viewed as totally acceptable morally, provided that the interpersonal circumstances under which it occurs are considered moral. However, using a categorical yardstick, the same act might always be considered immoral, since it does not meet the single, crucial, and prespecified condition: marital status. Other kinds of sexual acts—such as oral or anal intercourse or homosexual behavior—might be considered situationally acceptable to someone reasoning with the first yardstick, but never acceptable to someone using the second.

## Starkly Different Strategies

These two approaches offer starkly different strategies for guiding moral choices. In recent decades, U.S. society has become increasingly tolerant of a more contextual approach; witness the gradual but steady acceptance of unmarried couples who live together and even those involved in openly gay and lesbian relationships. To a degree, some of this newfound acceptance is a matter of simple resignation ("it's going to happen anyway, so we might as well just go along with it"), but undoubtedly our culture has experienced a sea change in how people think about questions of sexual morality. Many no longer tend to base their views exclusively on traditional religious or family beliefs, as in previous generations. Instead, they want to think through matters of right and wrong on their own and within a broader ethical context. They are also more inclined to think that this approach would be acceptable for their children to adopt as they become young adults.

Some Americans view this shift from categorical to contextual thinking as a dangerously slippery slope, aiming us toward rampant moral relativism. Where will it all end? they worry, adding that pretty soon there will be no standards at all.

I do not share their pessimism; people have not simply replaced a system based on many standards with one based on fewer standards. They may have dramatically altered the way they think about questions of right and wrong, but that does not mean they necessarily ascribe to lesser moral standards.

## Again, Teens Are Vulnerable

As we have said, making fine moral distinctions, based on the careful weighing of complex situational issues, is way beyond the intellectual reach of most adolescents. They certainly can rattle off right-sounding values—like the importance of being really in love; of being open, honest, and trusting; of taking responsibility for your actions; of being sure you're "ready" and "able to handle it"—but if you ask them to explain what these concepts mean in any depth or detail, they are often at a complete loss.

Therefore, the current emphasis on personal decision making versus more prescriptive modes of determining right and wrong is not at all a good fit for many adolescents developmentally, particularly in this culture. Absent extraordinary amounts of adult support, it can make them intensely vulnerable to negative social pressure. And in a society that constantly depicts sex as a recreational pursuit devoid of moral considerations, it will be too easy for them to confuse a morally sound contextual approach with a basically amoral "whatever you think is right, is right" approach.

## Step Three: Levels of Values Education

Quite possibly, your reaction to the last few paragraphs was a yawn, a stomachache, or a trip to the refrigerator. These subtle and intellectually challenging philosophical distinctions are complicated and potentially confusing. If you are tempted to give up, stop and think for a moment what it must be like to try to decipher them as a child or an adolescent growing up in the United States today.

As the late Mary Lee Tatum, a pioneer sexuality educator, used to say, unless adults actively shepherd children and adolescents every step of the way through U.S. culture and become in effect their own personal cultural interpreters, young people grow up like little transplanted Martians, trying to make sense out of the many meanings of sex without knowing any of the rules or even the basics of the language. To test this, pretend you have just landed here yourself. Spend some time looking at the pictures, not the text, in magazine ads, or watching commercials on TV with the sound turned all the way down, and see what conclusions you might draw about the meaning of sex in our society.

To be successful guides, we need to be skilled in helping young people not only to think critically about important values, but also to recognize different kinds of values and different types of value systems. Let's look at them once more, this time reorganized into various "levels" of values.

### Core Human Values

The first is the level of core human values. These values are broad, abstract, and nearly universally acceptable. Examples include the preservation of life, health, and safety; care and concern for others; personal, family, and community responsibility; respect for the worth and dignity of each individual, for diverse ethnic and religious groups, and for families; and self-determination; equity; privacy; honesty; and truthfulness. As adults, most of us consciously strive to live by as many of these values as we are able and to reinforce, model, reward, and otherwise instill them deeply into our children's consciousness and behavior.

These types of values are called "core" and "human" because they are cherished nearly universally as the Golden Rule and the basis of just and humane societies. They also form the core of most of the world's religions, as well as the U.S. Constitution and the Bill of Rights.

Core human values also typically constitute the foundation or yardstick of the contextual approach to ethical decision making. In this system of thought, the morality of an individual decision or action is determined by whether the decision or action, or its consequences, reflects affirmation of one or more of these core values. Far from an anything-goes or a relativistic view of morality, as it is sometimes characterized, the core human values approach requires careful and disciplined reasoning, since complex choices, motivations, and potential outcomes must be constantly evaluated against a demanding set of abstract principles.

In practice, core human values are relative, *but only to each other*. In a given situation, a person may ethically choose to sacrifice the worth he or she ascribes to one of these values, if another one, at the moment, seems more ethical or humane. Telling a lie to preserve someone's health, permitting an abortion because someone becomes pregnant against her will, or even taking a life in an act of self-defense might all be considered moral acts by a person who also dearly cherishes honesty and the sanctity of life. However, for the same person, telling a lie, let's say, to achieve a huge personal gain, even in a situation in which no one else could possibly get hurt or even know about it, would never be considered a morally correct option.

## Culturally Controversial Values

The second level of values education pertains to issues that I refer to in my teaching as culturally controversial values. These are values and value-laden issues about which, in American culture today, there exists great disagreement. Unlike core human values, about which individuals in our culture tend to at least verbalize universal approval (even if they don't always live by them), these issues—such as premarital chastity, the absolute sanctity of fetal life, homosexuality, adult pornography, and condom availability for teens—are continually and hotly debated. Each issue is complex and many-sided, and each side has its followers and detractors among those who come from all walks of life, practice many different religions, and adhere to very different systems of thought in resolving values dilemmas.

Though deeply controversial, these value-laden issues are also crucially significant to many people. Some embrace their particular point of view so absolutely they believe it to be *the* fundamentally right one—so correct, in fact, that it should be assigned to the category of universal or "core value."

## Core or Controversial?

I vividly recall a clear case in point, at a workshop in Appalachian Ohio. Halfway through my talk, a high school teacher jumped to his feet, clenched his fists, and responded furiously to the distinction I had just drawn between core and controversial values. He was especially incensed by its implications regarding the issue of abortion.

The man argued eloquently about the rights of unborn fetuses, declaring in no uncertain terms that the sanctity of fetal life was absolute and in no way controversial or relative to the rights of the mother. He asserted that his point of view was inherently moral and should be obvious—or should be made obvious—to everyone and therefore should become the official position of the public school system where he was employed. How dare I suggest otherwise?

By this time the audience, nearly four hundred teachers and administrators strong, was barely breathing. Neither was I. Incredibly moved—not to mention more than a little intimidated—by the man's passion and remarks, I collected my thoughts and thanked him for his honesty and for his willingness to take what seemed like an enormous risk in speaking out. I responded that as an individual, I too held beliefs about certain issues, including abortion, that were heartfelt and, according to my conscience, objectively right. I too wished at times that I had the power to impose them on others. But, as an educator teaching in a nonparochial school—in an increasingly pluralistic democracy, which depends for its continued existence on respectful and open debate—I felt I had to draw a different conclusion: My professional obligation was to teach my students *how* to think (using core human values as a guide), not *what* to think (even if I were certain that my view was the right view) about complex and deeply controversial issues.

On second thought, I quickly qualified my opinion by stating that if it so happened that an entire community of parents and teachers were to aim for and reach consensus about a particular controversial issue—and abortion would be a good example—it might then become appropriate to present the issue to the student body in the black and white terms he had described. (I would recommend, nevertheless, that the reasons for the consensus be made very clear and that the conflicts in the larger culture about the issue be carefully explained.) I asked for people in the audience to raise their hands, first if they had agreed with the man's statement about abortion, and then if they had not. About half the group responded affirmatively in each case, and it became clear that in this community, about this issue, consensus in no way existed.

## Personal, Parental, and Religious Values

In addition to reinforcing core values and clarifying culturally controversial ones, parents and other adults need to be clear on three other important levels as well: personal, parental, and religious values.

### Personal Values

Our personal values are reflected in all of our thoughts, assertions, and actions. They include our unique set of cherished instrumental and abstract values, attitudes and opinions toward core and controversial issues, and distinct approaches (contextual and/or categorical) to resolving values dilemmas.

Values, of course, are only a part of our total affective life, which can be considered the sum of all our personal attitudes, beliefs, feelings, and values at any given moment. Since our affect exists in a state of constant change, many of our personal values are also enormously fluid. Even so, at any given time, each of us could take our affective temperature quite easily by asking ourselves the following questions: What are, at this particular juncture, my thoughts, feelings, opinions, and behaviors in regard to issue *x, y,* or *z,* and what values do they reflect?

### Parental Values

Parental values can be defined in two ways. The first is purely descriptive and consists of the unique set of personal values held by one's parent (i.e., "My mother or father values. . . . "). The second is prescriptive and consists of those values that a parent not only cherishes but also works actively to inculcate, with the expectation and hope that these values will eventually become internalized guides to children's independent choices and behaviors (i.e., "My mother or father wants me to value. . . . ").

Particularly about subjects as complex and relevant as sexuality, children and adolescents, especially, profit immensely from knowing clearly their parents' personal (within appropriate bounds of privacy) and prescriptive values. Not knowing these values, children are left to guess at or worry over their parents' views. This disconnect can create problems in at least three different ways.

First, without clear knowledge of their parents values about sexuality, children will likely enter their earliest sexual decision-making situations minus the benefit of a caring and responsible adult voice and perspective to draw upon. In sorting out the implications and meaning of these formative experiences—which often encompass the very first questions of right and wrong that adolescents will face independently—they often are completely on their own, with only the surrounding peer and media cultures for guidance.

Second, they may carry unnecessary guilt and even shame about the choices they do make. If parents have not shared their parental values or standards or even brought up the subject, as children they begin to become involved even in very limited sexual activities, they inevitably will feel they are doing something sneaky or wrong, if only because it will happen behind the parents' back. Moreover, although they may not admit it openly, virtually all adolescents care deeply about having their parents' respect. When they must make decisions in a vacuum created by their parents' silence—and I find the majority are in exactly this position—they almost always infer parental disapproval and undergo internal turmoil and even pain, at least to some degree. (They might also cavalierly conclude that their parents' views are probably "stupid" anyway, and easy to disregard, but that is most often bluster and rationalization.)

Paradoxically, many parents, raised themselves in an atmosphere of guilt about sex and not wishing to instill those same feelings in their children, do precisely that, albeit much more indirectly. They don't want to communicate about sex in a negative way, but in truth, they're also afraid to be too positive; not knowing how to strike the right balance, they put off the conversation indefinitely. In my generation, we *knew* that parents thought sex was bad, because we were *told* so; in one of the ultimate ironies of post-sixties United States, children in today's younger generation often *infer* that parents think sex is bad, because they are not told much of anything at all.

Finally, parents who do not share some sort of prescriptive sexual values with their children actually impede the normal process of adolescent growth and development. One of the most central and important psychosocial tasks that all healthy adolescents must successfully complete is the construction of an internalized code of personal values to guide their actions and decisions, one that is influenced by, but unique and separate from, their parents'. This is difficult and crucial developmental work. It requires ongoing opportunities for adolescents to push and pull against parental views, so that they can gradually evaluate and select the values and attitudes that best fit their evolving, independent self and discard those that don't. How can they do that at all efficiently or effectively, if they don't even know what those views are?

## Religious Values

A fifth level of values education applies to those families (and schools) affiliated with a particular religious faith. In addition to providing opportunities to learn about core, controversial, personal, and parental values, these parents and schools have the additional job of educating their children and students about the unique sexual values held by their faith community.

Religious values can be shared effectively with young people in a wide range of ways, depending on the beliefs and orientation of the individual family. They may be presented as required and moral absolutes that all young people are expected to adopt, or offered somewhat less dogmatically as very positive goals toward which everyone should at least aspire. Other parents may choose to describe them simply as important options and views to which their children are asked to give serious consideration.

In school settings, approaches can also vary dramatically, depending on the beliefs and practices of the specific religious group, the nature of the particular institution, and the makeup of the student body, their parents, and the staff. Some parochial schools present their own religion's view exclusively, whereas others additionally encourage discussion, even debate, about values and beliefs held by other individuals and groups in the larger, pluralistic society. In still other schools, students are permitted and even encouraged to challenge and debate the particular points of view espoused by all religious groups, including those held by the school's own affiliated religion.

Each of these kinds of discussions can be important, not only for the children, who will come to better understand the place of religious values in people's lives, but also for the adults, who will learn how to articulate clearly—and argue persuasively for—the values of their particular faith.

## Too Little, Too Vague

In my experience, disappointingly, religion is not nearly the positive support it might be for young people as they struggle to develop clear and viable sexual values. Most can tell me only vaguely what their particular faith teaches about sexual topics, and what the students can articulate is almost always framed in negative and unappealing terms: "Religion teaches that sex is bad, or wrong, or sinful and you'll be punished if you do it." Moreover, they are usually unable to tell me on what *basis* sex is considered to be bad or wrong (except, maybe, that God or the Bible says so), and although they know that marriage somehow automatically makes it "right," they're not sure why or how a "mere piece of paper" can make such a huge and transformational difference.

Totally devoid of real or sophisticated understanding and ignorant of even basic theological arguments, sadly, many children easily conclude that religion is shallow, arbitrary, and completely out-of-step with the reality of their lives. If parents and clergy want their religious beliefs to be taken seriously, they must make a much more disciplined, positive, and articulate contribution in the marketplace of competing values and value systems to which children and adolescents are constantly exposed.

## It Takes a Village

Although extreme in the utmost, the traditional Orthodox Jewish community in my home town provides a clear and wildly successful example of a culture in which nearly everyone works together to create a twenty-four-hours-a-day, seven days-a-week culture within a culture that supports Jewish values. This burgeoning community of several thousand people is tucked away in a small geographical pocket of the city. Since Jewish orthodoxy prohibits driving on the Sabbath, families live in one of several adjacent neighborhoods and within walking distance of their closest friends, extended relations, and places of worship and study. Apart from work (many adults leave the area for jobs in other parts of the city), the center of everyday life for the entire community is the synagogue and other nearby Jewish-run communal, educational, and recreational organizations. Since the kosher dietary laws are observed strictly, local Jewish merchants operate many of the community's food stores and restaurants. The majority of children attend ultra-traditional Jewish day schools, most often segregated by gender, where they participate in both secular studies and intensive Jewish learning from kindergarten through twelfth grade. The children's dress is very modest, and their social activities are carefully monitored.

In astonishingly high numbers, children raised in this community remain in the fold, growing up to assume a way of life that mirrors closely the traditional values of their parents and grandparents. On the whole, they remain unfazed and uninfluenced by the social values of the larger secular society, and they embrace and adhere totally to centuries-old, strict Orthodox beliefs and practices concerning marriage, sex, and reproduction. Remarkably, even today, many still elect a modified arranged-marriage route to matrimony, in which a young person is introduced to another young single person, selected carefully for them by friends, family, or their personal rabbi. The couple then participates in an elaborately scripted courtship procedure, at the end of which they mutually decide if the marriage will take place.

During the entire process, including the period of engagement, it is forbidden for them to be alone, except in a public place, or to touch each other in any manner whatsoever. In fact, even while married, there are periods of required abstinence. Contrast *that* with prevailing American norms!

For most Americans, this way of life would seem an impossible anachronism, very far removed from the life they might choose for themselves and their families. The example certainly illuminates, though, the kind of monumental and community-wide commitment it would take to preserve such a cherished but out-of-mainstream way of life and to shield growing children almost totally from perceived counterinfluences in the larger society.

## Positive and Relevant Messages

There are certainly less extreme strategies that parents can pursue to increase the chances that children will be favorably disposed to a religious "take" on sexuality. Some children and adolescents can clearly articulate the views of their particular faith, and most importantly, hear and accept these ideas as reasonable, positive, and relevant guideposts. More often than not, these youngsters regularly attend afternoon and/or weekend religious school programs, in many instances from elementary all the way through their high school years. The most important ingredient may not be longevity, however, but context: Teachers and clergy in these programs know how to present religious precepts in a context that makes sense in the reality of today's world, and that taps into the larger developmental and cultural contexts in which children and adolescents experience that world.

A case in point: Some years ago I was hired to teach human sexuality education in a Modern Orthodox Jewish school. Modern Orthodox synagogues adhere strictly to ancient Jewish law, but accept the realities of contemporary life. The hallmark of a modern Orthodox Jew is someone for whom secular education and the world at large have inherent value and are seen as a means to understand God's world in the deepest sense. As a result, this brand of orthodoxy, because it attempts to integrate worldliness with religious practice, tends to attract a membership that is somewhat more heterogeneous, both geographically and in regard to the degree of ritual observance and engagement in the secular world. Since I am not an Orthodox Jew, and since most of my teaching occurs in secular settings, I remember asking immediately for clear guidance about how I was expected to handle the issue of sexual values.

The response of the school head was positively brilliant. First of all, she implored me to emphasize to the students two values above all: taking personal responsibility for one's actions, and showing total respect for each other, as people and as male and female sexual beings. Next, she suggested that I spend a good bit of time discussing with the students the range of sexual attitudes and values within the larger culture and helping them to think critically about the positives and negatives of each of those views. Finally, she said, with a twinkle in her eye, we'll send the rabbi in for the last class, and he'll explain the Jewish point of view.

The first time I heard the rabbi speak to the students, I understood the twinkle. His lesson, delivered with great warmth and wisdom, came straight from his heart. The children, seventh-grade boys and girls, were enthralled. Although I don't remember his exact words, their meaning was unforgettable: "My dear children, I'm so glad to be here with you today, because there are two things I love and care about more than anything—you and Judaism! I understand you have been talking about different attitudes and values that you may have heard about sex. I'm here because I also want to make sure you know that Judaism has truly *wonderful* things to say about this subject, and I want you to understand exactly what they are and how they compare to other ideas you may come across. As you continue to grow up, your parents, your teachers, and I all hope that you will make these Jewish values your values, because we know and believe in our hearts that they are right and healthy."

What the rabbi and the school head accomplished in this approach was a masterful blending of core, controversial, and religious values, in just the right proportions for an early-adolescent audience. Students were taught the importance of living by core values and learning how to analyze conflicting secular value systems to which they are exposed. At the same time, the values of their religious heritage became highlighted in the most positive of ways.

"Our religion has many rules about sex not because sex is not bad," said the rabbi, "but because it is so good! In fact, it is so good and so powerful and so important, that our tradition regards it as sacred and holy. We must always treat it, therefore, in caring, loving, and respectful ways, and in accordance with the laws of God."

Parents cannot assume that their child's religious school actually tackles the subject of sexuality in its curriculum, let alone that the topic is being handled skillfully. If that is not the case, parents must become advocates. In any case, parents must also educate themselves so that they can speak articulately and confidently in conversations at home. Most crucial is to make sure their messages are framed positively and that they give clear reasons explaining why these beliefs are important, for them and their children.

## Putting It All Together

Unless we intend to model our parenting after Baltimore's ultrapious Jews or in some other way erect a culture-proof shield around the lives of our children, we'll need to step up to the challenge in another way: We will need to become our children's own personal cultural guide. And, we will need to be constantly vigilant about it. (The average American, for example, sees more than twenty thousand sexual acts, references, and innuendos annually, *on network television alone!*) If we are skilled enough, however, we can transform these and many other everyday experiences, into endless teachable moments about sexuality and values.

## Enlisting the Media

Although there will be more media literacy tips in later chapters, one example here will demonstrate the insidious power of media messages and how we can use them as important teachable moments. Recently, a new offering during the premiere week of the fall TV season had received enormous hype and looked pretty interesting, so I checked out the preview. In the second or third scene, a handsome man and a beautiful woman are lying in bed together, and it appears to be early morning. The man's pager goes off. As he reads the message, a worried look crosses his face. He apologizes sincerely to the woman, but says he has to go to the office to deal with an emergency. It becomes clear by the way he searches for his things around the room that this is her place, not theirs, and that he has not been there before. She, looking hurt and disappointed, but not entirely surprised, tries to coax him to stay a bit longer. The promise of sex (again) is definitely in the air. He lingers for a moment, kissing her with passion, but retains his resolve and says, "I'm really sorry, but if you'll give me your phone number, I'd like to call you."

The entire scene took less than two minutes. The next day in my seventh-grade human sexuality class, we spent more than twenty minutes deconstructing it, carefully considering its messages and implications about sexual values and about other issues relating to health, safety, and gender: How long have these people known each other? Is this typically what happens in adult relationships? Do you think it's what should happen? How long—and how well—do you think people should know each other before putting themselves in a position where they are totally alone? Do you suppose there was any discussion of pregnancy or STI? Do you think these characters may have had "one-night stands" before? If so, what risks were they taking for HIV? What kinds of message does the scene give about the kind of relationships—and the kind of power—that exists between men and women? Does this relationship have anything in common with teenage relationships today?

It was very good timing; we had just finished our "Sex should be . . . " activity, and we had a long list of values to work from.

## Using Everyday Experiences

Not long ago, my cousin called me in a panic. She had been driving a car pool, with her nine-year-old son and his buddy in the backseat. Oblivious to her presence, it seems, the friend informed her son, with a measure of excitement in his voice, that two of their classmates, Joseph and Susie, were "having sex." Her son sounded very interested in the details. Horrified at this sudden turn of events, but having no idea at all where to go with it, my cousin nonetheless felt she had to say *something*. Interrupting the conversation, she asked, "What does that mean, that they're 'having sex'?"

"Oh," said the boy, "that's when a boy and girl take their clothes off, and the boy lies on top and rubs her titties."

Luckily, my cousin was able to keep the car on the highway. But all she could manage to say at this point was, "I don't think I want to talk about this anymore."

She was disappointed in herself and knew she needed to reopen the discussion, but didn't know how. We talked about what was keeping her stuck and unable to work through this problem on her own. She was simply stunned that children as young as nine would know and talk about such things, and she was overcome by the idea that maybe they would even try it. We decided it was probably just talk, and that was reassuring, but not enough to end her discomfort. There were other important things going on in the boys' conversation; we needed to look beneath the words at the values lessons these children were teaching one another.

It took some conversation—it was hard for her initially to think in these terms—but by first looking at her own personal values about sex, she eventually identified several clear and important parental values that she knew she needed to share and reinforce very directly with her son. The language the boys had been using was offensive to her because it was sexist and demeaning, and she wanted her son to understand the importance of showing respect to girls and their bodies. She also wanted him to appreciate that sex is private and that somebody's sexual experiences should never be the topic of gossip or public conversation. Moreover, she wanted him to recognize that the story was more than likely not true (or at the very least was an exaggeration), that telling the truth was very important, and that it was not OK to make up or spread stories to make yourself look grownup or cool. And, she wanted him to know, in no uncertain terms, that nine is too young to begin having sexual experiences of any kind.

Most importantly, because she learned to translate her concerns into the clear and direct language of personal, parental, and core values, she had gained the ability and confidence she needed to become her son's own personal cultural interpreter and guide, now and for the future. She could now close the earlier disconnect she had experienced with him and continue to help him make connections between values and behavior.

## Being a Mentor

Several years ago, I was asked by a colleague if I would have a chat with his sister, another teacher in her late twenties, who was having some sort of relationship problem. He didn't know exactly what the issue was, but he thought maybe I could help in some way.

We agreed to meet not long after, and the woman explained that she was feeling very confused about herself and her relationship with a man she had been dating for several months. She knew she was falling in love with him and wanted very much for things to work out. He was sensitive and giving, they loved being with each other, and she was happier than she had been in a very long time. She shared that she'd been hurt badly in two or three earlier romances when she was much younger, and this was her first healthy and serious attachment in several years.

The problem was sexual. Because she'd had such little dating experience in her twenties, physical intimacy was not a prospect she had faced as an adult. Feeling very confused about her sexual morals, she was annoyed with herself for feeling like a teenager all over again. She felt silly and embarrassed even talking with me about it. It was almost as if the last ten years of her life had never happened.

I asked some questions about her upbringing. When she was growing up, she told me, her mother and grandmother had only made vague, but very negative references about sex, especially about what happens to girls who "give in." Her dad said little on the subject, but when she was in high school and college, he would bring home church pamphlets about abstinence for her and her brother to read. She thought of herself as a fairly religious person, and although she'd always felt a slight tug from her religious upbringing whenever she found herself in sexual situations, she couldn't put her finger on any specific religious teachings that really seemed to fit. Her friends had always been much more sexually adventuresome than she; they considered her quite prudish and frequently told her so.

Although she insisted that she wasn't feeling pressured by the man she was dating in any way (in fact, he'd make it clear that the decisions were hers to make), she really wanted to make him happy. She couldn't understand her anxiety, and she was terrified she was really going to mess things up. So far, she'd just been pretty much "letting things happen."

It was clear to me that she wasn't at all "hung up," just not quite yet *grown up.* Like many girls and boys coming of age in United States, she simply had missed out on the kinds of learning opportunities that all young people need to successfully grow into sexually healthy adulthood. In her case, it was her moral development—her ability to determine what she herself believed to be sexually right and wrong for herself—that had suffered most. She felt like a teenager because, in truth, she was still thinking like one.

What she needed was some serious mentoring. The first step was to help her separate out all the various people in the mix she was trying so hard to please; as long as gaining the approval of anyone else—friend, boyfriend, or family—was her bottom-line instrumental value, she stood no chance of solving or even identifying the issues at stake for her on a personal moral level. Next she needed to discover what kind of moral thinker she was: Did she think sex outside of marriage was a categorical or a contextual question? If contextual, what were the core abstract values that she would absolutely need to insist on as nonnegotiable moral criteria? And what about her religious values? She needed to take another truly honest look at what her religion beliefs required of her, and why. Then, she needed to stop just "letting things happen"; she had to take responsibility for her values and choices and to open up conversation about them, even if there might be scary emotional and relationship risks ahead.

## Taking Your Affective Temperature

The young woman's confusion, in this last example, is not too different from the angst experienced by many adults when it comes to counseling their own children about sexual values. The solution is similar as well: To find clarity, we must begin by looking inward, at our own personal attitudes, feelings, beliefs, and values.

We will return to the topic of values in Chapter 11. In the meantime, you might want to think about or write about the following questions:

1. Think about your day today. What were the three most important decisions you made? What three activities occupied the largest portions of your time? What three or four important instrumental values do your decisions and activities reflect? How do you feel about what you have just discovered?

2. To what three or four abstract values or ideals are you most committed in your life? In what way are these values reflected by your behavior and choices?

3. When it comes to questions of right and wrong sexual behavior, what kind of moral thinker are you—primarily categorical or contextual?

4. If your perspective is primarily categorical, what sexual behaviors do you believe to be inherently right and wrong? Why? Where do your ideas come from?

5. If your reasoning is more contextual, what values matter to you most in guiding your thinking? What criteria would you insist on in determining the morality of a sexual act?

6. What are your views about controversial sexual and reproductive issues, such as abortion, adult pornography, gays in the military, condom availability in schools, gay marriage, abstinence-only versus "comprehensive" sex education, gay adoption, and embryo research?

7. What is or will be your best parental guidance about sexual behavior? What three or four values or messages do you most want to impart?

8. What are your religious views concerning sexual and reproductive issues? What is the "official" position of your particular faith community regarding these topics? Why? How important is it to you that your child adopt these views? What is your plan for inculcating these values?

**5**

# Sexuality: More Who We Are Than What We Do

...................................................................................................

When I was a very young teacher, my school head stopped me in the hall-way one morning to ask an important question. Since, after all, our courses did cover much of the same material, how did my program—an upper school elective in human sexuality education—differ from the required biology course taught just down the hall?

I remember answering that the sexuality program had an entirely different focus, with the emphasis not on biology per se, but on understanding the biological facts in relation to sexual health decision making. When we studied hormones, for example, it was in the context of explaining topics like pregnancy risks, oral contraceptives, pregnancy testing, fertility drugs, and menopause—not directly for the purpose of mastering the intricate workings of the endocrine system.

Although the head looked reasonably satisfied, I knew I wasn't. I was still mulling the question over several days later, when I spotted some of my seventh-grade students. They were sitting outside my classroom, studying for an oral quiz on reproductive anatomy and physiology scheduled for next period. I stood back for a moment, watching them frantically quiz one another.

"Orgasm, orgasm. What is that again? Do only men have them, or women too?" "What's the difference between ejaculation and erection?" "Is it *cli'-tor-is* or *cli-tor'-is*? Is that the same thing as an orgasm?" "How do you make identical twins?" "Oh, quick—here she comes!—what's a hymen?"

I knew right away I had my answer. The difference between a sexuality course and a biology course, I realized, is that in a sexuality course, it's not so important that the students learn the subject matter, but that they learn to become more comfortable *saying the subject matter out loud.*

Listening to them talk about sexual and reproductive organs in the same tone of voice and with the same lack of embarrassment and self-consciousness with which they might discuss kidneys or elbows, I knew it didn't really matter whether we had the quiz that day or not. They had already passed! (We did have the quiz anyway because knowing the facts is of course important, too.) Their comfort and confidence meant they were on their way to becoming sexually literate people, able to think, reason, communicate, problem-solve, and make decisions competently about the sexual parts of life, just like all others. Helping them to develop these skills was my responsibility, as the sexuality educator, not the responsibility of the science teacher, whose job was to teach them biology.

## The Narrowest Possible View Of Sexuality

Enabling adults—and students—to understand the process of sexuality education, as distinguished from sex education, is a huge challenge in American society. Ask just about anyone to describe the topics one might find in a sexuality curriculum, and the list probably will include something like the following: anatomy and physiology of the male and female reproductive systems, pregnancy, puberty, menstruation, wet dreams, abstinence, STI, AIDS, teen pregnancy, and birth control. Clearly implied is the notion that sexuality is about all those things in life that have to do directly with "having sex" (that is, having intercourse). Or, as a colleague likes to point out, the average American thinks of sexuality education as being about four things: the kind of body parts you have, how they work, how they are used, and the kinds of trouble they can get you into if you don't use them carefully!

This cultural tunnel vision places our children at serious disadvantage, even jeopardy. As long as we continue to see sexuality—and sexuality education—in these very narrow terms, we will continue to overlook at least 90 percent of what the process is really about, and thereby end up forfeiting our largest and most important roles in supporting children's healthy sexual development.

## Sexuality Is About People, Not Body Parts

Often, one of the first things I'll say to a new group of middle school students is, "Why are we here?" "To talk about sex," some brave soul will announce, and then I'll say, "OK, if we're here to talk about sex, then exactly what is sex?" (Later I'll explain that we're really here to talk about sexuality.) After about twenty minutes of processing the ensuing giggles—and analyzing the intriguing observation that although everyone in the room knows the answer, absolutely no one is willing to supply it—another brave soul will finally declare, "Sex is when a man sticks his penis in a woman's vagina." The room always erupts with palpable relief and usually spontaneous applause at this monumental act of courage.

What these youngsters are reflecting back to me is what they have absorbed thus far from culture, not only about sex and the collective discomfort we feel about it, but about the context in which it is held. Just think, for example, about the language they use to explain "the act" and what it communicates: This is something a man *does to* a woman—or more accurately, something that his body part does to her body part. And that word "sticks" (which is almost always the verb of choice, even though their facial expression usually reflects they know it doesn't seem quite right), does it in any way communicate that this is an experience of love, intimacy, caring, or mutuality—or, in fact, any kind of humanity at all?

On a much broader level, what they are mirroring as well is a societal understanding of sexuality—and not just sex—that is altogether limited and limiting. Sadly and predictably, and probably well before middle school age, they have already been conditioned by culture to comprehend sexuality merely as a matter of genitality, genitality in turn as a matter of sex, and sex as simply a matter of sexual intercourse.

Put most plainly, what both we and they need to understand is that human sexuality—and therefore human sexuality education—is essentially not about body parts. It is about the people, the thinking, feeling, valuing, experiencing, growing, changing, decision-making, relationship-building people, who are attached to them. And, envisioned as broadly as possible, it encompasses utterly every facet of human life that is connected not only to the issue of sex, but also to the issue of gender.

Both as an intellectual construct and within the scope of human experience, it is hugely complex and interwoven and infused deeply with personal and interpersonal meaning. And yet, in American culture, our sexuality is an aspect of our lives that few of us can even pinpoint, let alone adequately describe. Throughout this chapter, indeed throughout this entire volume, we will be attempting to step back far enough from ourselves and our lives—and from our children's lives—to see this elusive concept in operation.

## Six Sides of the Sexuality Puzzle

One way to make the very abstract concept of human sexuality more concrete is to envision a six-sided cube, like the palm-sized Rubik's Cube puzzle so popular in the 1980s. Imagine that the six faces of the cube, each painted a different color, are in turn composed of nine square facets. Each facet may be rotated around the cube in myriad ways so as to become intermingled with facets on the other sides of the cube, thereby enabling countless variations of multicolored designs. (The object of the original puzzle was to scramble the colors together randomly and then figure out how to manipulate the facets back to their original matched-color positions).

Our sexuality can also be thought of as a multifaceted cube with separate but intricately connecting parts. By picturing the six-sided whole that is our sexuality, we'll be less likely to continue to think about sexuality simply in terms of sex. The six sides, or dimensions, of sexuality—health, values, development, intimacy, sensuality, and gender—are introduced briefly below, and will be discussed further in later chapters.

### Health

Sexuality is about people and their sexual health and safety. This aspect of sexuality is probably the one about which we tend to be the most attentive and discerning, especially since the emergence of HIV/AIDS. The very phrase "safe sex," as its use has evolved in American society over the last two decades, is practically synonymous with such topics as AIDS, STI, abstinence, and condom use.

In reality, the health dimensions of sexuality are much larger than any one specific health problem. (Ironically, as discussed in Chapter 13, the way we have gone about AIDS education in this country has in some respects actually disempowered young people in their ability to protect themselves against other sexually transmitted infections.) They involve a huge array of knowledge, attitudes, and skills related to preventive sexual health care—from finding the courage to bring up hard-to-discuss topics with partners and health care providers, to undertaking periodic self examination of breasts or genitals, to understanding the importance of acquiring early and adequate prenatal care, to fully accepting oneself as a person potentially at risk for a variety of sexual and reproductive health problems.

Even still, we've only yet uncovered the tip of the iceberg. As the World Health Organization asserts and as everyone knows intuitively, health is far more than simply the absence of disease. It is the attainment of optimal health and well-being along all of life's dimensions—physical, social, emotional, intellectual, and spiritual. Therefore, we must work to consciously broaden our understanding and our conversations about "safe sex" to include these other aspects of health and safety as well. In other words, besides asking ourselves and our children if a particular sexual act might be physically safe or unsafe, we must also recondition our thinking so that we proactively consider other dimensions as well: Is it emotionally safe? Is it safe interpersonally? Morally? Ethically? Legally? Is it safe in regard to my future, and to my overall health and well-being?

## Values

Sexuality is about people and their personal conduct and character. Sexual behavior is a powerful force in people's lives. Ethical sexual conduct, therefore, requires careful moral thought about one's values and choices, as well as a sensitive and respectful attitude toward the needs, values, and feelings of others.

Just as it is important to underscore that ethical considerations about sexual behavior go beyond the singular act of sexual intercourse, it's also vital to reflect on the many other moral and ethical dimensions of sexuality. In contemporary society, for example, debates rage continuously about a whole host of controversial sexual and reproductive issues: abortion, post-intercourse contraception, school-based sex education, minors' rights to contraception and abortion, religion and politics, sex in the media, fetal tissue research, cloning, infertility technology, ownership of

frozen embryos, gender and marital roles, sex and the Internet, sexual harassment, homosexuality, hate crimes, same-sex marriage, gay adoption,
government and private sector funding of family planning services, gays
in the military, gay/lesbian and transgender civil rights. Formulating and
voicing opinions about these cutting-edge issues, the disposition of which
will affect our children's adolescent and adult life in many practical ways,
is important for us and for them.

Finally, we must realize that our children confront sexual conduct and
character issues daily, in school and elsewhere, on much more direct and
personal levels that beg for our attention. Listen in to their conversations
in hallways, in car pools, on playing fields, or at the mall, and you will
hear constant chatter about sex. Much of the language they use in this
bantering is coarse, demeaning, and sexist. Although most of the time it's
"just talk," undoubtedly a myriad of negative and potentially destructive
attitudes receive reinforcement and sanction in the process. Worse still, in
middle and high school cultures, degrading and humiliating sexual labels—slut, fag, wimp, pussy, bitch, ho, and gay and lesbian (used pejora-
tively)—have become the epithets of choice in targeting unpopular
individuals or groups. Virtually every adolescent and preadolescent is involved regularly in these incidents, as either a perpetrator, a victim, or a
bystander; even more disturbing is that adults rarely intervene. We must
learn how.

## Development

Sexuality is about people and their lifelong development. Human beings
change and develop as sexual and reproductive people throughout their
entire lives. Again, we tend to think of sexual growth and development
primarily in physical terms, but we are all products of continuous and cumulative emotional and social development as well. I'm quick to make
this point should older students grumble, when I catch up with them in
the classroom after teaching them in an earlier grade, "But do we have to
talk about this, *again*?" "The facts of life and sex may be the same," I remind them, "but it's *you* who are different. You're a very different person
than you were two or three years ago, and that's what we're really here to
talk about."

At every stage of life, there are new sexual and reproductive developmental challenges—physically, emotionally, and socially. For example,

people in their twenties and thirties and now even well into their forties are at their peak years for courting, coupling, marriage, childbearing, and for managing the acute pressures associated with balancing work and domestic roles—particularly for two-income families. Many individuals, of course, also find themselves during these years having to handle the additional challenges presented by divorce, single parenting, reentry into the dating scene, remarriage, step-parenting, and blended families.

Witness as well the tremendous interest in all aspects of menopause and midlife change that has developed in tandem with the aging of the baby boomer generation, and the burgeoning medical, educational, and commercial enterprises it has spawned. Consider, too, the enormous hype and hysteria over the drug Viagra—followed predictably by the sobering realization on the part of many couples and physicians that rekindling "good sex" in the later years is more than a simple matter of hydraulics. Long-standing relationship patterns, feelings, and issues are at least as important as the easy availability of a sure-proof erection.

Of course, the years from infancy through late adolescence are especially marked by an obvious and predictable timetable of sexual and reproductive learning needs, interests, behaviors, and milestones. The complexities and characteristics of these developmental stages will be the subject of Chapter 9.

## Intimacy

Sexuality is about people and their intimate physical relationships. Physical intimacy is of course central to sexual fulfillment, but it is probably the aspect of sexuality that is discussed least openly between parents and children and even in ongoing couple relationships. Topics such as sexual stimulation and arousal, orgasm, erections, and vaginal lubrication are not only supremely uncomfortable and embarrassing to many of us, but also highly intimidating—even in long-standing relationships—because they require revealing such personal information about ourselves. On the parenting front, many mothers and fathers find it almost impossible to find the "right" words and phrases to explain even sexual anatomy, let alone sexual functioning, to their children.

Although profound emotional intimacy is a natural outgrowth of many of our relationships throughout life, sexual intimacy offers a rare and unique combination of physical and emotional connection, enjoyment,

and affection. It also creates unique vulnerabilities, since at its most fulfilling it requires intense physical, social, and emotional risk taking and
trust. And yet, we usually come to these kinds of relationships, especially
early on, with very little in the way of adequate preparation or even basic
information. (I wonder how many of us, for example, could correctly label a diagram of the external female genitalia!) Suggestions for providing
adult guidance about these difficult and sensitive issues are discussed in
Chapter 8.

## Sensuality

Sexuality is about people and their *sensuality*, that is, how they see and experience their bodies. How we regard and experience the sexual and reproductive parts of our bodies—our sexual self-image—underlies every
other aspect of our sexuality. Our level of personal comfort or discomfort
with body parts and bodily functions, the positive and/or negative attitudes connected to our body image, and the degree to which we grant
ourselves permission to accept and enjoy feelings of sexual pleasure and
arousal are essential determinants of our well-being as sexual people. Others include our unique physical desires, fantasies, and attractions; our pri-
mal need to be touched, caressed, and held; and our individual issues and
concerns regarding fertility, sexual desirability, and physical attractiveness.
All of these aspects of sensuality are fundamental to who we are and we
how experience our sexuality.

## Gender

Sexuality is about people and how they experience their gender. If the preceding discussion has helped convince you of the impressive depth and
breadth of the notion of sexuality, particularly in comparison to the concept of sex, you might want hold onto your hat and put on your seat belt.
We haven't yet even touched upon the most far-reaching aspect of all—
the role of gender in shaping who we are as sexual people. So focused,
even obsessed, are we as a society on the genital components of sexuality,
we fail to understand that the largest part of who we are as sexual people
has to do with our gender, not our genitals.

**Sexuality = Genitality + Genderality.**   It was Mary Calderone, founder
the Sexuality Information and Education Council of the United States,

who first made clear that although *sex* is something that people do, *sexuality* has more to do with who people *are*. In other words, *whereas sex is an issue of genitals and genital behavior, sexuality is fundamentally an issue of personal identity*—encompassing the multitude of ways we think, feel, and act because we are either male or female. To coin two rather clumsy but illuminating new terms, sexuality includes both our "genitality" and our "genderality."

In order to foster healthy sexuality, parents and teachers must communicate and educate about the parts of sexuality directly related to genitals and genital behavior. However, they must also recognize and better understand the more elusive and invisible aspects of sexual development. Issues of genderality, meaning those aspects of identity and personality that are gender-based, must take their place alongside other more explicitly sexual and biological concerns on the cultural and parental radar screen.

**Genitality.** Certainly, body parts and functioning are a significant part of sexuality. It's interesting and fun to ask a group of students to list those aspects of life that are related to the concept of genitality: bras, jock straps, other underwear, tampons, pelvic exams, prostate exams, self-exams of breasts or testicles, sexual intercourse, masturbation, contraceptives, sexually transmitted disease, pregnancy, labor, childbirth, breast-feeding, menstrual periods, wet dreams, pubic hair, orgasm, ejaculation, erections, circumcision, and hymens.

Another neat way to understand the concept of genitality is to think about the sexual and reproductive events in our lives in terms of their unique personal meaning. My favorite examples, which everyone relates to and which most adults and even teenagers willingly share, are people's stories about the experience of having their first period or wet dream. Although the physiology of these milestones is pretty much the same for everyone, no two personal stories—and I've heard hundreds of them—are ever the same. Some boys and girls are embarrassed and confused by these events, others relieved and excited, while still others are frightened half to death. Some dared tell no one, others gleefully told everyone, and many are sorry they had told anyone (especially if it was their mother or father or sibling or friend at school, and he or she told the rest of the immediate world!). For many it was a momentous experience and an important turning point, whereas others can hardly recollect any details at all. No matter what the experience, it was uniquely *their* experience, unlike anyone else's in the world. And, the same would be true in recollecting our first kiss, first sexual touch, first intercourse, first gynecological or testicular exam, first pregnancy—or our last.

Many years ago I was amazed to see this topic woven into the story line—with great sensitivity and unusual candor—on the popular TV hospital drama *St. Elsewhere*. In this episode, a young adolescent boy, seriously ill, had been hospitalized for cancer treatment. His disease, until recently in remission, was suddenly back in full force. The boy had endeared himself to the hospital staff by facing his terrible misfortune with remarkable grace and courage. However, one day he was discovered barricaded in the bathroom, totally despondent and unwilling to come out.

Kindly, knowing Doctor Westphal was called in to help. Sitting calmly by the bathroom door, he finally got the boy to talk. The boy was absolutely certain that his cancer had spread all over his body, and he was terrified that he was about to die. When asked why he thought this was so, he recounted how during the night he'd had a strange sensation in his sleep, and then fluid had escaped from his penis. This fluid, he assumed, was a manifestation of his ubiquitous cancer. All was lost, and there was no point in going on with his treatment.

The good doctor (himself dying of terminal cancer) sweetly explained to him that what he had experienced had nothing whatsoever to do with his illness. Quite to the contrary, it was a sign that he was growing up to be a normal, healthy young man, and that someday he would be able to become a father. The doctor then elaborated the details of puberty, which, clearly, the boy had never been told before. He came out of the bathroom, ready to resume his treatments.

I've always marveled at this scene, not only because it appeared at all, given the period in which the show was produced, but particularly because the writers chose to send the hospital's elderly patriarch to the rescue. What a wonderful message—even grandfathers can (or at least *should*) be there for you if you need information or reassurance about sex. It also struck me as a marvelous example of what I attempt to elucidate with the word "genitality," and of how it is the meaning of the sexual and reproductive events in our lives, not the events themselves, that constitute the essence of our sexuality.

**Genderality.**   Whereas genitality denotes those life experiences related directly to our sexual and reproductive organs, its twin concept, genderality, refers to those that are connected indirectly.

The piece of news anticipated most eagerly at the time of our birth—second in importance only, perhaps, to the health of mother and baby—is the pronouncement of our biological gender. Based, of course, on the appearance of external genitalia, in reality, the perception of a baby's gender remains a purely biological issue for only a split second. Instantaneously, thousands and thousands of personal, interpersonal, and cultural associations connected to the concepts of "boyness" and "girlness" will coalesce and begin to inform the lenses through which he or she is perceived by others. These multiple associations, projected consciously and (primarily) unconsciously onto the blank screen of an infant's psyche, will shape in large measure how he or she will someday see himself or herself—in ways that will have little or nothing to do directly with sexual anatomy. This last point was once made convincingly by the six-year-old son of a friend. When told by a playmate that women could not be doctors, he replied that was completely untrue, since being a doctor had nothing to do with having a penis. Therefore, for each of us, what begins as a direct, simple statement of biology, eventually becomes an indirect and powerful determiner of identity.

## Sexuality as the Most Fundamental Part of Identity

Our sexuality—the sense of how we see ourselves and how the world sees us as males and females—is a fundamental component of our total personality. In fact, it is arguably the most fundamental. Pronounced the very second we were born, it is the part of our psychosocial self that is so close to our biological core that it exists right on top of our naked skin; every other component, including our self-perception of race, nationality, ethnicity, and religion, and so forth, develops on top of it. Affixed to us even before we were named or clothed, held or comforted, spoken to or fed, our sexuality may well have determined more about our future course than any other single aspect of our lives—and all before we had even left the delivery room!

The power of this idea first hit home when I read about a study involving newborns in a hospital maternity unit. The authors of the study had played a trick on visitors coming to the unit to look at babies through the glass enclosure. Instead of being shown the particular baby they were expecting to see, all visitors were shown the very same baby. A researcher stood behind a screen nearby, and unknown to the visitors, wrote down the statements they made while observing the newborn. The comments made by the visitors were highly stereotypical, depending on the gender of the baby they thought they were viewing. About "boys," they consistently "observed" strong cries, muscular movements, and bigness; about "girls," just the opposite—sweet faces, delicate gestures, gentle form.

These preconceptions and differentiations according to gender are reinforced in countless other ways in the earliest months of life. We are all of course aware of the most obvious examples: name choice, birth announcements, clothing, room decoration and color, and gift and toy selection. In fact, today, with raised consciousness about the importance of these early gender-typed messages, many parents, relatives, and friends of the family expressly try to minimize their impact by deliberately making choices that are more gender neutral. Despite good intentions, though, this effort is often much easier in theory than in practice. Ask anyone who has ever searched for a congratulatory new-baby card that doesn't make some stereotypical point about gender!

These obvious examples, however, tell only a small part of the story. Research studies have identified much more subtle and powerful ways in which babies are treated differently according to gender. For example, girls when held are placed closer to the body than are boys and are spoken to more often and in softer tones. Baby boys, on the other hand, are more often encouraged to engage in active play (like reaching for an object) with a parent, whereas girls are more often encouraged to engage in verbal play (like word recognition).

Some researchers and psychologists argue that there are significant brain differences present at birth that may account for later male and female divergence. They argue that these inborn differences themselves condition adults to respond to infants in discrepant ways, which we then improperly interpret as culturally stereotypical. I have no doubt that scientists will continue to more fully unravel these intricacies. Regardless of the cause, however, the available evidence documenting these early experiential differences is powerful and dramatic. It is difficult to believe that these rudimentary experiences won't in themselves become important precursors of later gender differences—in personality, interests, and abilities, and the like—of the kinds often explained away as self-evident, folk wisdom proof that "boys will be boys" and "girls will be girls."

## Making Sexuality "Real"

So close to the surface of our naked skin is this early learning about gender, and so intellectually abstract is this aspect of our sexuality, it is hard for us, both children and adults, to be in touch with its full meaning in our lives. One quick and effective way to help people appreciate how pervasively the stamp of gender affects their lives is to ask them to think about or write out a list of at least ten ways their life would be different if they had been born the other gender. (I have totally eliminated the phrase "opposite sex" from my language; it makes us all sound as if we are mortal enemies or from an entirely different species!)

The resulting conversation is always fun, energetic, and eye-opening. A group of seventh-grade boys and girls can generate easily a collective list long enough to fill several blackboards, with examples that leave no aspect of their lives unmentioned: grooming, clothing, hobbies, interests, aspirations, athletics, belongings, free time, religious rituals, friends, room decoration, telephone talking habits, Saturday afternoon activities, favorite gifts, taste in music, the way they talk, walk, sit, and even curse and belch (remember, these are twelve- and thirteen-year-olds!).

The most enlightening examples are always the personal and interpersonal. We discover that boys and girls often have very different ways of handling conflict, emotions, and stress. They have different kinds of relationships with their parents, siblings, grandparents, aunts, uncles, teachers, same- and other-gender friends; different attitudes, values, and even language about sex and dating; different approaches to competition, approval, success, failure, and school work. Although girls and boys may be very much the same on the inside, we conclude, the way they are trained to present themselves on the outside is vastly different.

Adults have an even easier time getting the point; just a single example can lead to twenty minutes of intense conversation. When someone remarks, for instance, that she would not have been able to give birth, the women in the group begin to speculate on what life would be like without periods, pregnancies, labors, or deliveries. (One student once figured out that a forty-five-year-old woman will have spent fully seven years of her life menstruating!) Men share their envy or their relief at missing out on these experiences and remind the women that at least they don't have to shave every day. Everyone begins to contemplate the multitude of ways that the experience of fathering might differ from that of mothering.

Someone else in the group alludes to occupation, and we're off on a long tangent of other related issues, like parental expectations, educational opportunities, earning potential, or the experience of sexual harassment on the job. The mention of relationships with one's parents, children, boss, or in-laws; images of attractiveness; awareness of physical safety; or even household chores prompts dozens of other examples. In these times of changing perceptions of gender and gender roles, everyone's experience in the group is different. But no one concludes that life would have been the same—or even close—had he or she been born the other gender.

## Redefining Sexuality Education

Changing our perceptions about human sexuality also means changing our perceptions about the nature of sexuality education. Since our sexuality grows and changes throughout our whole life, sexuality education, too, is a birth-to-death proposition: It encompasses virtually everything we experience that affects our development as sexual and gendered people.

Our earliest sexuality education is entirely nonverbal. As discussed, it begins the instant we are born in the perceptions, reactions, and actions of others regarding our biological gender. It continues day after day, even moment by moment, through other countless interactions with these central male and female figures in our lives. The development of our genitality, or how we experience the genital and reproductive parts of ourselves, is equally primary. It too begins to develop immediately—as soon as we experience being held, touched, bathed, diapered, and dressed.

Later, as we become increasingly receptive to attitudes and feelings expressed through behavior and body language, we begin subconsciously to pick up dozens of other important cues about sexuality. The nonverbal reactions of others around us—to nudity, masturbation, toilet training, sex-related words and conversations, and so forth—become important sources of instruction. An embarrassed look, a slapped hand, a face filled with disgust, a suddenly hushed tone, teach a powerful lesson, as does a reaction that is relaxed and accepting.

There is, of course, a direct, verbal component to sexuality education. It begins later still, with the labeling of body parts (although if we grow up in families where arms are called "arms," but penises are called "ding-dongs," there are important indirect messages as well!). It continues through our preschool years, with the answers to our earliest questions about body differences, conception, and sexual behavior. As discussed in Chapter 3, these questions typically surface between the ages of four and six.

Ideally, these early conversations will be encouraged, and dialogue will continue throughout childhood and adolescence, as new developmental questions come to mind or as the important adults in our lives decide to bring other topics to our attention. Even in these primarily verbal interchanges, however, nonverbal messages will remain paramount. Critical attitudes, feeling, beliefs, and values about sexuality are communicated constantly through our voice tone, facial expressions, body posture, and choice of language, which may contradict or even belie what we say with our words. A comment intended to be open and inviting—"be sure to come with me with any questions you have"—may not have the intended effect at all if we sound or look uncomfortable, tense, or guarded when we say it.

## Redefining Our Goals and Our Roles

Redefining sexuality education this broadly—in ways that acknowledge its verbal and its nonverbal components, its richness and complexity, and its birth-to-death course—also forces us to redefine the goals of the process and our roles within it. When sexuality education is defined narrowly as the giving of sexual and reproductive information and related topics, its goals can be defined simply. When it is conceptualized broadly, our roles as adults become infinitely more complex. We ultimately have little choice about these roles, since sexuality education just happens in the process of life itself. Our only real choice is to become acutely aware of it and proactively involved in it, or not.

Understanding sexuality education as a lifelong process that is fundamentally continuous and incidental also changes our perception of who participates in it and where and when it unfolds. If it is defined solely as the giving of information, then there is only one adult role to consider: who will do the giving and when. The only discussion—and in the United States, often the argument—is over who can best fulfill that role, families or schools, and precisely when it should happen. However, when its course is understood within a broad (and inevitable) developmental framework, the when and the who become moot concerns. And the real question emerges: Since all significant adults in children's lives, especially parents and teachers, have important roles in promoting healthy sexual development, what are the most logical and appropriate roles for each, and how can they best work together to lend each other ongoing support and reinforcement?

We continue to have much difficulty sorting out the right answers to this question, but the options will become clearer once we begin to recognize the solution as a matter of context, not content. Choosing the most appropriate roles and responsibilities for families and schools is best accomplished by focusing on the unique characteristics of each as institutions.

Families, on the one hand, are small and homogeneous and ideally provide intimacy, security, and consistency. They are, or certainly should be, the ever-present safety net in a child's life, always available for support, guidance, and backup. Families, obviously, also provide parents or parental figures, who offer constant role modeling and ongoing attention and know the child and his or her unique needs better than anyone else in the world. They also have access to countless teachable moments, in which informal learning can take place.

Parents also have the critical role, which they alone can assume, of making clear to their children their own particular set of values and beliefs about sexuality. This information is crucial to children as they become aware of alternative values and value systems and try to sort out the vastly conflicting ideas to which they are exposed in this highly pluralistic and media-dominated society. Later, as they struggle in adolescence to separate their own from their parents' values, knowing clearly what their parents think and value is crucial to the process.

Schools, on the other hand, are large and diverse and provide endless opportunities to confront a bigger, more heterogeneous, and less personal world. They are a microcosm of the larger society and an important intermediary in preparing children for their future. Schools have teachers, who are trained to do the formal instruction in a child's life and who have access to curricula and other important education resources. Also, as communities of caring, competent adults with an ongoing presence in the child's world, schools can provide an additional support system, with the advantage of having somewhat greater emotional distance than do parents.

Finally, schools, unlike families, have groups of students, who can be engaged, through skilled teaching, in constructive conversation with one another about critically relevant developmental issues. As only peers can, they alone provide for one another an accurate mirror of their own hidden feelings, experiences, and reactions. Extraordinary opportunities for feedback, validation, and normalization can result.

Clearly, schools and families have complementary, but unique and non-interchangeable roles; neither schools nor families are in any way substitutes or replacements for one another. No teacher can tell your child what you, as the parent, think and value. Nor can or should a teacher be there to process your child's feelings or experiences after a particularly wonderful, or particularly awful, evening. You, on the other hand, should not have to instruct your child about such things as follicle-stimulating hormone and other intricacies of the reproductive system; you may well get lost somewhere inside the fallopian tube and never come out again! Nor do you have at your disposal (thank goodness?), for forty-five minutes, five days a week, a roomful of your children's peers.

We have, of course, been speaking in ideal terms. In reality, we live in a culture in which neither families nor schools have handled their respective roles particularly skillfully or consistently. As a result, far from having the experience of working creatively and successfully together, parents and teachers often find themselves at odds or having to try to make up for gaps and deficiencies created by the other or by the frequently manipulative and exploitive advertising and entertainment industries only too happy to fill the void. Unfortunately, many children grow up with inadequate guidance from either families or schools.

If sexuality is about who we are, sexuality education is about who we are becoming. For children, it is about who they are becoming as sexual youngsters, adolescents, and adults. As the adults who love and guide them, it is up to us—parents and teachers—to work together to support that "becoming" in optimal, healthy ways. Creating these kinds of partnerships will be an ongoing theme in chapters to come.

# Gender: Girls Aren't from Venus, Boys Aren't from Mars

I often describe sexuality education in schools as a remedial discipline. By the time the students get to me, I spend almost as much time helping them unlearn things—misinformation, stereotypes, embarrassment, and other communication barriers—as I do teaching them anything new.

And the confusions! After years of ingesting bits and pieces of sexual information haphazardly from here, there, and everywhere, many come in lacking even the basics. Hand them a rudimentary list of vocabulary words, and, remarkably, most can barely discern sperm from semen, ejaculations from erections, vaginas from vulvas, ovaries from uteri. As for the urinary, reproductive, and digestive systems (you know, the ones "down there"), well, they've got those particular body parts so hopelessly enmeshed, entangled, and overlapped, I wonder, truly, if they'll ever get them disengaged.

Next to their sexual parts, what has them mystified most are their "gender parts"—those multiple components or dimensions of self that have to do with our maleness or femaleness. Although most of us think of gender as primarily biological, that is truly only the beginning. The broad human dimensions of gender are also a complex amalgam of cultural constructions, social learning, and self perception. Unfortunately, the three major

components of gender—biological gender, gender roles, and gender identity—are often muddled and misrepresented in our society. My students
universally mirror these confusions. Just as I find it imperative, always, to
recap their genital "plumbing," I find it equally necessary and even more
important to explain, or rather reexplain, the components of their gender.

## A Culture as Confused About Gender as Sex

As Americans, our cultural understanding of gender-related concepts is
pathetically narrow and underdeveloped. Often we fail to adequately distinguish intellectually between what are unique and nonoverlapping dimensions of gender. We are prone to think in absolute, categorical terms
about gender traits, which, in reality, exist along a smooth continuum of
human experience. Moreover, even as we continue to give unclear messages about gender, we also greatly exaggerate it—along with sex—as an
immensely important indicator and determiner of happiness and success.
As a result, we create unnecessary pressure and confusion for young people as they come to terms with their own personal, sexual, and gender development.

In today's media-saturated world, children and adolescents are exposed
constantly to simplistic and sensationalistic presentations of sex and gender. My students come to class all the time asking about the most out-
landish situations imaginable—involving transsexuals, bisexuals, drag
queens, cross-dressers, female impersonators, transvestites, and just about
every other sexual and gender variation possible—which they have seen
played out shamelessly on daytime talk shows. These distorted and damaging representations only fuel existing confusion about the components
of gender makeup and create gross misunderstanding about people who
do not conform to society's traditional view of gender norms.

Especially for young people who do not fit the typical or the stereotypical gender profile—and even for many who do—grave social hardships
and handicaps result from our cultural preoccupation with and misperceptions about gender. In fact, the glut of books in recent years addressing
the unique difficulties faced by girls and boys growing up in the contemporary United States all indict these unhealthy gender attitudes and expectations. In this chapter, we'll focus on identifying (and correcting)
these misperceptions at their source. We'll examine their impact on how
young people come to see themselves and each other, and offer specific

strategies for creating a healthier and more nurturing cultural and social environment.

## The ABCs of Gender

As psychologist Erik Erikson first pointed out, the central psychosocial task of adolescence is the formation of one's own unique and separate identity. Since gender constitutes the most primary and fundamental aspect of identity (see Chapter 5), if we don't consciously and actively assist young people in understanding the dynamics of gender and gender development in their lives, we hamper rather than help them. To lend the proper and necessary guidance as they make their way through the muddy terrain of the American gender landscape, we should start by clarifying our own understanding of the three fundamental dimensions of gender: biological gender, gender roles, and gender identity.

The most basic part of gender is biological. As most people define it, biological gender refers to whether we are physically male or female. Determined and assigned to us most commonly at the moment of birth, our biological gender is pronounced immediately upon observation of a newborn's external genitalia.

Gender roles, in contrast to physical gender, are determined not by biology, but by society, culture, and family. They consist of the full complement of intellectual, social, emotional, and behavioral—and in some instances, legal, moral, and religious—expectations ascribed to individuals on the basis of their assigned biological gender. As young children, even as infants, we learn our gender role effortlessly and largely unconsciously, through our moment-to-moment interactions with other male and female figures. Because they continuously express and model their own gender role beliefs and expectations, they inform and shape the process through which we develop our own.

Whereas biological gender is determined objectively and gender roles are molded socially and culturally, gender identity is constructed or construed personally. It exists solely within the experience of each person and is defined as the gender with which that particular individual identifies or experiences himself or herself to be. Gender identity typically solidifies within a person's conscious awareness by the age of seven, in concert with other normal maturational processes. From that point on, the child understands intellectually and emotionally that he or she is, always has been, and always will be a boy or a girl. Although that concept is intuitively obvious to older children or adults, for the young child it is realized only gradually. Children of five or six, for example, may still wonder if they should be a mommy or a daddy when they grow up, since they can't yet intellectually grasp the concept of gender constancy. Once gender identity takes shape, like any other aspect of core identity, it becomes a part of one's self-concept that is deep-rooted and immutable.

Although on the surface these concepts may seem clear and distinct, in reality each is exceedingly complicated in its own right. Moreover, as indicated earlier, these three dimensions of gender are frequently misaligned with one another and also with the completely separate and independent issue of sexual orientation. (Sexual orientation is a sexual issue, not a gender issue; in determining a person's sexual orientation it is not the person's gender that is of concern, but the *sameness or difference* of the gender of that person's object of desire.) We'll tackle the complexities of each gender dimension separately, then identify areas of confusion among and between them.

## Biological Gender

What could be simpler or more straightforward, one might assume, than biological gender? People are born decidedly one or the other gender. In fact, males and females are so uniquely distinct from one another, at least biologically, that we are correct in referring to each other as the opposite sex. Right?

Well, not necessarily. Although most people are unquestionably male or female from a biological perspective, it may surprise or even shock you that about three million to ten million Americans are not. Many of these individuals—approximately 1.7 percent of all newborns—are identified immediately at the time of birth, because their external genitals are ambiguous in appearance. It may be unclear to the observer, for example, whether the baby possesses a clitoris or a penis, since the size and shape of the organ in question are somewhere in between the two. Or, when the external genitalia are examined, they may present clearly as a mixture of both male and female organs.

For other *intersexed* people, as biologically ambiguous individuals are referred to clinically, identification comes later. Whereas at birth the external genitals appear normally differentiated, in later years sexual development does not proceed as expected. When the child reaches pubescent age, virtually nothing happens, or the changes that do occur appear abnormal in some respect. At this point a medical workup might determine, for example, that the child raised all of her life as an anatomically correct girl is in actuality a chromosomally correct (XY) boy, whose mixture of internal male and female genitalia includes two testicles. In the world of intersexual phenomena, a variety of anatomical and chromosomal configurations is possible.

Imagine the upset and upheaval that these kinds of events precipitate. We live in a society not only where a strictly binary classification of gender is the norm, but where most people do not realize that anything else is even—quite literally—humanly possible. So what's the story here? How can this happen? How can "opposites" be the same?

## We All Start Out the Same

The answer to these questions is that males and females are not opposite at all. Anatomically, we all start out the same.

If we could take a good look at the genitalia of a growing embryo, we would discover that up until the sixth week of development, it is impossible to discern its gender. This is not because, as most people guess, the genital organs have not yet taken form. In fact, the genitals at this stage are quite clearly distinguishable, even to the naked eye. The reason that we cannot discern gender is that up until this particular developmental juncture, the embryo is not discernibly male or female, but discernibly male *and* female!

Remarkable as it may sound, each of us begins our human journey with a combination of both male and female anatomical parts. A close examination early in the first trimester would reveal four separate areas of genital tissue: decidedly male organs (precursors to the prostate gland, seminal vesicles, and sperm ducts), decidedly female organs (precursors to the vagina, uterus, and fallopian tubes), and two additional areas of undifferentiated tissue, which at this point are neither male nor female in form or function.

At approximately six weeks of development, the XY chromosomal makeup of a male embryo, inactive thus far, begins to exert its influence on the previously undifferentiated portions of genital tissue. Upon instruction from the Y chromosome, the first of these areas differentiates and begins to develop the form and function of male testicles. The newly generated testicles in turn begin to secrete the male hormone, testosterone, which then enters the bloodstream and stimulates the final development of the embryo's sexual and reproductive organs. Under the influence of testosterone, a three-step process takes place: the prostate, seminal vesicle, and duct tissues will become fully developed; the female parts will wither and eventually disappear; and the second area of undifferentiated tissue will evolve into fully formed external male organs—the penis, foreskin, and scrotum.

The development of a female embryo, in the absence of a Y chromosome, will follow an exactly opposite sequence: ovaries will form instead of testicles, the precursor male organs will vanish, and the fledgling fallopian tubes, uterus, and vagina will grow. And the external female genitals—which we think of as being so utterly different from male anatomy—will develop form, shape, and to a large degree, functions that are directly analogous to the penis, foreskin, and scrotum. The same embryological tissue that becomes foreskin in the male, for example, becomes the inner labia in the female, forming a hood over the top of the clitoris just as the foreskin provides the covering over the head of the penis. The clitoris, the most sexually sensitive organ of all the female genitalia, has the same basic design as the ultrasensitive male penis (though much smaller); it also has the same embryological origin as the penis and is located in precisely the same spot on the pelvis. Finally, compact the scrotum, shift it upward, arrange it around the inner labia, and it's not difficult to understand that the male's testicular pouch comes from the same original tissue as the female's outer lips, or labia.

Understanding these processes provides an important window into understanding ourselves—and others who may seem categorically different or even freakish. First of all, none of us—not even those of us who consider ourselves normal males or females—are truly "opposite" sexes. We are, rather, flip sides of the same bigendered embryological coin. Second, virtually everyone starts out on this earth as "intersexed." Some individuals—roughly between four and ten million Americans—are born with both male and female biology in some form or another, as the result of one of many possible developmental variations. These people are living reminders of the bigendered origins of the entire human species, as well as the supremely complex and ultimately fragile processes that govern our growth in utero.

Biologist Anne Fausto-Sterling, of Brown University, and other leading experts argue that the significant numbers of individuals born intersexed should cause us to rethink our strictly binary understanding and classification of biological gender. Fausto-Sterling conceptualizes at least five genders, which exist along a smooth biological continuum. At the left and right poles of the continuum are people who are definitively "male" or "female"—chromosomally, hormonally, and anatomically. At the very center are "herms," or true *hermaphrodites* (the term derived, interestingly, from the combination of the mythological male and female Greek figures Hermes and Aphrodite), representing the particular intersexed variation with which people are born with both testicular and ovarian tissue. In between each pole and the center is the remainder of intersexual possibilities: To the left of center are those individuals Fausto-Sterling calls "merms" (born with testicles, but a varying degree of female anatomical parts), and to the right are the "ferms" (possessing ovaries, but external genitalia that tend toward the male pattern).

Most people will have a difficult time accepting that biological gender is not strictly an either-or phenomenon. In the past, the standard and unquestioned medical treatment for babies born with genital anomalies has consisted of early surgical intervention, utilizing available tissue to approximate definitive male or female anatomy, whichever is easiest to accomplish. The baby's gender is then assigned accordingly, regardless of chromosomal makeup. According to Fausto-Sterling, this knee-jerk reaction—which she labels "surgical shoehorning"—is a misguided attempt at forcing intersexed infants into rigid, culturally biased categories that simply do not respect the wide diversity of human experience. Instead of altering anatomy, we should alter attitudes, by devising new classification schema more closely aligned with biology and reality for the estimated 4 percent of our population who do not fit the prevailing, mutually exclusive, bipolar system.

Although the aforementioned is certainly a controversial view, many intersexed individuals would agree. As more and more have come forward to share their stories as adults, they have begun to assert the view that the steps undertaken to "normalize" their bodies were unjust and damaging, not only physically, but developmentally, socially, and psychologically as well. Most had no say in the matter, and many grew up with little or no explicit information about their medical or surgical history. (With modern advances in surgical technique and an increasing emphasis on joint decision making between parents and professionals, intersexed babies to-day typically receive a much higher standard of care.) Organized through the Intersex Society of North America, they are challenging us to revisit the ways in which we currently conceptualize and compartmentalize our notions of gender. Although a more fluid understanding of biological gender would clearly benefit people born intersexed, as we will see later in the chapter, it may prove a healthier attitude for those at the "anatomically correct" poles as well.

## Gender Roles

Gender roles are a subclass of a larger set of roles, or rules, known as social roles. These are collectively and mutually defined expectations regarding how each of us is to behave in relation to others in various social situations.

Allow me to elucidate, by means of the relationship between me, the author, and you, the reader. Although ours is not strictly a social relationship, our respective roles of author and reader operate in a fashion similar to the multitude of complementary social roles in which all of us engage routinely with the day-to-day people in our lives.

Each of us brings to this book all our previous perceptions, experiences, and learned expectations about our respective roles of reader and author. My expectations about you include that you are probably a parent or an educator. I expect (and hope) that you will be motivated to read the work from cover to cover, but probably not all at once; hence, the chapters are of fairly equivalent length. If another of my assumptions is correct, you will start at its beginning and end at its end. Therefore, I gave careful thought to the chapter sequencing. My expectation is also that before you even purchase the book, you will probably check out the table of contents (thus, the attempt at engaging chapter titles) as well as my professional credentials (hence, the jazzy book jacket) to see if it's something you want to buy in the first place.

You, on the other hand, probably expect that I know a good deal about my subject matter, that I can put a coherent and reasonably well written sentence together, and that I can tell you something worth knowing, equivalent, at least, to the amount of money that you paid for the book and the measure of time it took you to read it. If I can't, I expect that you will react with some combination of confusion, annoyance, or disappointment—and if you're really mad, contempt and derision—all typical and expected reactions in cases of unmet role expectations.

Complementary roles serve crucial functions, both in society at large and within smaller social groups such as couples, families, friendships, and work and business environments because they prescribe, in advance, what is expected of us. These roles enable us to efficiently and confidently enter a huge variety of relationships and situations, since the applicable roles and rules are largely transferable from one similar situation to the next. As a result, we are rarely required consciously to stop and negotiate new rules each time we enter a novel locale or circumstance. Complementary roles, therefore—especially our day-to-day social roles—give our lives security, predictability, and solidarity; they are crucially important to the effective functioning of societies, groups, couples, and pairs.

## A Very Short History of Gender Roles

Across many societies during much of human history, male and female gender roles were clearly delineated and prescribed. In large measure, biology was in fact destiny, both for men and for women; the female's prolonged reproductive and nurturing roles, and the male's greater relative size, strength, and social mobility consigned them each to the fairly rigid and mutually exclusive, yet complementary roles of caretaker and hunter-provider. We know that for hundreds of thousands of years, these gender divisions and expectations were enormously functional, since they have certainly passed the ultimate tests of time and human survival.

Even with the advent of modern agriculture approximately ten thousand years ago—which enabled and required men to stay closer to home and hearth, and women to tend to farming as well as domestic responsibilities—the divisions of labor, roles, and status between the genders remained clear. With the evolution of the concept of property ownership and the consequent bestowal of power, authority, and wealth through the male line, patriarchy gradually emerged as the dominant theme of societal and family life. Men, with few exceptions, were positioned at the helm of family, commerce, government, and worship. Buttressed by these powerful and enmeshed forces of economics, religion, tradition, and, eventually, secular law, this paternalistic system—and the rigid gender role classifications it reinforced—endured throughout the next several millennia.

Enter the industrial revolution. (My students always want to credit the sixties for all the sexual, gender, and social revolutions associated with modern times. They may be right, I tell them, but the decade they mean is probably much closer to the 1860s than the 1960s.) During the last century and a half, the United States and many other nations have witnessed an ever-escalating movement into centralized, factory-based manufacturing, and the parallel decline of a system based nearly totally on domestic industry. With this upheaval has come an irrevocable shift not only in the fundamentals of economics, but in the basic makeup and fabric of all aspects of society. As one societal pillar—its economic base—has reinvented itself, others with which it is intimately aligned have been required to adapt.

Increasingly, as the manufacturing shift occurred, the father found himself no longer head of the family business, but a worker alongside others, in a job that (though it probably wasn't) may just as well have been performed with equal skill and success by a woman. With the father away from the family domain for long hours at a time, his physical and psychological presence and influence in the family unit consequently decreased. As he became less directly involved in day-to-day matters, his role in the upbringing of children—especially in regard to discipline, vocational training, and character development—became more limited, whereas his role as breadwinner became paramount.

As male roles shifted, of course, so did female roles. Mothers began to take on more of the primary responsibility for the family unit, just as women were gradually assuming more and varied roles in the workplace (a trend supported by the increasing availability of reliable methods of contraception). In today's world, especially as we have entered the information age or the so-called second industrial revolution, there are fewer and fewer jobs that cannot be performed interchangeably by men and women. With the advent of two-career families, we are also witnessing a gradual re-negotiation of domestic roles, with fathers increasingly involved in day-to-day housekeeping, child care, and nurturing, and seeking to find a more satisfactory balance between the pleasures of family and the pressures and responsibilities of work. The evolutionary movement in society toward greater flexibility and equality between the genders—as reflected in our changing laws, politics, traditions, workplace, and religious practices—parallels these developments on the domestic and economic fronts.

## *What Does All This Mean for Our Children?*

This unduly brief overview of the evolution of gender roles throughout the millennia is necessarily simplistic. It does at least point out the mind-boggling rate of social change that society endured in the nineteenth and twentieth centuries, especially when compared with the thousands and thousands of years of relative stasis that preceded it.

This rapid rate of social change also explains the ongoing confusion and heated debate about gender and gender roles in contemporary society and much about the widely touted gender and culture "wars" of the late twentieth century. As mentioned earlier, social roles provide the rules that make our lives simpler and more predictable. They also embody and reinforce the prevailing political or power dynamics within any given relationship and in some cases (historical gender roles as a clear example) within society at large. Whenever underlying social roles undergo significant change (absent explicit and systematic opportunities for re-negotiation by all parties involved), social upheaval is the inevitable result. Predictably, there will be a period of confusion, disappointment, and anger; accusations of betrayal and irresponsibility; statements of contempt, derision, and ridicule; and active attempts at denial and resistance. We could all probably identify many examples of each in our recent cultural (or personal) history.

Think of gender roles as being like a deck of cards, let's say, with twenty-six representing traditional female roles, and the other half traditional male roles. It's as if someone has suddenly thrown them up high into the air, and we men, women, boys, and girls must wait to see where they will all eventually land, so that we will know what our new roles can and should be. The gender role revolution is one of the most significant legacies of the twentieth century and a daunting challenge that we need to actively prepare young people to successfully manage in the new millennium.

# Gender Identity

One of the few things that most of us can take for granted throughout our whole lives is our gender identity. No matter what else is going on, we wake up every morning knowing exactly who we are gender-wise and knowing that everyone else knows exactly who we are, too.

We simply get up, eat breakfast, put on our clothes, and go about our business. Never once do we have to think, question, or worry about publicly confirming (or hiding) our gender, except in some special or silly circumstance—if a caller mistakes our voice on the phone, or if we dress or wear our hair in an unexpected way and someone becomes momentarily confused, or if our parents give us a name usually associated with the other gender and we're sent to the boys' gym instead of the girls'. In these situations, we'll either laugh it off or maybe become momentarily embarrassed or annoyed. Then we'll explain the mix-up, and that will be the end of that.

That's the way it is for most of us. For others, those who commonly refer to themselves as *transsexual* or *transgendered,* the issue of gender can never be taken for granted. Imagine what it would be like to know that when others look at you (even when *you* look at you), people never see the gender that you know yourself to be. In other words, what do you suppose life would be like if your biological gender, and therefore the gender you were assigned at birth ("It's a boy!" "It's a girl!") simply did not match your deep internal conviction about which gender you really are?

For one thing, you could never simply get up, eat breakfast, dress, and go about your business—not without first considering how you were going to get through yet another day having to playact a life that did not feel like your own. Instead of the life you knew you were meant to lead, each moment would feel like an endless charade; how you were forced to look, act, communicate, and relate as one gender would have to be superimposed on top of the way you were *really* supposed to look, act, communicate, and relate as the other. To understand the dilemma, imagine what it would be like to be living your own life and then suddenly having to successfully present yourself to the entire world—right now and forever—as the other gender.

Such is the excruciating predicament of those who suffer from various forms of gender incongruence or gender dysphoria, in which the self and the body are seemingly in hopeless opposition to one another. Although the etiology of gender dysphoria is under investigation and multiple biological, genetic, environmental, and psychosocial theories have been proposed, there is no general scientific agreement about why or how this condition develops within certain individuals.

Though the words *transsexual* and *transgender* were not coined until the twentieth century, there is compelling historical and anthropological evidence that these gender-blended individuals have existed throughout all of history and among hundreds of cultures throughout the world. Although in some societies, like U.S. society, transsexuals have been the subject of misunderstanding and ridicule, if not out-and-out persecution, in many cultures they have been not only accepted but even highly respected and revered. In more than 150 Native American societies, for example, such individuals were thought to have unique spiritual powers, and they enjoyed an honored status in the community. In many other cultures, they played prominent and unique roles in religious rites and rituals, folk celebrations, and communal ceremonies.

In Western cultures, transgendered people have lived largely in hiding for hundreds of years. Strict prohibitions in the Judeo-Christian tradition against gender cross-dressing, as well as rigid separation of the sexes in regard to religious and family roles and responsibilities, eventually made even slight cross-gender behavior or expression seem a virtual abomination. Even in the new millennium, despite many earlier decades of social upheaval and gender evolution, we persist in describing and understanding one another as "opposite" sexes. Therefore, for most of us, absolutely secure in our own gender identity and supposedly assured of everyone else's, the idea of male and female as anything other than absolute, discrete, and dichotomous categories is simply unfathomable.

The study of transsexualism and transgender culture is a blossoming field in medicine and psychology. Interestingly, much of its progress has been stimulated and encouraged by the power of Internet communication. As more and more closeted transgendered individuals have found each other through support groups on the Net and as they have shared their life stories and their common needs and concerns, they have helped not only to affirm and inform each other, but to educate and reeducate the medical and mental health professions as well.

Increasingly, the transgender community is beginning to challenge the notion that gender identity is necessarily fixed and dichotomous. Certainly the vast majority of people are gender congruent, and a small percentage is definitively gender incongruent (these are the likely candidates for "sex-change" or sex-reassignment surgery, because they are certain that they will only feel at home with themselves in a body that is aligned with the true gender they know themselves to be). However, still others find themselves comfortable and fulfilled living a life that is both masculine and feminine. More accurately called *transgenderists* than transsexuals (the latter being those who desire or who undergo sex reassignment surgery), they live their lives and present themselves to the world as the other gender, without feeling the emotional or psychological need to alter their anatomy in any way. Others may consider themselves truly androgynous and feel no need to identify physically or emotionally with any specific gender; others still find that their identity is actually quite fluid and fluctuates from one gender to another and back again over time. As in the case of intersexuality, then, it is becoming increasingly clear that gender identity also manifests itself along a continuum of human experience rather than in universally discrete categories.

## The More Things Change . . .

If these transgender variations seem bizarre or discomforting, remember that U.S. society itself has transgressed many previously hard and fast gender rules, as the strict bipolar gender roles of a century ago have been steadily relaxed. Although these changes are perhaps most apparent in the workplace—where women now enter occupations and achieve positions of authority and responsibility once thought utterly impossible—changes are evident in all aspects of private and public life. To realize the starkness of this transformation, as psychologist and writer Dallas Denny points out, one need only recall that the casual dress typical of American women today was patently illegal less than one hundred years ago—when it was routine for women to be arrested for wearing pants in public—and would have been considered scandalous even a short fifty years ago. By the same token, many men are crossing over traditional gender lines as well and are considering a much fuller range of work, family, and lifestyle possibilities.

It is truly ironic that the gender revolution, which has so dramatically altered the face of work, family, and relationships in our society, has yet to really reach the one population ordinarily most amenable and susceptible to changing trends. Anyone who spends any time in school buildings, recreation or sports events, shopping malls, houses of worship, or any other place where young people congregate will confront large numbers of boys and girls acting out tightly scripted male and female roles in their dress, speech, body language, and nonverbal communication. The atmosphere in these places is palpably supercharged with updated and unselfconscious renditions of classical gender stereotypes, unfettered "macho" posturing, wily feminine flirtatiousness, and above all, the need to be seen as constantly and unequivocally cool. As I walk by these spectacles, I always feel sad and disappointed at the painful artificiality and superficiality of it all; it makes me want to call out, "Get a life! Deal with it! Why don't you just get real?" or any of those other barbed expressions teenagers are so good at throwing in the faces of adults when *we* just don't get it.

Certainly what these young people are acting out in part is a modern-day version of the mating dances that have kept us coupling for eons. By all means, ritualized roles and rules are probably essential to emotional survival in such risky and intimidating social circumstances. But, I think we have to ask ourselves if these ways of relating are right and healthy for young people, if they are as inevitable as we might assume, and what we might do to bring about change.

## New Patterns, but Built on Old Concepts

Many young people are stuck in a more stereotypical gender world than they need to be in. Increasingly, their life—at least their social life—exists in a generational time warp that can only slow or even hamper their assimilation into an adult world that is increasingly gender flexible, if not gender neutral. Gender is the one area of social change in which adults, ironically (and probably because of necessity), are way ahead of them.

Why this paradox? One explanation is certainly the effect of mass-media entertainment and advertising. Billions of dollars are spent each year, targeting young people with thousands of images, selling just the right masculine or feminine look. Women are to be small and thin, men big and muscular; females are to be meticulously groomed, males are to be attractive, but rugged and more relaxed; men are the dominant players, women the passive sex and beauty objects. It is these particular expectations, the advertisers tell us, that determine our worth as males and females, as well as our ultimate chances at success, popularity, and happiness.

Understandably, insecure preteen and teenage boys and girls—just coming into their own identity in a popular culture that ubiquitously glorifies sex and accentuates gender—are enormously susceptible to these caricatures of narrow, outdated, bipolar expectations. Moreover, as Mary Pipher points out in the landmark book *Reviving Ophelia,* all adults should be deeply concerned about raising children in any culture that seems to most value *looking* good, not *being* good. In her work with teenage girls in particular, Pipher struggles mightily to cultivate active "intelligent resistance" to these limiting and damaging messages.

The second and vastly more subtle and complex influence involves not *what* we think about gender and gender roles in American society, but *how* we think about them. Even though the *content* of our day-to-day gender roles has changed, the *context* in which we continue to think about gender issues has not. Limiting and misleading attitudes—cultural myths, really—still determine our fundamental orientation about the true nature of masculinity and femininity. Largely unconscious, and therefore invisible to most of us most of the time, these myths help create and perpetuate our children's (and our own) susceptibility to outdated societal and media-promoted stereotypes. Even more significantly, the extent to which we lack sexual and gender equity in our society today is at least in part attributable to their continued endorsement. By bringing them to more conscious awareness, we'll be able to evaluate and alter these beliefs, to better suit the realities of twenty-first century life.

---

## Gender Myth Number One: The various components of gender are categorical and bipolar in nature.

---

Challenging strict, bipolar assumptions about the nature of gender has been a central theme of this chapter. As we have seen, biological gender, gender roles, and even gender identity are expressed along a wide continuum in the reality of human experience.

Understanding the gender continuum concept is especially important in relation to the issue of gender roles. After all, most people are decidedly male or female, and most do experience congruence between their gender anatomy and psychology. However, most people probably don't naturally or neatly fit the rigid, bipolar expectations of men and women as prescribed by traditional gender roles. In fact, given an unbiased social environment (which, of course, is impossible, so we will never know for sure), the personal qualities, interests, talents, occupations, and proclivities of boys, girls, women, and men would likely approximate a bell-shaped curve of social, emotional, intellectual, and behavioral characteristics.

Any bipolar view of appropriate and inappropriate gender roles artificially accentuates true male and female differences and de-emphasizes and diminishes the common humanity we share. However, not only have we depicted the sexes historically as inherently different (e.g., males as intellectual, females as emotional; males as workers, females as nurturers), but the normative view has embodied significant personal and political power differentials as well: males as powerful, females as less powerful; males as aggressive, even violent dominators, females as passive, even subservient helpers; male traits and accomplishments as inherently positive and valued, female traits and accomplishments as inherently less positive or devalued.

Certainly, realignment of power among women and men—in almost all personal, economic, and political spheres—has progressed continuously in the last half century. But, even while our children continually experience firsthand the manifestations of these changes in their daily lives, the media continue to feed them a steady and seductive diet of macho tough guys and waiflike beauty/sex objects. We will see in later chapters some of the destructive ways these gender stereotypes can play themselves out in the dynamics of teenage relationships.

---

### Gender Myth Number Two:
There is a right and correct, or wrong and incorrect, way to be a man or a woman, a boy or a girl; one can even be considered a failure in fulfilling one's gender.

---

This belief follows logically from the assumptions embedded in the first myth. If the dimensions of gender are seen as bipolar and precisely defined and if gender is culturally and socially promoted as an all-important aspect of identity, then meeting these gender expectations "properly" becomes a continuous test of social competence and a decisive measure of personal success.

The social dynamics at work in many middle schools and high schools in the United States provide proof positive of the pervasiveness and deep-rooted tenacity of this particular cultural myth. Almost invariably, the students whose personal and social characteristics most closely approximate stereotypical gender attributes find themselves, often quite effortlessly, at the top of the social status pyramid. These are the kids whom everyone knows and can identify as the "most popular"—not popular, necessarily, as in preferred, respected, or even well liked by lots of other kids, but popular as in celebrated, acceptable, prestigious, and therefore socially powerful. Either implicitly by simple comparison, or explicitly by deliberate acts of inclusion or exclusion, these kids hold and jangle the keys to the local teenage country club; it is they who determine who is "in" (i.e., those who are like them) and who is "out" (i.e., those who are different).

Even in late elementary school, characteristics like wealth, physical size, athletic ability, attractiveness, and having the just the right look and the right personality (funny, seemingly impervious, verbally quick, and above all, cool) often rule. Although kids who are kind, talented, conscientious, helpful, or smart may be well liked or respected, it is not they who typically set the social dynamic and tone, because, sadly, as the kids have already learned, those aren't the attributes that really count. Although those at the top of the social pyramid may well also be bright, caring, and hardworking, that's probably not what got them there.

The psychological toll on those nearer the bottom of the social hierarchy can be devastating, particularly in the middle and early high school years, when kids are most insecure emotionally and most concrete intellectually. Although we probably did not think explicitly in these terms as adolescents, many of us can probably remember the awful feeling that, no matter what else we might have had going for us, no matter how many math or science or Spanish tests we passed or papers we wrote or hurdles we overcame, we were still out-and-out failures at gender. If only we could have realized that we were desperate contenders in a bogus competition, in an arena whose rules were never fair and whose playing field was anything but level. There can be no sense of fairness, no measure of real accomplishment, no meaningful striving to do better, when a small minority of people automatically gain social status, power, and popularity simply because they fit naturally into a narrow, arbitrarily favored stereotype. And, in keeping with the social dynamic, lower worth and status automatically await those free spirits who do not fit the stereotype. Lost in the ongoing struggle is the elemental fact that gender is not even a contest; it's simply an expression of who we are.

The setups here for both groups are obvious. For those assigned effortlessly to the in crowd, there is an artificial aura of superiority, the illusion created that social and life success come naturally, without pain, hard work, or struggle. (How many of us have ever gone back nervously to a high school reunion only to discover that although the favored few peaked out long ago, it's the hardworking "nerds" and "geeks" who continue to really make it in real life?) For the perennially excluded, there may be many quiet, lonely times; ongoing feelings of worthlessness, hopelessness, and powerlessness; or premature cynicism and a sense of resignation about life. Some will suffer the very obvious and public effects of complete stigmatization: name calling, humiliation, intimidation, fear, anxiety, anger, and even rage. Is it an accident that the Columbine High shooters were among the most marginalized students in the school community and that many of their intended and targeted victims were among the most accepted?

For everyone in between, there are plenty of fresh reminders to hover as close as possible to the edges of the stereotypical: the labels of choice for gender transgressors—words like wimp, fag, sissy, slut, ho, lezi, bitch, whipped, and dog—keep most people effectively well within proper and acceptable male/female gender boundaries most of the time. Adults and outsiders will look in and say, "Isn't growing up tough! It was just like that when I was a kid." They'll have it almost right. Being a kid is only the half of it. It's having to be just the right kind of girl or boy kid that's the really hard part.

## Gender Myth Number Three:
## Biological gender, gender roles, gender identity, and sexual orientation are overlapping concepts.

Because we are undereducated as a culture about the dimensions of gender (i.e., biological gender, gender roles, and gender identity), and because they are intricate and complex, we tend to badly confuse their meanings. My students, as I have said, constantly mirror these mix-ups. Although they've learned most of the proper sexual and gender jargon in one place or another, the concepts behind the words are hopelessly muddled. They'll constantly refer to homosexuality as if it means androgyny, they speak of bisexuality when they really mean transsexuality, and they'll tell you that transvestites (cross-dressers) are the same as hermaphrodites. The only way to unravel it all is to lay the concepts out visually, along separate and nonoverlapping continua, just as was done earlier in this chapter.

For adolescents, this process is by no means a strictly intellectual exercise. Their confusion has a direct impact on how they will come to understand and judge themselves and how well they treat one another. For one thing, unless they can appreciate the full spectrum and complexity of human gender expression, they, like most Americans, will fall into the faulty logic of assuming that biology, gender identity, sexual orientation, and gender roles are normally bipolar and always tightly linked. Our universally held assumption—unless we explicitly find out otherwise—is typically that a biologically male (female) person is someone who (1) always identifies as male (female); (2) always finds himself (herself) attracted exclusively to females (males); and (3) always prefers to enact predominantly masculine (feminine) gender roles.

How, then, to explain a chromosomally correct male who self-identifies as a woman, is sexually and romantically attracted to other women (even after sex-reassignment surgery), drives a truck, and loves football? (Although the preceding example is fictitious, I wouldn't be surprised at all to find out that such a person exists.) Learning about the wide possible range of gender variations and how very independently these "gender parts" find expression in different people can help young people become more understanding and accepting of the relatively minor (compared to the previous example, certainly) sexual and gender differences they see in themselves and one another.

There is a very short leap between the presumption of universality, no matter how incorrect, and the presumption of correctness or normality: If we really believe that this is the way everyone is, it then seems logical and right to assume that this is the way everyone should be. Of course, once we have taken this leap and made it known, those who don't fit our presumptions will likely respond by remaining hidden or closeted to avoid our negative judgments. As a result, we'll become even more falsely reinforced in our misperception that everyone really is the same as us. Throughout history and even today, much of the persecution of people who are simply "different" is based on this perilous leap of logic. The developmental danger for young people is that they will attempt to shoehorn themselves and others (to borrow and broaden Fausto-Sterling's helpful metaphor) into destructive, false identities, roles, and orientations that simply do not fit who they really are and how they are meant to live their lives.

Perhaps the most common and most problematic of examples is the nearly universal confusion in American culture between the distinct issues of gender roles and sexual orientation. Even in early elementary schools today, the labels *gay* and *fag* are common epithets of choice. Targeted often at boys who do, or like to do, "girly" things (crying publicly, playing with "girl" toys, or enjoying "girl" games and activities), or who simply lack athletic prowess, the message is clear: Boys don't do that. That is, boys don't break the gender rules—at least not without inviting swift and severe social payback. By observing what happens to the rule violators, boys learn quickly that to break the gender rules is to risk social suicide. Many, if not most, react by psychologically walling off—even burying, perhaps forever—their own perceived "female" inclinations, in whatever ways "female" may be defined by the prevailing social forces that surround them. How sad.

Similar pressures set in for girls, but typically not as early; being called a tomboy is not nearly as damning as being labeled a sissy. Fortunately for them, girls typically will be allowed fuller expression of their "masculine" and "feminine" sides—until they visibly enter pubescence and begin to become both sexualized and "genderized" by society, advertisers, and the girls' peers. We are not as threatened by their crossover behavior as little girls (versus little boys), probably because it's logically understandable given the higher status and respect still accorded males culturally, and because the misguided connection between homosexuality and gender role transgression is not as strong in the case of lesbianism.

Although, arguably, young children do not fully comprehend these complex social dynamics and may not yet understand the concept of being "gay" in specific sexual terms, many clearly have an underlying gut sense of what is going on. One example comes to mind. A kindergarten teacher was approached by one of her students, a girl, in tears. A boy in her class had called the child gay, and although she reported that she didn't know what the word meant, she did know by the way he said it that it was meant as a serious insult. The incident had badly hurt her feelings. Later, when asked if she knew *why* the boy had said this to her, she replied, "He said that he called me gay because I was acting like a girl."

This boy is certainly confused, and he doesn't quite have the entire picture just yet, but he surely understands pieces of it. The three parts he knows so far are pretty stunning: (1) that gay is somehow bad; (2) that gay somehow means acting like a girl; and (3) that acting like a girl is somehow bad. Remarkably, although he's not even in first grade yet, he's already learning the basics of homophobia and sexism and the implicit connection between the two. And, since his earliest intellectual understanding of the concept of gay is associated, falsely but nonetheless powerfully, with cross stereotypical gender role behavior, he has already beginning to assimilate (and spread) the myth that the issues of sexual orientation, gender role behavior, and perhaps even gender identity are one and the same.

---

### Gender Myth Number Four:
### Being a "real" man or "real" woman goes beyond biology; therefore, one can and must continuously prove or demonstrate one's masculinity or femininity.

---

The existence and the terrible burden of this particular myth is palpable in any school environment or any other place where young people congregate. It can be identified more easily among boys, partially because in group settings, boys just tend to be visibly more "out there," and partially because the pressure to perform, to demonstrate, and to prove is in itself an essential ingredient of the stereotypical male role.

Although it may feel extremely important to many girls, for example, to embody virtually just the right sexual or gender "look," failure to achieve it is not exactly the same kind of assault to one's "femininity" as failure to perform is to one's "masculinity." Since the essence of traditional femininity is to please, not to perform, and since a girl or woman can almost always figure out better and better ways to please, she can't really ever "lose" her femininity—that is, unless she does something considered outrageously masculine, like constantly cursing or belching in public, going totally "butch" in appearance, or trying to take too much power or control away from men in her life. (Rumors started circulating about Hillary Clinton being a lesbian shortly after her political activities began to imply to some that it was she, not the president, who was really wearing the pants in the White House.)

Masculinity—on the other hand—is not judged quantitatively, but proven qualitatively. You've either got the "right stuff," or you don't. Even one slip-up, and no matter how many times you've proven it before, you can become an immediate low-life wus, wimp, fag, or "girl." (If the worst thing a guy can be called is still "a girl," especially if adults aren't stepping in to challenge them, what exactly are our boys learning from one another about fundamental gender equity and respect?)

Watch just about any group of boys interact with one another, and these dynamics will almost invariably surface. My first dose of it was more than twenty years ago, the first time I ever taught an all-male class of high school juniors. One boy tossed a pen to another, because he had forgotten to bring one and the class was about to take a quiz. He missed the throw, and it fell to the floor—this in front of the entire class, already feeling threatened and totally uncomfortable being in a sexuality class with their sixteen-year-old friends and peers. I remember the awful pain of it as if it were yesterday. So relieved to have something or somebody to focus on besides sex, and so happy that it was he and not they, the boys giddily joked, jeered, pointed, and attempted to make emotional mincemeat out of him at virtually every opportunity for the remainder of the period. Worse still, I did the absolutely unforgivable: I tried to protect him from them. That of course made him an official wus. I didn't want to imagine the treatment he might have received on a "real" playing field.

What I didn't know then is what I know now like the back of my hand: The thing to do is to go with it, not criticize or try to stop it. If I had the period back, I'd wait for a few quick examples of serious torture, get the class's attention (that's the really hard part), and simply ask them to describe what had just happened, and why. Sooner or later, somebody would be brave enough to begin reconstructing the events, others would explain that the boy was just an easy target, not a total loser, and eventually someone would acknowledge the discomfort in the group that had caused the whole thing to happen in the first place. We'd probably have ended up agreeing about how trivial, obnoxious, immature, and totally unnecessary it had all been. And then we would have gone on to have a really great class.

In their important book about boys, *Raising Cain,* authors Dan Kindlon and Michael Thompson warn us about expecting too little from our young men and about expecting too much. It's too much to expect them to walk into a situation like the one just described and not become threatened or act out their insecurity in some disruptive way. But, it's also expecting far too little of them if we don't then require them to rise to the occasion, take responsibility for their cruelty, and figure out a better way of owning up to and working through their feelings of vulnerability. My ultimate message to those boys years ago should not have been that their conduct was bad, but that it was beneath them and that I expected them to act in a manner that affirmed the best they could be, not the least they could muster.

## Reviving Ophelia *and* Hamlet

In 1994, Mary Pipher's *Reviving Ophelia* delivered a stunning wake-up call about the emotional suffering and turmoil experienced by adolescent girls in the United States. It has become required reading not only for parents, but for girls themselves; even many of my middle school girls carry well-worn copies with them to school and can quote from it by heart.

The harsh indictments in *Reviving Ophelia* are targeted not at parents, but at culture. Parents are not the issue, Pipher vehemently contends; most are doing everything possible they can think of to provide healthy experiences for their growing daughters and to actively combat the negative messages and influences that surround them. The problem lies instead in the toxicity of a junk culture that works against the best efforts of parents and other positive forces in a young girl's life at almost every turn.

Pipher's central and compelling argument is that the nosedive in confidence and self-esteem observed so often in early adolescent girls is rooted in a society that delivers relentlessly punishing and destructive messages about the nature of femininity. Younger girls, before they have become sexualized by culture, says Pipher, are allowed to be marvelously androgynous and adaptable; they can choose almost always to be their assertive and energetic selves without worrying whether their behavior will be labeled as feminine or masculine. But when they enter adolescence, and as popular culture begins to overwhelm them with ubiquitous and unhealthy messages about what it means to be a successful and attractive young woman, "the selves of girls begin to go down like ships in the Bermuda Triangle."

As media values and images begin to take firm hold in an enveloping and all-important peer group, girls begin to experience intense psychological conflict between their autonomous selves and their need to be perceived as acceptably feminine. The great danger is that they will stop wondering, "Who am I, and what do I want?"—the central developmental questions of adolescence—and start fixating instead on what they need to do to please and acquire the approval of others. As a result, in Pipher's words, many girls split themselves into "true halves" and "false halves" and end up with two conflicting selves: the *authentic self* (the person you really are, including those parts of you that might not be socially acceptable), and the *socially scripted self* (the parts you show in public because that is the person you are supposed to be). Since self-esteem is based on acceptance of all thoughts and feelings as one's own, girls caught in this trap begin to lose more and more of their self-confidence as they "disown," and thereby become a diminished version of, their former selves.

This "sacrifice of wholeness," a term borrowed by Pipher from writer and therapist Alice Miller, is at the heart of the matter. Conversely, it is the permission and encouragement to become "whole" again that strongly attracts adolescent girls toward Pipher's work. Many girls are intuitively aware that they are being pressured in ways not good for them: Their premature sexualization makes them feel anxious and out of control; the snobbishness and cruelty of social cliques, even the ones they may aspire to join, bother them deeply; they may want to be pretty and popular, but not at the high price they may feel is demanded of them. Pipher's words and stories help them figure out the answers to the pivotal developmental questions they face: How do I care for myself, but not be selfish? How can I be honest and still be loved? How can I achieve and not threaten others? How can I be sexual and not a sex object? How can I be responsive but not responsible for everyone? She calls this internal work "intelligent resistance" to the culture's relentless assault on girls' personal and social integrity.

Partially in reaction to the growing attention placed on the special needs of girls and to a gradually increasing public consciousness about the unique problems of boys in today's society (violence, alcohol and drug abuse, attention deficit/hyperactivity disorder, school problems), a deluge of publications about their special needs has followed the publication of *Ophelia*. It has become the boys' "turn."

Two of my favorite books in this genre—William Pollack's *Real Boys,* and Kindlon and Thompson's *Raising Cain*—articulate eloquently the flip side of Pipher's classic polemic about girls. Boys, Pollack argues, are trained by culture to wear a "mask of masculinity" in order to hide their true inner feelings; despite the image of toughness and strength they feel they must project to the world, they too are suffering internally. Society's stereotypes, he says, place them in a veritable "gender straightjacket," by judging them constantly against rigid, outmoded, and ultimately impossible definitions of manhood and masculinity. Like Kindlon and Thompson, Pollack argues that these cultural pressures exact an enormous toll on boys, making them ashamed of normal feelings and vulnerabilities, and ultimately disconnecting them from their "true selves." Kindlon and Thompson label this process, by which a boy is steered by culture away from his inner world, "emotional miseducation."

Like girls, boys feel trapped in an emotional and behavioral no-win situation. Because they know they will be shamed by other boys for failing to act and feel in stereotypically masculine ways, they become determined to hide the parts of themselves that might make them appear "weak" or "feminine." As a result, they too experience a painful erosion of confidence and self-esteem, as they begin to fear and perhaps even loathe the parts of themselves that do not fit the supposed masculine ideal.

Unlike girls, however, boys face an additional bind: The very same expectations that create the unhealthy and unrealistic emotional constraints in boys' lives also prohibit them from seeking the help they need to begin to feel better about themselves. (I have yet to see, nor do I truthfully ever expect to see, well-worn copies of *Real Boys* and *Raising Cain* being toted and quoted at school by adolescent boys.) Being a "real boy" means that you just tough it out; telling someone about the pain you feel only magnifies it, since it proves you are weak—the very thing you were worried about in the first place. Instead, boys develop a mask of coolness—a facade of bravado, stoicism, and control—and a behavioral repertoire of defensive postures and aggressive orientations that deliver a clear message of imperviousness to other boys: "Don't mess with me, I've got what it takes." Moreover, boys typically face these gender conformity pressures at earlier ages than do girls, often by early elementary school age or even before. (A father called me just last week to say that he knew it was OK for his fifteen-month-old son to prefer playing with dolls instead of cars and trucks, but did *I really* think it was *really* OK?)

The ones who can't muster the "right" facade—in other words, who can't sufficiently hide or disguise their very human and very normal vulnerabilities—pay dearly. They become the targets of unrelenting teasing, taunting, and retaliation for having done the unforgivable: for breaking what Pollack calls the unspoken "Boy Code" of invulnerability. According to Kindlon and Thompson, however, *all* boys suffer deeply as a result of the destructive emotional training that our culture imposes on them, and virtually *all of them need help.*

Some of them are beyond help. Writing about the Columbine High School shootings, psychologists Jackson Katz and Sut Jhally argue that the experts who harp on the same tired old issues—accessibility of guns, media violence, inadequate adult supervision, peer group pressures—are missing the point. What the rash of school shootings reveals, they tell us, is not a youth problem or a violence problem, but a masculinity problem—which we will not solve until we recognize it as such. Only then will we understand the cultural forces that coalesce to produce hundreds of thousands of physically abusive and violent boys every year; only then can we begin to deconstruct the notion of violent masculinity as a cultural norm and a means of proving or maintaining manhood.

## The Gender Straightjacket
## Is a Unisex Garment

We should not be surprised that both our boys and our girls are in such emotional turmoil. It also no great surprise that so far our approach has been to look at boys' and girls' troubles separately—as if girls really are from Venus and boys really are from Mars, as if we needed to aim our telescopes in entirely different directions in order to see them each clearly. It is just another indication of how we have seen them (and ourselves) all along as separate, as different, even as opposite. But, might that not be the real problem here? What might happen to our children's troubles if we were to look at them as people first, and—oh, incidentally—as boys or girls second?

It is no coincidence that Pipher describes our girls, and Pollack, Kindlon, and Thompson describe our boys, as divided right down the middle of their very being into their "true" and "false" selves. This is the "sacrifice of wholeness" to which Miller refers, the bargain with their inner selves, which both boys and girls conclude they must make in order to pass the exacting and relentless gender exams administered by peer and media cultures. To pass—to be real boys—boys must sacrifice their "feminine" half; to succeed—to be acceptable girls—girls must separate themselves from their "masculinity." Young people take daily lessons from each other and from culture on how to become "opposites," on how to define themselves and each other by their differences. It is a waltz they learn to do together.

For every unspoken regulation in the Boy Code, there is an exact flip-sided Girl Code version, and neither set of rules can exist—or be changed—without the other.

Boys and girls are not opposites. They come into the world whole and alike in many, many more ways than they are distinct. Certainly there are inherited differences, and researchers have identified slight, measurable disparities—for example, in language development and spatial abilities—between the statistically average boy and the statistically average girl. But, other than reproductive capacity, in the words of psychiatrist Frank Pittman, author of *Man Enough,* there are truly not enough of these differences to make a gender out of. "Masculinity" and "femininity" are two artificially constructed halves of the same whole, and that whole is our common humanity. Our children are telling us that although exaggerating or highlighting these few distinctions may well have been functional in the past, they do not fit today's world. Our children want and need for us to allow them to be whole.

## Cultivating "Intelligent Resistance"

Pipher's "intelligent resistence" work with adolescent girls may be her most important gift to parents and teachers who want to help boys and girls remain whole. "It is what we cannot see that makes us sick," she teaches. For this reason, girls and boys must be helped to see the impact of society on their development and to understand the effect of culture in their lives. Once they do understand, she says, they can fight back, and their intelligent resistance will keep the "true self" alive.

Make no mistake, intelligent resistance is not about making boys and girls the same. Even if that were the goal, it would be impossible anyway. As discussed in Chapter 5, there are thousands of ways—primarily unconscious—in which newborn babies are nurtured differently according to gender. That is not about to change. No matter how much or in how many ways we alter our consciousness about gender, many real differences in style, interests, attributes, and abilities will undoubtedly continue to emerge (as well as many cross-gender overlaps, even when average differences are still apparent).

The real goal of intelligent resistence is to make everyone very different. Or rather, to *keep* everyone very different. If we raise children to know that their gender does not need to define arbitrarily who they must be like and who they must be different from, then they will be free to develop into their own totally distinct, totally unique, totally whole self. Not only will we begin to see boys and girls who allow themselves to be more alike, we will also see boys and girls who accept a greater range of differences among themselves. In other words, we may begin to see less diversity *between* the genders, but much more diversity *within* them. (If the rule is that boys and girls must be very different, then girls and girls, and boys and boys, must be the same.)

Remember, too, that some boys and girls seem to present themselves to the world as if they'd just spent nine months in the womb studying the traditional-gender-role handbook. We've all known parents who swear they've tried their best to be fairly, or even very, gender neutral in raising their kids, but their boys have just been "all boy," or their girls have been "all girl," practically since the day they were born. Who knows what the subtle influences in these babies' lives have been? But it should not surprise us that some children—boys determined to be adventurous or rough and tumble, girls who are very aware of pleasing or taking care of others—seem naturally to fit a more stereotypical mold.

According to Michael Gurian, author of *The Wonder of Boys* and *A Fine Young Man*, it would make perfect sense that many girls and boys are programmed genetically for propensities as good nurturers and able adventurers, since these attributes were once so necessary for survival. He believes that there most certainly are inborn differences, which he believes are hardwired into male and female brains, that we must value, honor, and nurture. Moreover, he worries that boys, especially, are being trained away from their basic nature, and that normal, inborn male characteristics and behaviors are increasingly being defined in pathological terms. He sees too many of us concluding that "if only boys could be more like girls," our problems with them would go away.

No matter where we might come down as parents on the nature-versus-nurture controversy (increasingly science will discover, I am convinced, that nature and nurture are intricately linked), the point is to respect, support, and normalize our children's natural proclivities, whatever they may be. Just as we should be wary of attempts to shoehorn our children into narrow, culturally defined stereotypes (especially the hypermasculine tough guy and the hyperfeminine, waiflike images depicted in the media), we should be equally vigilant about prejudicial attitudes toward anyone for whom traditional roles and behaviors are a good, healthy, and natural fit.

To be effective, we adults need to educate ourselves in the art and skill of intelligent resistence and other counter-culture tactics and then teach them to our children. That in itself is a difficult and revolutionary concept. Throughout most of history, one of the primary roles of adults has been to socialize children *into* the ways of culture. When it comes to gender, ironically, our role as parents and teachers is to steer them away and even to protect them *from* culture, in at least two ways. First, we must actively challenge endemic cultural myths about the basic nature of sex and gender, and second, we must raise children's consciousness about the unhealthy ways in which popular and peer culture continuously play on these fallacies. The rest of this chapter describes some important places to start.

*Understand the distinctions between biological gender, gender roles, gender identity, and sexual orientation.* Remember that if sexuality is the most fundamental part of identity, and if identity is the central psychosocial task of adolescence, then having a clear understanding of the components of gender is vital for healthy development. It's important for all adults to firmly grasp these distinctions so that they can correct the many misconceptions to which children are exposed. (There will be suggestions later on how to communicate about these topics in age-appropriate ways.) A helpful way to remember how they differ is to recall that biological gender is something that people *have;* gender roles are primarily learned and are *performed;* gender identity develops from within and is *experienced;* and sexual orientation concerns the gender of the person (same, different, both) to whom an individual is sexually, affectionately, and romantically *attracted.*

*Make sure that young people are aware that sexual orientation and gender roles are entirely different elements of a person's sexual and gender makeup.* Confusion between the issues of sexual orientation and gender roles is omnipresent in the lives of children and adolescents. As concepts, they are not even in the same ballpark or the same section of the produce department: Biological gender (apples), gender roles (oranges), and gender identity (pears) are *gender* issues, whereas sexual orientation (celery) is a *sexual* issue. The false connection between gender roles and sexual orientation is made by children when they are quite young—as we have said, whenever they begin to police one another for stepping outside traditional gender roles, by calling each other "gay." Since, at the same time, they are also clearly sending the message that gay is "bad," they give and receive a very effective double dose of gender-role dogma: First, acting like the other gender means that you are gay, and second, being gay or even perceived as gay is social suicide. As a result, boys especially begin to feel that they must hide—and maybe even psychologically wall off entirely—what they think of as their "feminine" parts. Without intelligent adult resistence, this dynamic will become a powerful and far-reaching lesson in what Kindlon and Thompson call the "emotional miseducation" of boys (and ultimately girls, because girls will become misled about the true emotional range of boys).

*Strike the phrase "opposite sex" from your vocabulary.* As shown in Chapter 3, language is not only a communicator of thought, but also a major conditioner of thought. Every time we repeat certain words or phrases concerning sex and gender ("opposite sex" certainly being one of them), we inadvertently teach and reinforce certain very specific culturally based values, attitudes, and assumptions. Therefore, changing our language to reflect more accurately what we really think about gender whenever we talk about it—for example, by saying something like the "other gender" rather than "opposite sex"—is a direct and powerful way of changing culture, at least within our children's immediate world. It is also a way of speaking that directly contradicts basic beliefs underlying the need for boy-versus-girl codes of gender behavior.

*Help young people understand the difference between gender and sexual diversity, and sexual "deviancy" or "perversion."* Throughout history and across cultures, a broad range of sexual and gender diversity has existed, and there have always been sexual and gender minorities. This diversity persists all over the world today. In educating our children about human sexuality, we have two choices: We can accentuate how different *we* are from *them*—perhaps even labeling *them* as sick, immoral, deviant, perverts, or freaks—or we can emphasize instead our common humanity and remember that complexity and diversity are inherent in being human. If we choose the latter, does that mean that everything is OK, that down the road we will begin to accept all forms of "deviant" or "perverted" gender and sexual expression? Of course not. True deviancy or perversion—meaning deviancy from, or perversion of, the core human values that must remain firmly at the base of a just and caring society—can never be tolerated, let alone accepted. Rape, sexual exploitation, child molestation, pedophilia, and child pornography are not forms of sexual or gender diversity, but failures of human decency. And, one's capacity for decency—

or indecency—does not reside in one's particular body parts, sexual orientation, or gender identity.

*Teach children directly about the intellectual concept of social roles.* By the time they are three or four, children are very aware that human interactions are governed by roles, or rules, of social conduct. Just as children learn most of the rules of language through observation of and participation in speaking, they learn innumerable social rules simply by observing and participating in relating. As they grow older, we help them realize what they already know and will need to know about language through formal teaching in schools and teachable moments at home. We can (and should) also take the time to help young people understand just as explicitly the concept of social rules and roles—particularly about gender. This kind of teaching is enormously empowering; it enables everyone to step back and realize that gender roles are not inevitable or immutable, but are primarily learned. With this in mind, people can reevaluate and, when appropriate, change these roles and choose whether to enact a particular role, or not.

*Model flexibility in your own attitudes toward gender roles.* The rate of change in our society has been breathtaking during the past fifty years, and we can assume that the pace will only quicken. As we prepare children and adolescents to assume their rightful adult roles in twenty-first-century United States, it behooves us to encourage them to develop an open attitude toward the unique capabilities of every individual, regardless of gender. Exposing young people to individuals whose vocational or other choices are nontraditional, and modeling an openness toward flexible rather than restrictive gender rules or roles (even though the roles we may assume at home or in the workplace are fairly traditional) is key.

*Raise children's awareness about the destructiveness of sexist and demeaning sexual labels.* Children and adolescents often use sexual language—fag, slut, wimp, ho, bitch, gay—that is either inherently sexist, heterosexist, or spoken in a demeaning way. All these words, especially as they are commonly used, perpetuate gender-based attitudes and beliefs that are unhealthy and even destructive. It is another example of how, unless adults intervene, young people are reinforced in buying into the toxicity of popular culture. Later chapters will provide many suggestions for helping adults feel comfortable and competent in addressing language issues with children and adolescents of all ages.

*Cultivate children's media literacy skills.* Adults must play the role of cultural interpreter in the lives of young people, helping them to translate and evaluate the unspoken media messages and images—not only about sex, but also about gender—with which they are practically bombarded hundreds of times a day. In my experience with middle and high school students, with even minimal effort from adults, teens and even preteens can become extremely sensitized to how they are being shamelessly manipulated as individuals and as consumers. Look to later chapters to provide tips on developing and passing on these media literacy skills.

*Explain that the way people express their gender is simply an extension of who they are, not a measure of their worth.* Gender is not a test or a contest. Our bodies, our gender identity, our sexual orientation, and the gender roles with which we are comfortable (or not) are expressions of who we are, not measures of how much we are worth. We cannot fail at gender—either individually or comparatively—any more than we can fail at race, nationality, ethnicity, or religious affiliation. We simply are who we are. Adults can help inoculate children and adolescents against the pressures to be the "right" kind of boy or girl by demystifying and deconstructing the American commercial myth that one can become—and at all cost, literally, should aspire to become—a "perfectly gendered" male or female person. At the very least, we can teach them to understand that this impossible and fraudulent pursuit of just the right look, just the right personality, just the right traits is merely an artificial fabrication. They may not be able to change the rules of the game all by themselves, and they may even play by them when necessary for the sake of social expediency, but they'll know deep down that that isn't who they really are.

*Remind children at every opportunity that all girls are real girls, and all boys are real boys.* Once, so that I could see more easily where everyone was sitting and then reseat them in a more gender-balanced arrangement, I said to a class of middle school kids, "Please raise your hand if you are a boy." The effect on the class was swift, dramatic, and contagious. Almost all the boys looked instantly uncomfortable. Three of them pointed at two others mockingly, as if to say, "What's *your* hand doing up?" Two more singled out a third and just laughed; another kept putting his hand up and down, up and down, not wanting to commit himself until he saw what the other boys would have to say. The level of threat was unbelievable, and all I had done was ask them to identify themselves as being what they—and everyone else in the room—already knew themselves to be. It took me a while to figure out what was going on. I even repeated the question in two or three more classes to see if the effect would be the same; it was. These boys were under relentless pressure from each other about whether they could measure up, about whether they were "real" boys, about whether they had sufficiently proven their masculinity (they were twelve). Where and how did they learn this? I thought. What an unbearable emotional drain and burden it must be, just to be in the same building with one another, day after day after day. How very much we could accomplish by making sure that we confer on all our boys—and all our girls—the simple truth that they of course are already real, already OK, and already worthy, and that there is nothing whatsoever to prove.

# Partnership: Families and Schools Working Together

The first time I ever saw the word *masturbation* in print, I was a junior in college. I read it in a chapter on Freud in my abnormal psychology book.

I honestly don't remember if I previously had ever heard the word spoken, or if I had, whether I had any notion at all of its meaning. What little I then knew about sexuality I had gleaned from reading between the lines in my family's medical dictionary, or between the sheets, by flashlight, from a thumb-worn copy of the novel *Peyton Place* that belonged to the older girl up the street, which she had gotten from the girl around the corner.

The world in which I now work is light-years away from the world in which I grew up. I teach in settings, all in the private sector, where educators are encouraged, if not required, to deal forthrightly with sensitive and controversial subjects, including sexuality. A middle school textbook that I have used since 1978, for example, contains an entire chapter on the topic of masturbation.

In 1994, it was my elder son who was the junior in college. The product of a fairly restrictive public education and a witness to the controversies, sometimes vicious and ugly, that swirl just outside the seemingly safe periphery of my work, he called me late one Friday night from his dorm. He had just heard on the radio a verbatim, bleep-free recording of a conversation on the topic of masturbation between then–U.S. Surgeon General, Dr. Joycelyn Elders, and a reporter at a medical conference. Widely recognized for advocating honesty and forthrightness with young people about sexuality—and in some circles, widely vilified—she was fast becoming a serious political liability. President Clinton was furious at this most recent example of characteristic openness, although her statement on masturbation was mild by comparison to many earlier commentaries. He had taken the opportunity to ask for her resignation.

There was urgency and apprehension in my son's voice. How upset was I? How might the firing of the outspoken surgeon general and its implications affect me and my work? How did I feel about this escalating trend toward censorship and repression? What was I going to do?

"Not to worry," I said, with deep satisfaction and great expectation. "I have a feeling it's going to be a *wonderful* week."

I was not to be disappointed.

The next morning, the Elders story was in every daily I was able to get my hands on; by evening, it was the lead comedy routine on *Saturday Night Live*. Sunday's clippings were sticking every which way out of my mailbox when I arrived at school on Monday, with thoughtful notes from teachers and administrators who had saved them. By Tuesday, the newspaper editorials—conservative and liberal, pro and con, irreverent and solemn—were everywhere. A minor setback occurred midweek (alas, no cover story on *Time* or *Newsweek*), but by the weekend, right on schedule, the best of the best of the political cartoons were being reprinted.

I was in heaven.

I couldn't wait to get to class that first Monday morning after the Friday before. "Hi, everybody!" I almost shouted, waiting in the hallway and practically bursting with anticipation and unending questions. "Do you know about Doctor Elders? What did you hear? What have you read? What do you think? Did you have any interesting conversations about it with anyone? How about your parents? What did they think?"

We shared and compared, analyzed and argued. The more we talked, the less we were sure that we really knew all the facts.

More information, please, that's what we needed! By Thursday, we had collected mounds of newspaper articles, opinion pieces, and snippets of TV and radio news reports.

As we considered each, interesting side topics and questions kept distracting us. Who is the surgeon general, anyway, and what does it mean to have a bully pulpit? Why do they keep referring to Elders as the Condom Queen? What *is* a condom queen? And the guy before her—C. Everett Koop—he was controversial, too, right? Why was that? Tell us, what *was* the AIDS epidemic like (way back) in those early days? And by the way, what were those other opinions that Elders had expressed that made everybody so mad, which the articles keep mentioning? Really? She said *that* about *drugs*? What *is* the difference between legalization and decriminalization? Do you think clean needle exchange is a good idea or a bad idea? And so on and so on.

Soon enough, what really caught our notice was not the incident itself, but what was being spoken, written, and asserted about it. Perplexity and skepticism quickly set in: what to do about all the varying interpretations—not just about what Elders had *meant*, but even about what she had *said*. How can you know which interpretation is the right one? the students fretted, and how much can you really believe about *anything* you have just read? And what about the politics and the timing of the thing? Surely, this comment wasn't as bad as some of the earlier ones. Why did this happen *now*?

And, of course, interspersed throughout were all kinds of questions and conversations about the topic of masturbation: what it is, why people do it, why it's been such a taboo subject in our society, and why some people think it's better not to talk about it in school at all. (Since we in fact were talking about it, in a school, at that very moment, we stopped to debate that point too!)

We shared laughter about the myths that people once believed about its consequences (blindness, insanity, pimples, hairy palms, and the like), and shared relief that we are all lucky enough to be living in a more enlightened age. We discussed modern medical opinion that masturbation is healthy for people to do or not do, as they wish. And, medical knowledge aside, we acknowledged respectfully that because of deeply held personal, family, or religious values, some people believe that masturbation is morally wrong or at the very least inappropriate. We agreed that parents and other trusted adults would be good people to consult if students had further questions, feelings, or concerns.

Girls and boys in one seventh-grade section were asked to pen letters to the editor expressing their views on some aspect of the Elders story. Wrote one outraged student, "Elders didn't even bring up the topic! Someone else posed the question! I know she was warned by the White House to keep down the rhetoric, but everything she said was the truth. I don't see why Clinton fired her. She did nothing wrong." Cool, practical reasoning moved another student: "Mr. Clinton fired her because she went against what he said. You don't do what the boss says not to." Still another argued, "I do not think Joycelyn Elders is a good Surgeon General. She has stated things in ways that hurt other people. She has been pushing her luck too much. I am glad Clinton fired her, but the fact that she was fired for speaking about masturbation was not good."

Having read a provocative piece in the *Wall Street Journal,* another student contemplated that "Dr. Elders was an African-American appointee who happened to have very strong opinions and was not afraid to express them." Maybe Mr. Clinton did do the right *thing,* she allowed. "But did he have the right *reasoning?*"

Even Elders herself would not have known whether to laugh or cry. We had just spent an entire week using her own story to prove the very point over which she had just lost her job—that education works.

I was so proud and so excited to share the students' good thinking and good work at a training workshop I was to teach the following week. I especially wanted to tell the teachers how well the newspaper had served as an educational tool and how well the topic of sexuality had served to spark interest in newspaper reading.

Regrettably, the details of the lessons were soon lost, made irrelevant at once by the reaction of the teachers present: They were absolutely incredulous about the openness my students and I are permitted, utterly stunned by the conversations I described. As for incorporating the newspaper into their instruction, that was simply out of the question. Only material approved by county administrators the previous summer was permitted for use in their classrooms. I was sad and angry—for them and for their students—and sorry that I had only contributed to their frustration.

"What about the parents?" they eventually demanded to know. "Didn't they call? Weren't they upset?"

"No," I told them, by this time, almost sheepishly. "That was the very best part!"

All week long, at the spontaneous invitation of their children (it had not been required), fathers and mothers had helped to gather information and to find articles. They had answered questions and had discussed the issues. They had expressed honestly and openly their feelings, values, and opinions. I actually had not heard this directly from any of the parents. But it was easy to know how much they had been involved, because their thoughts and ideas cropped up everywhere in my classrooms. The trust that we place in one another, and our partnership in the education of their children, is most often simply taken for granted.

These are parents committed to literacy of all kinds, including sexual literacy. They believe that the more often their children are afforded opportunities to learn, hear, think, reason, read, communicate, share, and write about topics like sexuality, the more likely they will understand and manage their decisions, their relationships, and their lives in healthy, caring, and ethical ways.

To paraphrase the wise old proverb, they are also parents who believe that it takes a whole community to raise a sexually healthy child. And that it especially takes families and schools working together.

I called back my son at college to report that it had been a very good week, indeed.

## Too Controversial for Schools to Handle?

The incredulity of the teachers in my workshop, especially toward the openness in my classroom and the accepting parental reaction I described, disturbs me to this day. The perception that sexuality education is simply too controversial for schools to handle has obscured an important truth: In reality, parents are hardly ever opposed or even mildly resistant to school-based sexuality education. This sweeping parental support should not really surprise, since national polls have confirmed year after year for decades that the vast majority of American adults overwhelmingly favor comprehensive sexuality education in schools. However, it should confuse: Why, then, is the public perception otherwise? Why isn't comprehensive education in schools the norm across the nation? If parents approve, if the need is great, if programs are sound, and if students are responsive, why isn't it happening?

This was the enigma that grabbed me back in the 1970s, the illogic of it all simply too beguiling and important a challenge to ignore. Today, unbelievably, as we have entered a new millennium—and decades into the HIV epidemic—we're really no further along and in many ways, are farther behind.

## The Impact of the Religious Right

Of course, the cultural and religious forces that have coalesced beginning in the late 1970s to halt the progress of sexuality education in our schools make the riddle partially understandable, at least from a political perspective. During this time, the Religious Right has been enormously successful in projecting its particular view of sex—abstinence before marriage for all people, abstinence-only education for all schools—as the one, morally correct view. Moreover, by sheer single-mindedness, the Religious Right have been able to maintain public focus and attention almost exclusively on the issue's moral aspects (as this group defines them), thereby nearly subverting totally the health and social science levels of the debate. By shrewd, organized, tenacious, and often fierce targeting of individual school districts and sometimes individual schoolteachers, these "one issue" zealots, typically representing only a small minority of citizens, have time and time again frightened schools and communities away from finding a more appropriate, middle-ground approach.

In these ways, not only have groups aligned with the Religious Right succeeded unilaterally in limiting and controlling the terms of the public discourse, but they have managed, remarkably, to foreclose it altogether. By insisting that a truly moral person knows there's only one right position to take anyway, they project the view that there is nothing really of substance to discuss. By default, then, anyone who sincerely and legitimately disagrees runs the risk of becoming painted as immoral, amoral, or antireligion at worst and misguided at best.

The beliefs and tactics of the Religious Right, however, only partially explain its lock on this issue. After all, balanced, informed, and articulate voices are being heard loudly from all fronts on other stock concerns of the Right—homosexuality, abortion, euthanasia, school prayer, school vouchers. Sometimes a more liberal view prevails, sometimes a more conservative. But when the subject is sex education, I hear only the same tired, old arguments and the same lack of any genuine dialogue that I have heard for decades, despite a mind-boggling pace of social change. (I even heard them implied just the other day in the questions asked by a twelve-year-old in New England, who called me for help in researching her eighth-grade speech on sex education in schools.) The culture appears virtually incapable of movement, growth or even any kind of productive debate. We are simply stuck.

## Freeing Ourselves as a Culture to Meet Real Developmental Need

The tenacity of the Religious Right only partially explains the stalled movement toward more comprehensive sexuality education in a country that consistently and overwhelmingly professes to value it. Woefully undereducated ourselves about the process and even the subject matter itself, we may possess the will, but we lack the know-how. We may not like the watered-down programs our children are left with, but not knowing with what or how to replace them, we continue to support the current alternatives by default.

Freeing ourselves as a culture to embrace a more rational and sophisticated approach to sexuality education begins with an acknowledgment and understanding of the principles laid out in the previous six chapters:

1. Children, in ways that we have not previously accepted or understood, are capable and deserving of more education at earlier ages. Sexual knowledge is not dangerous, but empowering, and empowerment through education is far better than control through fear and ignorance.
2. Sex is far more than intercourse, sexuality is far more than sex, and sexuality education is far more than "intercourse education."
3. Sexual values and value systems in the United States are exceedingly complex. Parents and teachers must be constantly attentive and involved with young people in ongoing moral and ethical dialogue.
4. Sexuality education is not a didactic exercise, but a lifelong process in which virtually everyone participates. Families and schools, working in partnership, are the most important catalysts and allies in supporting healthy growth and development.

To succeed, any attempt at rebuilding or even reconsidering the programs in U.S. schools will require a firm and uncompromising commitment to these ideas. We'll revisit them here, with an emphasis on school-based settings.

## Age Appropriateness:
## Not Too Much, but Not Too Little

A few years ago, I was invited to make a presentation to the entire fifth-grade class at a large public elementary school. Since I had worked with parent groups at this school for many years, I was proud and pleased that they had asked me to spend time with their children.

A near fatal glitch occurred, however, when one of the school administrators called to prep me for the program. "We're really very glad you're coming," she explained, "but we need to let you know that while you are here in the building, there are three words you can't say."

"OK, let's have them," I said, as I held my breath.

"The words you can't say are *intercourse, fertilization,* and, of course, *sex.*"

"I can't even say the word *sex*? But I'm the Sex Lady. That's what all the kids usually call me. Heck, that's what their *parents* call me!"

"We're sorry," the administrator said, "but the county guidelines are very clear. The fifth-grade program is about puberty, adolescence, growing up, wet dreams, and periods—period. We're not allowed to change or add anything at all."

"So I *can* mention sperm and eggs, and penises and vaginas, right? I just *can't* talk about how the two get together, as in fertilization or sex or intercourse?"

"Right."

"But I know these are bright kids, and it's a very big class. Surely, one student or another will wonder how on earth the sperm and egg come together to create a new life, and they'll think to ask me a question about it."

"In a case like that, there are a couple of things you can do. You can say that that is not a topic we are permitted to discuss in this grade." (Teachers can answer questions about sex, intercourse, or fertilization later, in the sixth grade, the administrator told me, but they can't bring up the concepts directly until eighth grade.) She added, "Then you can encourage the student to go home and ask her or his parent about the information they want."

"I'm really sorry, but I don't think I can take on this teaching assignment," I said. "As an educator, I just don't think I can put myself in a position where I might have to tell a child that a perfectly intelligent, honest, and developmentally right-on question can't be asked and answered in a school building. After all, these are questions that six-year-olds are known to ask, let alone sixth-graders! No matter what else I might try to teach them, that's what I'm afraid they'll remember.

"Most of all, I don't want them to think that the immediate and most trusted adults in their lives—including, and especially, their teachers—aren't available to them for teaching."

The compromise the school came up with was a good one, and as it ended up, I was happy to do the program. A letter went home saying that a guest speaker would be at school expressly to review and directly support the approved fifth-grade curriculum, *and* that students would be free to bring up additional or related topics or questions for discussion or clarification, even those not specifically designated in the curriculum. Any parent who did not wish his or her child to participate was free to ask that the child be excused (none did). The letter went on to say, "Our children are growing up and entering a complex and confusing world. We want to do as much as we possibly can to prepare them before they leave us and go off to middle school. We hope you will encourage your child to participate."

## Whose Needs Are We Really Meeting?

As adults, we must be willing to ask ourselves what we are *really* teaching and communicating when we make decisions about school curricula. If we use a film or assign a reading without setting the proper climate for discussion with students afterward, are we communicating that we are just too plain embarrassed to talk to them about the subject? If we separate boys and girls for sex ed, are we telling them that we think they are entirely different creatures or that they can't—or shouldn't—learn about or talk about these things with each other? If we ask for permission slips from parents *only* about this topic, are we implying that sexuality might not be OK to learn about, or that there might be something inherently wrong or dangerous about the process of sexual learning? Or are we communicating that as educators, it is *we* who are not sure of what is OK and not OK to teach or learn?

Worse yet, if we tell children that we can't answer their personal or individual questions, because we're not allowed to answer them (either not yet or, in some schools, not ever), do we give the message that there is something wrong with them for being so "advanced" or for wanting to know about such officially forbidden or "bad" topics? And, if the most immediate, caring, and trusted adults in their lives project silence about this topic, while so many other adults—perfect strangers with nothing but crass, commercial interest—can't wait to get their attention about sex through the media, what exactly does that teach?

It is totally appropriate and essential for parents to be completely informed about the topics and approaches their children will experience in the classroom. Most importantly, parents should be encouraged to become involved in the dialogue with them. But everyone—parents and teachers—must become better educated and work much harder together to reach agreement about what is truly developmentally and culturally age-appropriate for children and adolescents, especially in the reality of today's world. If we can't all totally agree, for our children's sake, I would certainly vote for us to come down on the side of comprehensiveness. We could then make alternate provisions for the minority of parents who want less, not more (we've pretty much done the opposite to date, attempting to accommodate those who want less, at the expense of those who want more). Otherwise, we will continue to give destructive, mixed, and unintended messages about the importance, appropriateness, and meaning of sexual learning.

We must also be honest with ourselves about the evasions and miscalculations of the past. The school district mentioned earlier, for example, one of the largest in the United States, is *six to eight years* out of sync with real developmental need, according to the normal timetable of questions that young children typically ask. Imagine the howl and cry if the district were that far off the mark in the teaching of math! Whatever the causes of our missteps—ignorance, denial, embarrassment, discomfort, or the understandable desire to avoid unpleasant confrontations or community controversy—it has been the needs of adults, not children and adolescents, that have most often determined our curricular choices. Those of us involved in education must constantly ask ourselves, Do our programs *truly* meet expressed and observed developmental need, or do we teach what we teach because we are most comfortable with it or least afraid to teach it?

Too often the answer is the latter. How did we become so out of step?

## Is It Sex Education or No-Sex Education?

School-based sexuality education is by no means a new concept. As early as the late 1800s, mainstream organizations such as the YMCA, YWCA, the Child Study Association, the National Education Association, and the National Congress of Parents and Teachers began making the case for school-based teaching. During the first half of the twentieth century, the federal government, through several national publications and dozens of regional U.S. Public Health Service conferences, advocated strongly for sexuality instruction, as did participants in White House Conferences on Child Welfare in 1919 and 1930, and the Mid-Century White House Conference on Children and Youth in 1950.

A Joint Committee of the National Education Association and the American Medical Association furthered the cause of public instruction significantly in 1955, when it published and widely distributed five pamphlets designed to assist adults in understanding sexuality education. At about the same time, the American School Health Association launched a nationwide family life education program. Many of these pioneering organizations, even early on, supported a comprehensive approach to teaching about sexuality, that is, one not just biologically but also psychologically and humanistically oriented.

Despite escalating support for public instruction over several decades, there were, of course, always individuals who opposed school-based programs for a variety of personal and religious reasons. By the mid-twentieth century, however, the growing visibility and acceptability of sexuality education prompted some groups of opponents to organize themselves politically. They began systematically attacking local schools and school districts. Calling attention to themselves and their cause with provocative and moralistic acronyms, such as MOMS (Mothers Organized for Moral Stability), POSSE (Parents Opposed to Sex and Sensitivity Education), and CHIDE (Committee to Halt Indoctrination and Demoralization in Education), they began openly characterizing sex education as a conspiratorial scheme designed to "demoralize youth, divide parents from children, and increase sexual activity among adolescents." (These same charges are often leveled against school-based programs today.) In their view, since sex was an adult marital behavior, school-age children needed little in the way of preparation. Furthermore, they argued, whatever education was required belonged in the home and in religious settings, most definitely not in schools.

Successful through the 1970s at keeping many school districts on the defensive, these kinds of groups were able to create and maintain the image of sex education as potentially suspect and highly controversial. (On the contrary, studies for decades have demonstrated an approval rating for sexuality education of at least 85 percent.) As a result of their success, these groups found themselves unexpectedly well positioned to take an active role in the shaping of school-based sex education in post-AIDS United States.

Capitalizing on the fear of this terrible disease and the feelings of help-lessness and confusion it engendered, they judiciously shifted their focus in the early days of the epidemic from keeping sex education out of the schools entirely to a new single-minded purpose: instituting abstinence-only sex education throughout the country. Several highly sophisticated and nationally recognized groups—such as Concerned Women for America, the Eagle Forum, Focus on the Family, the American Life League, and the Family Research Council—have since worked tirelessly to promote public school use of highly restrictive (and according to many experts, highly biased factually) abstinence-only curricula, most developed by organizations associated with the Religious Right. Given the religious affiliation of many of these groups, it is only fair to wonder whether the fundamental concern here is truly abstinence education in the service of preventing disease and pregnancy or chastity education in the service of imposing religious doctrine. (There is nothing wrong with chastity education in a religious-based setting; as a disguised goal in a public school setting, it is disingenuous and a violation of the separation of church and state.)

The push toward abstinence-only education received a huge boost in 1996, when a rider to the Welfare Reform Act passed by Congress and signed by President Clinton allocated $250 million to fund abstinence-only programs throughout the country over a five-year period. Programs accepting these grants were compelled to teach the following: that "abstinence from sexual activity outside marriage is the expected standard for school-age children," that "a mutually faithful monogamous relationship in the context of marriage is the expected standard of human sexual activity," and that "sexual activity outside the context of marriage is likely to have harmful psychological and physical effects." In addition, grantees were required to prohibit the teaching of contraception, except for information limited to its risks, disadvantages, or ineffectiveness.

In late 1999, both the Alan Guttmacher Institute and the Kaiser Family Foundation published national data regarding the extent of abstinence-only education in the United States. According to their findings, 14 percent of public school districts actually have no formal policy regarding the teaching of sexuality education; 45 percent have programs that include information about abstinence *and* contraception; and nearly a third require the teaching of abstinence-only lessons. Only 9 percent of all U.S. secondary students attend school in districts where there is comprehensive sexuality programming, that is, in which both abstinence and contraception are presented as important topics among many others, in a broad educational approach designed to support adolescents in becoming sexually healthy adults. Significantly, these data were collected prior to the availability of federal funding for abstinence-only programming and therefore do not reflect its anticipated and considerable impact.

## What's Wrong with Abstinence-Only Sex Education?

That abstinence from sexual intercourse is the safest strategy for avoiding exposure to unwanted pregnancy and disease (in addition to abstinence from oral and anal intercourse for preventing sexually transmitted disease) is indisputable. All people, young and old, must know and fully comprehend this reality.

However, it is not the only important reality to contemplate. Consider the following additional realities:

- Although the logic of the abstinence-only approach is clear—if no intercourse occurs, pregnancy and disease can be avoided—*more than half of teenagers attending schools in the United States right now have already had sexual intercourse.* By the time they reach the age of twenty, 80 percent of boys and 76 percent of girls have engaged in this behavior. No educational program, no matter how effectively delivered, is likely to significantly reverse this entrenched and long-standing behavioral pattern (the rates of sexual behavior among teenagers and unmarried adults began to increase in the 1970s), at least not anytime in the near future. Therefore—by default—schools that adopt abstinence-only programming *immediately place millions of American teenagers at additional and unnecessary health risk, by denying critical prevention information.*

- In the middle of the nineteenth century, young people reached puberty at the average age of sixteen, near the age at which they were also likely to marry. Today, the average age of puberty for girls is twelve and a half, and for boys, thirteen and a half, whereas the average age of marriage is in the mid-twenties. Moreover, teenagers today have less adult supervision and more freedom and mobility than ever before. An abstinence-only approach requires a delay of intercourse ten or more years beyond biological maturity, an outcome that is contrary to practice in virtually all societies—unless there is a strict tradition segregating unmarried males and females and chaperoning women. Developmentally sound programming must take into account these hugely important societal and biological realities.

- There are absolutely no studies in the professional literature demonstrating the efficacy of abstinence-only education (despite glowing promises and predictions by its proponents). Quite to the contrary, a comprehensive review of thirty-five controlled studies, conducted by the World Health Organization, documented that the most effective programs address a combination of topics: abstinence, contraception, and methods of STD prevention. For example, students educated in these types of combination programs are more likely to delay the onset of first intercourse and to use protection more consistently and effectively when they do become involved.

- There is no documentation whatsoever that a comprehensive approach to sexuality education encourages teenagers either to engage in sexual intercourse or to increase its frequency. Promoters of abstinence-only education often characterize programs that include information about contraception as directly promoting teenage sexual activity, thereby attempting to create the unfair, false, and dangerous perception that prevention information is harmful.

- More than 74 million American adults are presently unmarried. The majority of these individuals report that they have experienced intercourse during the last twelve months (approximately three-quarters of the men and two-thirds of the women).

- There is no available data to support the assertion that sexual activity outside of marriage is likely to have harmful psychological and physical effects. To the contrary, the majority of American adults have engaged in sexual intercourse prior to marriage (fewer than 7 percent of men and 20 percent of women aged eighteen to fifty-nine report that they were virgins when they were married), with no proven inherent or universally negative effects.

- Some abstinence-only curricula mention contraception, but only in the most negative of terms. Health experts warn that this distorted approach may backfire dangerously, by discouraging teenagers at risk of pregnancy or disease from using forms of protection that they have been led to believe are ineffective.
- More than 80 percent of U.S. adults believe that young people should be given information about abstinence and methods of preventing sexually transmitted infections and pregnancy.

It is no wonder, as the Sexuality Information and Education Council of the United States has warned and as the 1997 National Institutes of Health's Consensus Panel on AIDS concluded, that the abstinence-only approach "places policy in direct conflict with science and ignores over-whelming evidence that other programs [are] effective." Even more ironic, an approach that so stunningly ignores the realities of everyday life will likely invite the disrespect of many of the young people it purports to help; tragically, some will decide to discount adults entirely as credible sources of information and advice.

## Deep Flaws Conceptually

Unquestionably, many people, for personal or religious reasons, sincerely disapprove of sexual intercourse outside the context of marriage, and their views are to be heard and given unqualified respect. Moreover, the major-ity of adults would likely advise young people to delay sexual intercourse if not until marriage, at least until they have reached an adult level of ma-turity. Strong proponents of abstinence, by helping to validate a decision that flies directly in the face of popular culture, have helped many young people realize that as teenagers or even as unmarried adults, they do have a real choice about whether to become involved in sexual intercourse.

However, abstinence-only curricula go way beyond consciousness raising or sound, sincere advice giving: *They have at their foundation the implicit goal of denying at-risk adolescents potentially life-altering, if not lifesaving in-formation.* In the context of contemporary American society, this tactic is not only exquisitely ironic, but as many would argue, morally indefensible. After all, it is adults who have created or who tacitly support the sexually obsessed culture in which we live, a culture that overtly encourages, even di-rectly entices, young people to become sexual and sexualized at every turn.

Now the same adult community—from the federal government on down—is attempting to enforce on young people an ineffective and unrealistic educational standard and an absolute behavioral code that they themselves clearly (and hypocritically) reject in their own personal lives.

The abstinence-only approach also lacks academic integrity and rigorous intellectual thought. Sexual abstinence is a complex behavioral concept involving multiple religious, moral, health, and developmental aspects. Rarely are these distinct layers of the abstinence question adequately clarified or even articulated in deliberations or public controversies regarding school-based curricula. Policymakers need to train themselves to ask: Why are we choosing abstinence as our goal, and should it be our only goal? What are the various and distinct arguments favoring abstinence? Which of these possible arguments do we wish to make to our students, which do we think are appropriate for our educational setting, and how should they be framed?

The various arguments in favor of abstinence are based on important developmental, medical, moral, and religious concerns, but the arguments for each are not one and the same. In fact, unless these positions are presented carefully and distinctly, they may have the unintended and negative effect of seeming to contradict or undermine one another.

A developmental-based argument might caution, for example, "Wait until you have reached an adult level of maturity before even considering this behavior," whereas a safety argument might warn, "Do not participate unless appropriate precautions are taken." A moral take on the question might be, "This behavior is wrong, unless and until certain ethical criteria are met," and a religious one, "First and foremost, in the eyes of God, the couple must be married."

Just as being married does not guarantee safety, physical safety does not require a marriage certificate. Likewise, unmarried adults—some of whom may even consider themselves very moral or religious people—make sexual choices without feeling the need to consult religious doctrine. And, although adults can and do make immoral decisions, many teenagers are capable of courage, sensitivity, and wisdom well beyond their years.

Older teenagers especially are quite capable of identifying these kinds of subtle contrasts and discrepancies, and they deserve an honest and nuanced presentation of facts and concepts. Otherwise, we run the risk of losing our credibility entirely, as a direct result of our sloppy thinking.

Suppose, for example, that we have made the statement "The only safe sex is no sex or marital sex." As soon as they learn or figure out the real truth—that in the real world, not all marital sex is monogamous, not all monogamous sex is marital, and not all sex is intercourse—where have we left them? (More on how to talk about these issues effectively with your children in later chapters.)

Parents, too, should be able to expect an equally high level of sophistication. For some, especially those whose religious beliefs teach them very specifically that premarital sexual intercourse is an affront to God's laws, there can be no such thing as "safe sex" under any circumstances outside of holy matrimony. To them, therefore, the moral, religious, developmental, and medical reasons for remaining abstinent—or more accurately, for remaining chaste—constitute one and the same argument and, within their frame of reference, rightly and logically so. Schools should have the freedom and flexibility to acknowledge the great importance of religion in determining sexual mores for many people, and teachers should be encouraged and trained to explain clearly and nonjudgmentally that many families consider religious values essential to right decision making. Religiously observant parents should be able to expect that, in this way, schools will lend support to the legitimacy of their beliefs.

However, for many if not most other American families, these various levels of concern are not so easily aligned and deserve adequate differentiation, exploration, and consideration by policymakers and curriculum writers. For a considerable number of parents, for example, sexual morality is not defined by a particular scriptural interpretation—and perhaps not by any one particular religious conviction at all—but by personal and contextual moral values, such as the fundamental concepts of respect and responsibility. What they hope for in a sexuality education program is that schools will provide ongoing support and reinforcement of these core values as guiding principles in their children's lives. To other parents, health and developmental readiness are the important, overriding concerns in matters involving sexual decision making. They recognize and accept that sexual expression in some form is an inevitable—as well as a positive and healthy—part of their children's lives, and they look to schools for help in making sure that students have the tools to make those decisions as maturely and carefully as possible.

For these families, postponement, maturity, safety, self-awareness, relationship skills, and personal integrity, rather than abstinence or chastity, are the ultimate concerns. These adults may well value abstinence as a goal, particularly during adolescence, but as a means—temporarily, at least—to health and happiness, not as an end in itself. Programs that emphasize, or focus exclusively on, abstinence and chastity as the ultimate and only goals not only deny students important factual information, but also deny them support in making the kinds of decisions that are in concert with their own family's values and goals. Moreover, since the concept of abstinence in these programs often refers not only to sexual intercourse but to all forms of sexual expression beyond kissing or hugging, students are also denied important opportunities to think through their responsibilities in relation to other sexual experiences in which they may become involved.

A final concern conceptually about abstinence-only education relates to how it informs and reinforces a narrow, genitally based understanding of sexuality and sexuality education. As discussed in earlier chapters, sexuality as a concept and sexuality education as a discipline are infinitely more complex than issues concerning genital behavior. The notion of sexuality as a fundamental component of human identity—encompassing broad-based issues of health and safety, attitudes and values, human development, intimacy, sensuality, and gender—has been totally dwarfed by the push for abstinence education over the past decade.

Indeed, even in the current professional health education literature, sexuality curricula are most commonly categorized as either comprehensive (containing information about abstinence *and* contraception) or abstinence-only, thereby giving the narrowest possible meaning to the word *comprehensive*. In truth, neither of these approaches is sexuality education at all, but rather "sex (or no-sex) education." Calling either sexuality education is like saying that the history of the state of Pennsylvania is equivalent to the history of the United States, or confusing an apple with the whole produce department. The two subject matters are simply not the same. To the extent that we cannot appreciate the differences, we will not be able to support our children's healthy sexual development in the full and real meaning of the term.

## Whose Values? What Values?

One evening not long ago I happened to sit in on a PTA meeting at which a school head I've known for many years was explaining the school's sexuality education program to a group of parents. After listing the various topics covered, she ended by making the following statement: "And as far as sexual values go, rest assured that we leave that part to you at home."

I couldn't help but grimace. Later, I asked her to describe the classes in more detail. As I listened, it became clear to me that the school's program indeed had a very clear and very distinct values base. So what had she really been trying to say?

Parents (and educators as well) often express serious reservations and legitimate worries about how the issue of values will be handled in sexuality education classrooms. They typically identify three major concerns: that the program will somehow teach no values or the wrong values; that it will end up sending mixed messages about sexual values; or that the teacher or program will in some way impose values on children that differ from or undermine parental or family values. Confronted with these fears, the teachers, administrators, and school boards sometimes decide to counter with a program designed and publicized as being deliberately "values-free."

First of all, no curriculum can ever be values-free. In fact, what is a curriculum if not fundamentally a statement of values? Out of all the possible pieces of knowledge that could be taught about a particular subject, the task of a curriculum writer is to select the very few that are considered the most crucial. And, even if the goal of creating a "values-neutral" program were possible or desirable, curricula are taught by teachers, who, in the process of making moment-to-moment decisions in the classroom, are constantly modeling and reinforcing specific values.

I knew that my friend the school head understood these subtleties intuitively, because she is a fine educator and she runs a marvelous school, but like many Americans, her intellectual grasp of the concept of values was muddled. Although she wasn't able to sort it out at the moment she said it, what she had really meant to say was something like the following: "In all that we do here at school, as you know, we try to highlight and reinforce a core set of universal values—concepts such as honesty, mutuality, trust, responsibility, caring, and respect for self and others. Our sexuality program is no exception. When it comes to values-laden issues that are not universal, but are controversial, such as homosexuality, abortion, and premarital intercourse, we'll do our best to help students think critically about the many viewpoints to which they are exposed. We count on you, however, to make clear to your children what you think and value as well. That experience is a crucial part of their education and their healthy development as adolescents."

## How Clarity About Levels of Values Helps

The difference between universal and controversial values, first made clear in Chapter 4, is an essential distinction and often the missing link in resolving the debate over school-based values education. First, it enables all adults—faculty, administrators, parents, and those in the larger community—to clearly identify the specific values around which a program should be based, and it provides a common language for addressing concerns about values education. It also helps clarify specific yet complementary roles for parents and teachers.

In my own classrooms, for example, whenever a value-laden issue arises, I take time immediately to make a quick mental determination as to whether the value in question falls into the category of universal or controversial. If it falls into the universal group (for example, humane treatment of people with AIDS, or the prevention of rape, abuse, or harassment), I know that my role will be *reinforcer*, since unquestionably it is appropriate for all adults to assert, model, reward, and encourage the value of compassion. If the issue at stake is controversial, however, my aim will be entirely different: to encourage as much critical thought and analysis as possible, using core or universal values as a guide. For this reason, I will choose instead to play the role of *facilitator, moderator,* or even *devil's advocate*.

If the topic at hand is abortion or homosexuality, for example, I'll make a point of acknowledging that this issue is an extremely controversial issue in our society, and I'll ask everyone to identify, discuss, and debate the full range of views that exist. I may also ask if anyone would like to share his or her personal opinion about the subject, and also suggest that a topic of this importance is one that students might wish to talk over with parents or clergy. If I am teaching in a parochial setting, I'll also make sure that students understand how the issue is viewed by the affiliated religious group.

Distinctions between core and controversial values are not always this clear, since there are often crossovers among them. Also, as mentioned earlier, people often use core values as a base from which to draw conclusions about controversial issues. Others see little distinction at all between their own personal or religious values and core values. No matter how people's views may differ, all these shades of meaning make for exciting classroom discussion.

Moreover, many issues that relate directly to human values—and about which students and others may fundamentally agree—have highly controversial aspects. Arriving at an exact definition of sexual harassment, for example, even if everyone were in complete agreement about its inappropriateness, might involve long and heated debate. Finally, no matter what an individual's opinion might be about a controversial issue, teachers can remind students—and in fact should insist—that all points of view be expressed in ways that reflect core values, especially the value of respect for others. In my classroom, no matter what a student's opinion about homosexuality, for example, a word like *fag* would never be permitted if used in any kind of pejorative way.

Parents, too, can engage in these same kinds of discussions with children and adolescents, playing the same facilitating roles as teachers. But parents have an additional responsibility that teachers don't have. As a teacher, I can choose to share with my students my own personal view about controversial issues, or not, and if asked, I sometimes do. (I always make sure, though, that everyone else who wants to share has done so first, and that when I do share my view, I am seated in a chair as a participating group member, not towering above as the teacher/authority figure.) However, since knowing their parents' views is so critically important for children and adolescents, this kind of sharing is best seen not as an option for parents, but as a developmentally essential imperative.

## What About Schools Imposing Certain Values?

Often I ask teachers if it is ever OK to impose certain values on their students. I am still always amazed at the majority who emphatically say no. It is yet another revealing case of adults not knowing what they really think, because of our sloppiness as a culture in articulating about values.

"Please, please," I tell them, "do not hesitate to impose certain values on your students! In fact, you already do—all the time!" I remind them of what happens in their classes when students don't do their schoolwork: lower grades, calls to parents, having to repeat courses and even whole semesters of work. Schools stand for, and stand up for, all kinds of core values—in this case, the value of education and of taking personal responsibility for one's actions (or inaction). Teachers can and should impose core values not only in relation to academic concerns, but also in regard to the treatment of others. In my own classes, for instance, where very sensitive issues are frequently discussed, creating an emotionally safe classroom environment is essential. Students who persistently treat the viewpoints of others with disrespect are sometimes excused from certain class activities altogether, until they and I—often in conference with their adviser, principal, or parent—can resolve the problem. In other words, there is always the imposition of consequences whenever certain core or community values are violated.

I think our intellectual sloppiness about values comes partially from a good place; we have become a society that is increasingly sensitized to the goal of respecting individual differences. However, as a result we sometimes confuse *nonjudgmentalism* (the notion that people have the right to live their life without judgment from others about personal matters that do not affect them) with *lack of moral judgment* (the application of moral standards in judging human decisions and behavior). Too often we project an inappropriate "anything goes" or "it's all up to the individual" brand of morality. It's one of the biggest babies we threw out with the bath water in the 1960s.

I hear young people say all the time that there are no objective or absolute standards that we must live by—that people must decide for themselves what is right and wrong. Nonsense! Core human values such as honesty, integrity, responsibility, mutuality, caring, respect for life, and liberty are never relative, except to each other (for example, it might be ethical to tell a lie to save a life). This is a message that all adults, especially teachers and parents, must communicate unequivocally. They must also never hesitate to state that certain acts, such as rape, sexual harassment, child molestation, are always wrong.

What teachers should *not* impose in classrooms are particular personal or religious views about controversial sexual issues. That is a violation of the rights of our students and their parents, and in the case of religion, a violation of the separation of church and state. Teachers must remain nonjudgmental about controversial issues, and they must receive training in the skills required to maintain a classroom environment in which these diverse opinions are invited and heard with respect. Religious views most definitely do have a place in the classroom, but they cannot be imposed on others and cannot dictate curriculum. Because we have not understood their rightful place, we've either, sadly, left religious viewpoints out entirely or allowed them to rule—if only by default. School administrators too often allow themselves to be intimidated by individuals who insist that unless their particular religious perspective is held up as the right perspective, then the issue should not be discussed in school at all. (Parents whose children attend a public or private non-parochial school and who cannot tolerate that their particular point of view is presented in a less-than-absolute manner probably should strongly consider placing their child in an orthodox religious day school setting.)

## We Can *Find Common Ground*

The core value of preserving human life and health is at the foundation of all school-based health education. Consequently, we are morally obligated as teachers and caring adults to tell young people *everything we know* about how people can protect themselves and others against serious health problems. Although it is certainly in the interest of health promotion and disease prevention to highlight the strategy of abstinence, especially for teenagers, it is inappropriate to teach or emphasize only this strategy, unless it represents—which it most certainly does not—the sum total of what we know about prevention.

In other words, the right approach to teenage HIV prevention, for example, is not abstinence *or* condoms, it is abstinence *and* condoms. And abstinence *and* education. And clearer messages about sexual values. And better parent-child communication. And many other strategies—in fact, whatever it takes—to raise our children to become sexually healthy people. If ever a problem cried out for creative, expansive thinking, rather than an either-or mentality, it is certainly this one.

How tragic and ironic that adults on both sides of the sex education controversy have so much more in common than they realize because of all the shouting. All of them love their children. All want them to be safe and healthy and happy. All want their children to eventually understand their sexuality and learn to use and enjoy it as a positive life force. These are powerfully important shared values, the enormous and fertile common ground upon which we all stand, even as our disagreements about strategy blind us to it.

Were we to put aside our differences long enough to recognize, embrace, and articulate our common values, the result, I predict, would be nothing short of miraculous. It would enable us to frame a unified, crucial set of messages for young people about their developing sexuality. The message would probably sound very much like this:

"What we want you to know, dear children, because we love and care about you so deeply, is that your sexuality is a great gift." (Some will want to add the phrase, "from God.") "We fervently hope that it will become a positive and fulfilling part of your life.

"You must also know that sexual behavior, especially sexual intercourse, is extraordinarily powerful—emotionally, socially, and physically. In fact, sexual intercourse rightly can be viewed as the most fundamentally powerful behavior on the face of the earth, since it has the capability both to give life and to take it away. Therefore, decisions about sexual intercourse are always profoundly serious and always fraught with ethical questions. Only people who are capable of mature, responsible conduct should ever consider becoming involved.

"If, and whenever, people do become involved, it is therefore essential that they actively care for and protect themselves and others, emotionally and physically. Here are the ways in which you can do that."

In nearly thirty years of work with parents and educators in communities across the country, I have met few who could not comfortably sign on to this statement. It constitutes a kind of "big tent" values message, one that the vast majority of adults could agree to use as a starting point in their conversations with young people (if only we could just agree to agree). It would bring to the discussion clarity, consistency, and balance, all sorely missing from the current public discourse, and all sorely needed by young people trying to sort out the endless contradictions about sexuality that adult society now projects.

To many adults, the message as phrased above will seem inherently sound but woefully incomplete or insufficient. This poses no real problem, however, since other messages may be added without distracting from or negating the first message. For example, many adults will emphatically want to add this:

"Because of the seriousness of this behavior, or because of our deep [spiritual, religious, moral, etc.] beliefs, or for both reasons, we urge you not to engage in this act except within the context of a mature marital relationship. We believe this is not only the best way to protect yourselves and others, but also the best [or only] path to a fulfilling, happy, and righteous life."

Still others may wish to say: "Though we consider sexual intercourse wrong and [or] too serious for unmarried [immature] young people, we do think that some other types of sexual behavior may be right and healthy. Here are some of these, and some guidelines for deciding under what circumstances they might be right and healthy for you."

This layered sequence of messages, from the more generic and universal, to the more specific and controversial, allows adults to reach many important goals. First, it enables us to present a uniform front regarding a crucial set of universally held moral values and to state the various arguments for abstinence without confusion or contradiction. Second, it acknowledges the reality of teenage sexual behavior in today's world and respects the plurality of opinion in our culture about acceptable nonmarital sexual behaviors. (It is the argument over this behavior, and what to do and say about it, that keeps us from focusing on our larger areas of agreement.) Third, it encourages an active, positive, and open orientation to human sexuality.

Finally, by keeping us focused on the big picture of healthy sexual development, rather than the narrow goal of problem prevention, it enables us to avoid the worrisome trap of the mixed message. As one mother put it, "As parents we've got to do better than, 'Don't do that or I'll kill you. But if you do, be sure to use a condom!' Instead, the message should be 'Someday we hope this will be part of your life. But only under the best and right circumstances! Here's what they are.' Then we're really doing our job."

## Parents and Schools as Partners

As discussed in Chapter 5, sexuality education is an ongoing process in which virtually everyone in a child's life directly or indirectly participates. When its course is understood within this broad (and inevitable) developmental framework, the single most important question emerges: Since all the significant adults in children's lives, especially parents and teachers, have important roles to play in promoting healthy sexual development, what are the most logical and appropriate roles for each, and how can they best work together to lend each other ongoing support and reinforcement?

Deciding on the most appropriate roles and responsibilities for families and schools, as I have said, is best accomplished by focusing on *the unique characteristics of each as institutions.* You might want to revisit some of the specific suggestions made at the end of Chapter 5 about how best to think through these differences and unique opportunities.

What is most essential is that we come to see ourselves truly as equal partners, taking full advantage of our mutual but unique roles as *shapers and influencers* of how young people learn, think about, and manage their emerging sexuality. That kind of relationship can only develop under a set of three conditions: a mutual trust that we have all children's best interests as our first and only agenda; a mutual understanding of the true goals, purposes, and outcomes of comprehensive sexuality education; and a mutual common ground of core human values upon which we can stand united.

Let the dialogue begin.

## PART 2

*Raising Sexually Healthy Children*

# Sexual Health: Five Universal Needs Along the Way

The premise of the first seven chapters of this book has been that before we can anticipate a time when children in the United States are assured a healthy sexual upbringing, we will need to rethink the approaches we've relied on in the past. I have insisted that we go back as individuals—indeed, as an entire culture—to reconsider basic assumptions and beliefs about how children learn and what they need to know. Even more fundamentally, we must reconsider how we ourselves define and think about such basic topics as age-appropriateness, sex, sexuality, gender, and sexual values. Wherever it is we may want to proceed in the future, *we will not be able to get there from here* without a personal and cultural hiatus of self-discovery and reevaluation.

## *Now* We Can Get There!

Up to this point, this book addressed the most elemental and important questions: What is sex, really? What is sexuality? What is sexuality education, as distinct from sex education? How do children and adolescents learn about sex and sexuality? What do they need and want to know, and when and why do they need and want to know it? What are values, and how do we best think about sexual values? How does gender fit into the big picture of sexuality? How can families and schools work together to support healthy sexual development?

We've also examined basic assumptions about sexual learning, and I've proposed what are, in my best judgment, six essential truths or core principles that should guide us:

1. Sexual knowledge is good. Talking about sexuality is good, and good for our children. Acquiring sexual literacy is an essential goal for children and adolescents in today's world.
2. "Too little sexual knowledge, too late," not "too much, too soon," should be our biggest concern; if we listen carefully, children will teach us what we need to know about age-appropriateness.
3. Sex is not the same thing as sexual intercourse; rather, sexual intercourse is one of many kinds of sexual behavior that exist along a continuum of physical intimacy. The language we use about sex communicates attitudes and values, as well as information.
4. Values education is the heart of sexuality education. Sexual values are moral values. Sexual values education is a complex issue in contemporary American society.
5. Sexuality is much more a matter of who we are than what we do; the largest part of our sexuality has to do with our gender. If adults do not understand the "big picture" of sexuality, they cannot assume their proper roles in supporting healthy sexual growth and development.
6. Parental and school involvement in sexuality education is a moral responsibility. Ignorance, embarrassment, discomfort, and fear of controversy are no longer acceptable excuses for abdicating these roles. Parents and schools are not substitutes for one another, nor are their roles interchangeable; rather they are partners in sexuality education, with complementary but unique roles.

## The Ultimate Goal: What Is Sexual Health?

As discussed, once sexuality education is understood as an ongoing and interactive process of growth and development, not simply the didactic transmission of sexual information, it becomes evident that families, schools, and for that matter, every other individual and institution in a child's life all play a part. With this broad-based understanding and approach firmly in mind, the question for all adults becomes not *whether* to become involved, but *how best* to become involved. And, our ultimate goal—supporting children's growth and development toward sexually healthy adulthood—comes into clear view.

These realizations lead to a compelling but difficult question: If our goal is to help children grow up to become sexually healthy adults, what then is a sexually healthy adult? We must be prepared to explain the term in clear and specific language.

I'll never forget the first time I asked a group of students—juniors and seniors in an elective course on sexual health in the early 1980s—for their views on this very question. "The purpose of this course," I explained on the first day of class, "is to support your growth toward becoming a sexually healthy adult. So, we'd better define what that means. What is a 'sexually healthy adult'? How, exactly, would you know one if you fell over one?"

Groaning mightily at my feeble attempt at humor and muttering about how this was supposed to be sex class, and why did it already feel so much like work, my students put themselves to the task. Convinced I had given them an impossibly challenging assignment, I assigned them to small mixed-gendered groups, sat back, and waited.

Of course, I should have known better, since experienced teachers know always to expect the opposite of what they expect: they finished handily, in about ten minutes flat. And, each group, pretty much, had come up with the same answer. In composite form, the gist of it was something like the following: "A sexually healthy adult can be readily identified as having the following characteristics: a man or woman, with relatively large, attractive, clean, disease- and unwanted-pregnancy-free genitals, who uses them happily, satisfactorily, and a lot!"

"No, no, no, no, no!," I countered, horrified that I had practically stood on my head when they were in middle school trying to teach them—despite cultural messages to the contrary—that people, themselves included, are most definitely *not* walking, talking, genital organs.

Then I remembered where I was, and where they had just been. These kids, as smart and sophisticated as they were, had been swimming around in that very same sex- and genitally obsessed culture during the intervening three or four years since I had seen them last. Why would I expect that a one-time, albeit fairly intensive, counter-culture dose of messages—with no booster shot in between—would have inoculated them against such myopic thinking? I regained my typically more nonjudgmental composure, and we went back to the beginning, again.

Some days later, after interviewing parents, teachers, and other adults in our school community, we wrote the following definition together. (It was composed deliberately in adult language, since adulthood is the theme.) Years later, it remains the statement of purpose of all of my high school courses and programs and is still a powerful starting point for discussions with students, parents, and teachers-in-training.

## Philosophy of Sexual Health Education

As the World Health Organization has asserted, health is more than the absence of illness. It is a dynamic continuum expressing an individual's level of wellness along a variety of dimensions—physical, emotional, social, spiritual, interpersonal, and inter-environmental.

Within this philosophy of a holistic approach to health, the concept of sexual health, too, encompasses the total person and is a matter of mind, body, spirit, and relationship to other persons and the environment.

The purpose of preventive health education is to support the individual's optimal attainment of wellness, by encouraging the ongoing development of knowledge, self-awareness, and skills that promote healthful living. Sexual health is defined as including the following behaviors:

1. Taking active care of one's sexual/reproductive organs and systems.
2. Enjoying pleasure and satisfaction from one's sexual experiences and feelings.
3. Feeling a sense of comfort and fulfillment in one's gender.
4. Participating in or refusing participation in sexual behaviors in accordance with a consciously evolving, internalized value system.
5. Relating to others sexually in caring, supportive, and nonexploitive ways.

6. Communicating comfortably and effectively about sexuality, both verbally and nonverbally.
7. Taking responsibility for one's sexual behavior and its outcomes emotionally, physically, and interpersonally.
8. Taking responsibility for one's sexual and reproductive rights and freedoms.

*—The Park School, 1982*

What I like best about this statement is its remarkable clarity. As sexual people, we are defined by much more than what we do (or don't do) with our genitals: How we think, feel, plan, decide, learn, value, communicate, relate, problem solve, anticipate, enjoy, protect, care, and care for, are identified as the real issues. Also, there must be something generic and inclusive about its core elements, since each class I have taught over the past twenty years or so has generated a strikingly similar list.

Most importantly, as an educator and a trainer of parents and teachers, I appreciate the context that the statement creates for visualizing the ultimate purposes of sexuality education and for identifying corresponding adult roles. If this is what we hope our children are "becoming" and learning how to think and feel and do, then we adults in turn know what we must do to help make it happen. In addition, as I often tell my students and their parents, the statement actually doubles as a course syllabus and even more importantly as a life syllabus: It identifies the eight generic skills that we'll be learning about together in the classroom and that most of us will continue to work on for the rest of our adult lives. The focus, I explain, is not how to have healthy adult sex, but how to become a sexually healthy adult—as a person, a friend, a couple, a parent, and even as a citizen. (To work on this last goal, we create our own unique textbook in each of my upper school sexual health courses by screening two newspapers a day for sexual content.)

The statement points out as well that the characteristics of healthy *sexual* adulthood are very close to the characteristics of *healthy adulthood*—period. When we, as parents and teachers, help children develop a sense of responsibility, we are also enabling a sense of sexual responsibility. When we teach about trust, we are also teaching about honesty in sexual relationships. Whenever we encourage playfulness, spontaneity, assertiveness, compassion, integrity, or self-esteem, we are also gradually sowing the seeds for a healthy sexual life. If, however, we never explicitly make connections for our children between these values and the sexual parts of their lives, we will still have provided the ingredients, but our children will be left to make associations to sexuality on their own. They will do this probably by trial and error and at much greater potential cost.

As we've explored in earlier chapters, the role of schools in sexuality education has been particularly misunderstood and mischaracterized. School-based programs have often been perceived, at best, as providing a less-than-ideal substitute for parents who are not doing the job themselves, and, at worst, as attempting to inappropriately usurp parental rights, responsibilities, and prerogatives. The underlying assumption behind these perceptions is faulty—that sexuality education is an either-or proposition involving families and schools. If we take a thoughtful look at the eight characteristics or skills listed above, it becomes immediately apparent why both families and schools need to be involved, and how their characteristics and roles as institutions are neither interchangeable nor at odds, but complementary and unique. What's more, various components of these characteristics and skills can be nurtured and taught across the developmental spectrum, from preschool through high school.

Here are some examples. Although schools are best equipped to teach formally such topics as body systems, prevention behaviors, and health resources in the community, families are best suited to help children and adolescents incorporate positive attitudes and healthy behaviors into their daily lives (characteristics 1 and 7). Schools can make sure to teach about the sexual system—not just the reproductive system—and parents can encourage children and adolescents to feel good about their bodies, their bodily feelings and functions, and touch, affection, and physical intimacy (characteristic 2). Mothers and fathers at home can consciously nurture their children's self-esteem, and teachers can teach their students specific skills for communicating directly, assertively, and empathetically (characteristics 4 and 6). Parents can stay informed and make sure to express their opinions about current news events that affect our rights, choices, and responsibilities as sexual people and as citizens, and schools can routinely incorporate these topics into a variety of applicable subject matters (characteristic 8). Moreover, families and schools can work together continuously to dovetail each other's efforts, as they attempt to touch on important knowledge, values, and skills in age-appropriate ways across the entire developmental spectrum.

## From Daunting to Doable

Most parents—and especially, I think, those who like to consider themselves good parents—feel at least somewhat inadequate and unprepared
for the task of meeting their children's sexual education needs. It's a
process that can seem nebulous and overwhelming, particularly as children approach adolescence and parents begin to experience less direct
control over their lives and safety. These same parents usually have a very
clear gut sense of what they don't want to say or do about sexuality, but
not what they do want, and they can find that dichotomy unnerving and
even paralyzing.

For parents to regain a sense of control, it is essential for them to be
able to demystify the process of raising a sexually healthy child. They
must feel reassured that the sexual education needs of children and adolescents are neither nebulous nor overwhelming; to the contrary, these
needs are universal, predictable, clearly identifiable, and actually quite
similar and constant from birth through early adulthood. And, amazingly,
there are only five of them.

## Sometimes We Don't Know What We Know

For years, I have been telling audiences of parents that they can relax
more than they may think about meeting their children's sexual education
needs. Even if the process feels daunting, even if they are feeling helpless
or overwhelmed, they really can master it. *Moreover, they may already
know how, but not yet know what they know.*

A clear case in point. A friend once came to me unnerved about a recent incident in the family. He and his wife had tried their best to handle
it well, but were not certain they had done the right thing. At this point
they really didn't know *what* to think.

The father confided that their fourteen-year-old son had been clandestinely downloading and printing out pornographic pictures from the Internet. Not really horrible stuff, my friend relayed, but "pretty raunchy."
Interestingly (and not at all uncommonly), the boy had made the parents'
interception of this material relatively easy, if not inevitable, by leaving
the evidence sitting out at home, in more than one conspicuous spot. All
the more reason, the parents decided, for a direct and immediate response. They discussed when, how, and where.

The car, they finally realized, was the ideal place: No escape for anybody, and no necessity for uncomfortable eye contact. Treading slowly at first, on a family day trip, they announced their "find." Intriguingly, the son did not seem terribly upset or terribly surprised or angry at having been caught. He made no attempt to deny what he had done (except to soften his involvement a bit by saying the pictures were originally e-mailed by a friend), a reaction his parents took as a positive sign that he had wanted their opinions, and that this was his way of asking. The father began by relating that he certainly could understand his son's curiosity about pornography, as well as the excitement and allure of being able to access it so easily and secretly over the computer. And in truth, he acknowledged, images similar to these have been seen by millions of boys and men. As parents, however, there were things about the incident they found deeply troubling and worrisome, and it was their responsibility to say so.

Pornographic images can fill your mind with sexist and unrealistic ideas and expectations of *real* bodies and real-life sexual experiences, the father explained. Because these images can be powerful and seductive and so easily invite inaccurate and unhealthy comparisons, they can affect a boy or man's sexual fantasies in ways that can have a negative effect on his real relationships, now and in the future. (The father gave examples.) Moreover, both parents continued, they wanted him to realize that the pictures he had downloaded were part of a multi-billion-dollar industry that in effect exploits *all* women—his mother and sister included—not only by encouraging them to be defined and used as sex objects, but because it is primarily men who buy pornography and who reap its enormous financial profits.

What might have been the consequences, they asked, had his much younger sister been the one to discover the pictures—or some other downloaded material that was inappropriate for her age? Had he thought about that? What rules did they need to agree on as a family to make sure something like this didn't happen in the future? And—if as he had said the pictures had been sent by a friend—what indeed was being passed around his social circle, especially at school? Downloading can lead to the very tempting proposition of buying and selling, they explained; on school property, mere possession, let alone trafficking, would carry serious disciplinary if not legal consequences. "We forbid you," they emphatically declared, "to participate in any such activities."

"It was a good talk," the father told me.

"Then why are you both so insecure about what you decided to do?" I asked.

"Because we were just flying by the seat of our pants. And maybe we should have forbidden him to download or even look at pornography again. But we don't really believe in censorship, especially for kids who are high school age. Besides, you've got to pick your battles, and in this case, we knew we really don't have the power to make it stick."

Two things struck me immediately about my friend's story. The first was how marvelously he and his wife had handled a tough parenting dilemma. The second was how, despite their fine instincts and skills, they could not by themselves figure out what a good job they had done or even identify the correct criteria to use in evaluating what they might have accomplished. Ironically, because the issue was the common-sense-draining and discomfort- and anxiety-provoking topic of sexuality, like a lot of other good parents, *they didn't know what they already knew about good parenting.*

## The Five Core Needs of Children and Adolescents

Here's what my friend and his wife knew in their hearts but not in their heads: *Whenever children present us with sexual issues or situations, they are always expressing one or more of only five easily identifiable, developmentally based needs.* (One of the reasons this particular example was so tricky was because it embodied all five.) The art of good parenting, which my friend and his wife knew intuitively but not consciously, involves three basic steps: (1) knowing and fully understanding these five core needs, (2) correctly differentiating which specific need or needs are being expressed by a child in any given situation, and (3) skillfully drawing upon one or more of several developmentally sound approaches to meeting that particular need or needs for that particular aged child. Using examples from my friend's story, I'll briefly enumerate and clarify the five developmental needs and corresponding parenting skills (needs and skills truly are the flip sides of one another), with further embellishment later:

### Affirmation

*Children and adolescents need adults to recognize and validate their particular stage of sexual development.*

My friend and his wife—I'll call their son David—knew that interest in pornographic material is common for ninth-graders (and even younger boys) and is typically an expression of normal curiosity. They were also aware that David lacked the knowledge and maturity to properly evaluate the material he was viewing, and they wanted him to understand the negative, unrealistic, and unhealthy messages it portrayed. Sensing an important teachable moment and a chance both to gain his trust and to initiate a new and more adult-level dialogue about sexuality that they hoped would continue throughout his high school years, they decided together to treat the occasion as an opportunity for guidance, not discipline or punishment.

## Information Giving

*Children and adolescents need factual knowledge and concepts about sexuality, presented in ongoing and age-appropriate ways.*

David's parents explained to him how the images he had downloaded gave an artificial and unrealistic portrayal of adult sexuality, and that very few (if any) women and men in real life actually look anything like, or pose or position their bodies like, the models in the pictures. Appealing to his idealism and developing social consciousness—two emerging, positive strengths of many middle adolescents—they also provided him with information about larger social, economic, and ethical issues connected to the pornography industry that disturbed them.

## Values Clarification

*Children and adolescents need adults to share their parental values and to clarify and interpret competing values and values systems in the surrounding culture.*

David's exposure to pornography gave his parents an opportunity to clarify—by sharp contrast—their own deeply held beliefs about sexual values and about women's and men's sexuality. They were also able to help him interpret the implied values embedded in pornographic imagery, thereby bringing them to his conscious awareness and helping to diffuse the impact of these messages on his own developing value system.

## Limit Setting

*Children and adolescents need adults to create a healthy and safe environment by stating and reinforcing age-appropriate rules and limits.*

David's parents were aware of the importance of establishing rules—in cooperation with the child or adolescent whenever feasible—for the appropriate and safe use of sexually related and other material on the Internet. They also recognized that as children grow older, parents are wise to limit their hard-and-fast rules to those that are enforceable, are based in strongly held values, or are crucial for health and safety. In this case, they opted for guidance, where they felt they could not guarantee enforcement, and for a harder line on issues involving safety and ethical behavior.

## Anticipatory Guidance

*Children and adolescents need adults to help them learn how to avoid or handle potentially harmful situations, and to prepare them for times when they will need to rely on themselves to make responsible and healthy choices.*

As a middle adolescent, David has a fledgling but not yet fully developed ability to think through the implications of his actions. Without his parents' help, he might not have been able to identify possible future actions (trafficking) and consequences (trouble at school or with the law) that might have resulted from his present choices (downloading). They also helped him to understand and anticipate potential effects of his actions on others (a younger sister, who might inadvertently stumble onto something not kept carefully out of sight), and to better grasp the idea that something that he experiences today and may consider totally harmless might have a negative effect on his (sex) life later on.

In the next few chapters, I will highlight and clarify these core needs with many more examples. As we'll come to understand, being able to differentiate one need from another is the first step in knowing how best to proceed in any given situation, since different needs usually require very different kinds of responses. In fact, when a particular situation makes us feel really "stuck," it's often because we're being pulled in opposing directions by the conflicting needs we're sensing but can't clearly differentiate. (This was clearly the case for David' parents: They knew at once that they needed to be both open and supportive *and* clear and firm, and this seeming paradox confused them and made them feel insecure.) When we can accurately name each of the needs before us and delineate them from one another, the right set of responses usually emerges. We'll tackle the five needs, one at a time, in Chapters 9 through 13, but here they are once more described in general terms.

## Affirmation: Seeing and Hearing Children as They Are

As discussed, sexual development is a continuous process that begins at birth and continues throughout life. Our children need for us, as the most immediate, caring, and responsible adults in their lives, to both *see and hear* them as developing sexual people. To hear them, we must be available to them, always, as "askable," approachable adults, and we must continuously communicate and affirm our availability in direct ("Can we talk?") and indirect (open body posture, comfortable and inviting tone) ways. To see them as developing sexual people, we must fully comprehend and accept the notion of sexuality as a broad and intrinsic component of their identity from birth on, and be able to observe it develop as our children grow, much as we might observe the development of their racial, ethnic, or religious identity. In Chapter 9 we'll work on these communication and observation skills.

## Information Giving: Empowering Children Through Knowledge

Left to their own natural interests and curiosity, children and adolescents will ask a predictable sequence of questions and will grapple with a predictable set of issues about sexuality as they progress through each developmental stage, from early childhood through young adulthood. That's a reassuring concept for adults who feel clueless or insecure about the issue of age appropriateness, especially when it comes to the youngest of children. The constancy and universality of this sequence helps remind us that although society may have changed dramatically in the twentieth century, the internally based timetable that drives child and adolescent development has not. It's also comforting to realize that—as in the old tried-and-true social-work dictum "Always start where the client is"—if we remember to start where the child is, we can't go too far wrong. In Chapters 9 and 10, we'll identify and analyze these developmentally based issues and questions in depth.

## Values Clarification:
## Highlighting "Right" Thinking

Raising children in an open, pluralistic society presents supreme challenges for parents. As we have said, young people are deluged constantly with conflicting and in many cases deplorable messages about the meaning of sexuality and sexual behavior. Short of locking our children in the basement or the television in the attic, it is up to parents to become their children's own personal cultural interpreter and guide as they attempt to sort out what they see and hear around them. Chapter 11 will revisit the issue of values and provide multiple strategies for helping children discriminate the "right" values in the confusing quagmire that surrounds them.

## Limit Setting:
## Keeping Our Children Safe

Limits are those brackets that we place around our children's lives to keep them safe and healthy. From infancy, when our children are nearly totally defenseless, through college, when they may consider themselves totally invincible, they need clear limit setting. What changes as they change is the *content* of those limits. The fundamental *need* for limits, however, remains constant. We'll examine the concept of limit setting in depth in Chapter 12, moving from stage to developmental stage to understand how it both changes and remains the same as our children grow.

# Anticipatory Guidance:
# Making Ourselves Dispensable

Parenthood is one of those rare jobs whose ultimate goal is to put yourself out of business. From the moment they are born, we are preparing our children to leave us. We will spend the next eighteen years and usually even longer trying to fill them up to the brim with all the tools they will need as they eventually make their own way and begin to successfully lead their own lives. In Chapter 13, we'll define and consider those tools—the specific kinds of knowledge, self-awareness, attitudes, values, communication, decision making, and problem-solving skills our children will need to keep themselves sexually safe and healthy.

## The Five-Need Paradigm

Take a minute to glance through the parenting dilemmas listed below. You'll probably experience a range of thoughts and reactions in reading them, from "What on earth would I do in this situation?" to "Well, this one seems fairly straightforward." Read them again, and as you do, see what happens when you apply what I call the five-need paradigm. Next to each, put the letters "A" (affirmation), "I" (information), "V" (values), "LS" (limit setting), or "AG" (anticipatory guidance), or some combination of these, to indicate which of the five developmental needs and parenting skills you think apply. Then put a star next to the one need that strikes you as most immediate or fundamental. That step usually helps parents identify the best place to start their thinking about possible responses, and lessens the chance that they'll be overwhelmed or confused by seemingly conflicting needs. (Dilemma 8, for example, is the kind of situation in which parents can feel yanked in so many directions at once they become almost paralyzed with self-doubt.)

I hope you'll find the five-needs approach not unlike a doctor's process of differential diagnosis. It should help you determine the central or most important issues in virtually any parenting situation you may face. And you can feel secure about your selection, no matter what you decide. Since there are only five possible choices—and since you now know what they all are—you really can't go too far off. What's more, regardless of the most pressing need being expressed, all five are usually present in one form or another, so it may not matter much where you start. As you go through the list again, see if you don't feel a greater sense of confidence and clear-headedness than the first time around. (I've indicated my answers to a couple of them for you at the end of the chapter.)

Don't struggle too much with identifying specific responses to the child at this point. Those skills will come to mind much more easily as we proceed through the next five chapters.

1. You find that your twelve-year-old has been watching R-rated movies at the home of a friend.
2. A parent walks in on two five-year-olds playing "doctor."
3. A fifth-grader wants to go to the movies on a "date."
4. Your fifteen-year-old wants to know if you had sexual intercourse before you were married.
5. Your sons are playfully calling one another "fags."
6. A fourth-grader wants to know what a "blow job" is.
7. Your ninth-grade daughter is very level-headed and mature for her age, but the kids in her grade seem to be in the fast lane socially.
8. You are looking in your child's wallet to borrow some cash, and you discover a condom. (Try this one at ages fourteen and eighteen, and with a son *or* a daughter.)
9. Your fifth-grade daughter refuses to discuss puberty with you, even in the most basic of terms, and seems very anxious about the whole subject.
10. Your very good-looking son receives constant phone calls from girls in his grade. This seems to make him very uncomfortable.

## Some Sample Answers

*Your fifteen-year-old wants to know if you had sexual intercourse before you were married.* As we'll learn in Chapter 10, many times there are important questions *behind* the immediate questions our children ask. My hunch in this situation is that the child may be asking for the following kinds of dialogue:

- *Information:* How do people decide when they're ready for intercourse? What do they consider?

- *Values:* What were your views about premarital intercourse when you were a teenager? What do you think is right and wrong sexual behavior for a teenager, or before you are married? How will you feel about me if I make a different choice?
- *Anticipatory guidance:* What if I'm in a situation where I have to decide whether to have sexual intercourse? What's the best decision? How should I handle it?

*You are looking in your child's wallet to borrow some* cash and you discover a condom. This is a very different situation from the first, because it involves the parent's need to talk, not the child's. Also, the parent might want to address the issues differently depending on the age, and perhaps the gender, of the child.

**For a fourteen-year-old, for example, you might address the following needs:**

- *Affirmation:* The child's first need will be for us to recognize and be sensitive to the fact that we have entered into her or his private space without permission (even though we weren't snooping and perhaps the child was hoping subconsciously that we'd make this discovery). Regardless, most parents of a young adolescent will want to tell the child about finding the condom and will initiate or insist on a conversation about it. It will be important to start by ascertaining why the child is carrying the condom in the first place (maybe it's simply because others do, or "just in case") rather than jumping to conclusions. Parents should be aware that the child may also try to cover up the real reason to try to save face; they will have to use their best judgment about how far to press this issue.
- *Information:* The parent will want to make sure that the child has sufficient information about pregnancy risks and about the transmission, prevention, and symptoms of STIs.
- *Values clarification:* Parents can use the situation as an opportunity to state or restate their viewpoints about the appropriateness of sexual behaviors, including sexual intercourse, for teens this age, and to solicit the child's opinions. They'll also want to talk about the proper context— especially the kinds of relationships—in which they think those behaviors should and should not occur.

- *Limit setting:* Depending on what parents learn about the situation or decide about the adequacy of the limits they have placed previously around the child's social life, they may want to reset or re-negotiate the family's rules regarding curfews, adult supervision, and so forth.
- *Anticipatory guidance:* Parents can also be sure to stress the importance of prevention and planning ahead for circumstances that may arise (they can even let the child know that they are pleased that she or he obviously has given this issue thought). They may want to help the child anticipate and think through how to handle future situations that may call for sexual decision making or may create pressures to experiment.

Depending on the specific circumstances, many of the above suggestions will apply for an eighteen-year-old, especially if the parents previously have had few conversations with the child about sexual decision making and relationships. In some families, in which the parents are confident that an older teen is capable of approaching sexual situations in an adult manner, they may in fact consider this a private matter about which they will remain separate. In other families, regardless of the child's level of maturity, the parents' strong moral or religious views regarding premarital sexual behaviors or contraception, or both, may compel them to discuss the situation from the standpoint of values clarification.

# Affirmation: Seeing and Hearing Children as They Are

I can summon the memory as if it were last week. There we were, almost a hundredfold sitting in rows, mothers and daughters two-by-two. The window shades were tightly drawn, to keep out the afternoon light and the curious peeping of the fifth-grade boys, banished to the playground just outside the gymnasium wall to our right, but we could see and faintly hear them anyway. Pushing and taunting, they were congregated at a window where the shade was slightly torn. We prayed they would not be able to see in well enough to catch the really embarrassing parts, or else we knew we'd be at their mercy during recess for days.

The school nurse, very serious and medical in her starched white uniform, appeared before us. We couldn't understand her selection for this role, in place of our regular teachers, but their absence made it clear we weren't to ask. (Some days later we concluded that perhaps she had been the only menstruating woman in the building.) She greeted our mothers, then signaled for the lights to be turned off. We sat, motionless and silent, for the duration of the twenty-minute film. She signaled again for the lights, asking if there were any questions. We held our collective breath. Mercifully, not one soul said one word. After weeks of anticipation, dread, and rumor (a final poll revealed that most of us thought we were to be warned how we'd soon begin bleeding—from our breasts!), it was finally over.

As I look back, it's hard to imagine a less appropriate way of introducing the facts of menstruation and "growing up" to young and impressionable girls and boys (who, of course, managed to extort the entire story out of us by the end of recess). It was a classic case of adults trying to meet their own pressing need for avoidance, in the guise of meeting children's pressing needs for information and anticipatory guidance. As I've seen confirmed time and time again over the years, whenever adults are this far off in meeting children's real needs, *confusing adult needs for children's is almost always the cause.*

## Identifying Real Developmental Need

The first step in accurately identifying our children's real developmental needs is *the willingness to see and hear our children as they really are.* The more we know about their normal developmental processes—especially if we can learn to accurately frame them in terms of the five universal needs identified in Chapter 8—the easier it will be for us to discover our proper roles as parents and teachers.

### Birth to Age Two

The five universal developmental needs—for affirmation, information, values, limit setting, and anticipatory guidance—are constant from birth through adolescence. We can expect, however, that as children grow and develop, one or more of the needs will be primary at different ages and stages.

Our primary role in parenting newborns and infants in the first year of life is to nurture and protect. It is a role that we can't help but fulfill naturally and proactively, since their constant and insistent needs for sustenance, warmth, touch, rest, physical comfort, and safety require our constant and vigilant attentiveness. The affirmation we extend is therefore immediate and continual, communicated palpably by each of our moment-by-moment physical, emotional, and verbal responses to each cry, coo, and bout of crankiness. Our role as limit setter during this stage is absolute—we need only picture the confines of their crib to appreciate how little we trust them to care for their own needs when we're not there to protect them. Their need for anticipatory guidance is practically nil, since we are almost always by their side. At this stage, however, we are providing the prerequisites for fulfilling this need later on, since the confidence we instill in infancy enables the initiative they will need to take steps away from us later on. We also provide limitless information, although not of the didactic kind, as we help them appreciate the world around them as a fundamentally safe, nurturing, responsive, and loving place. And in turn, we teach them about our values, by demonstrating constantly how much we value them.

The acquisition of language and mobility changes their world and ours forever. The limits previously surrounding their lives and abilities—both intellectual and physical—become suddenly obsolete, and we begin to scramble (often quite literally!) to create safe ways for them to explore their ever-widening environment and to take on new challenges for expanding their intellect. We put up gates; take down knickknacks; hide the detergent; and buy new books, toys, and videos as we anticipate and attempt to guide their next physical and mental steps.

Whether we realize it or not, we are also providing a foundation for their later sexual life. The pleasure and comfort they come to associate with our loving touch and our physical warmth and presence will become their first and most important lessons in human intimacy. We can also enhance these good feelings and this positive foundation by consciously showing acceptance and approval of their body and its functions—including the sexual parts and their nearby neighbors, the urinary and digestive parts. Each time we give a bath or change a diaper, we constantly communicate messages about sexuality. Nonverbally (through our body tension, tone of voice, and facial expressions) and verbally (through the things we say and the words we choose), we speak volumes about how we feel about babies as sexual beings. If we can maintain the same affirming yet matter-of-fact attitude toward these parts and functions as we do to all others, we help them understand and accept their bodies as a positive and integrated whole. On the contrary, if we are suddenly tense or uncomfortable when our baby happens to touch his or her genitals, if we show extreme disgust or disapproval toward a messy bowel movement or an unexpected erection, if we use babyish or silly names for penises or vulvas, urine or feces, rather than the "proper" words we use for other body parts or products, we will teach just the opposite.

## Ages Two to Five

The years from two to five will require much less from us as constant nurturers and protectors, and our teaching about sexuality will become much more concrete and direct. We'll need to prepare ourselves to give accurate and straightforward information as we gradually help toddlers and preschoolers learn the names for a growing number of body parts and functions. To become a normal part of their everyday vocabulary, words like penis, testicles, scrotum, erection, vulva, labia, clitoris, vagina, urethra, urinate, anus, and bowel movement will need to become an everyday part of ours. And in case you're thinking that those big words are simply too long and complicated for small children to master, I am reminded of the time when one of my boys came home from preschool excited to explain how he had *laminated* all of his pictures in art class that day. Any three-year-old who can so effortlessly learn to say "laminate" can certainly handle the word *urinate*.

For many of us, this kind of openness and directness will necessitate homework and practice (saying the words over and over in front of a mirror, and naming body parts to our infants long before they will understand the meanings are two good tactics for overcoming residual discomfort from our own upbringing). We may also need to do some explaining to our children's grandparents, aunts, uncles, baby-sitters, and day care providers, and these conversations may well require a good deal of courage. Remarkably, even in the twenty-first-century United States, many of these words are considered taboo, if not explicitly counter-culture, terms. Said a woman in one of my parenting groups recently, "Oh my God, I couldn't *possibly* teach those words to my daughter. What if she were to repeat them in front of my mother, or worse yet, what if she were to say them at school! I can't be expected to change culture all by myself!"

Well, yes and no. For our children, especially when they are still very young, *we and our immediate family are their culture.* As discussed in Chapter 3, language is one of the most powerful conveyors of cultural attitudes and values, not just of information. Each parent must decide what attitudes and values he or she wants to instill and must recognize that his or her choice of language can either reinforce or contradict those messages in powerful ways. Parents must also reflect honestly on whose needs they are really attempting to meet—their own need to avoid embarrassment or recrimination, or their child's need to acquire an accurate, direct, and respectful language for thinking and communicating about the sexual parts of their anatomy, and eventually the sexual parts of their lives.

It helps to realize that there may be more than one developmental need at stake, each requiring a different kind of parental response. Parents who decide against giving children certain information, for fear of its being shared with the rest of the immediate world, are mixing up two very different sets of needs and solutions. Children have an absolute right for accurate and straightforward information, but they also need parental limit setting about how and when this kind of sensitive information should be shared, or not shared, with others. Denying information altogether is a solution that meets neither need. Fortunately, by the time children are old enough to form the thought, "This is neat, I think I'll tell everybody at school about it," they are also old enough to grasp the idea "This is really important information that parents like to tell their own children, so please don't share it." Also, once they are able to understand the concept of privacy—at roughly the same age they know to always keep parts of their body covered in public, or close the bathroom door, or knock before entering a room—they can also understand the admonition to "please keep this information private, because it is about private parts of your body."

**Body Differences.** Two- to five-year-olds are curious not only about their body parts and functions, but also about male and female body differences. It's helpful to allow or create natural opportunities for them to observe and learn the names for the body parts of the other gender. Bathing with a younger sibling, watching a diaper change, reading a book (*Belly Buttons Are Navels,* by Mark Schoen, is a good one), showering with mom or dad—if mom or dad is comfortable—are all great examples. For children in this young age group, body differences can be explained in very matter-of-fact tones and terms, before other youngsters or adults, perhaps, have an opportunity to communicate or instill their own attitudes, discomfort, or embarrassment. And parents, if they choose, can also build on the notion very early on that even though some parts of boys and girls are different, we and our bodies are mostly all the same.

Learning about body differences also sets the stage for responding much more easily to the sequence of developmentally based questions that young children typically begin to ask about their origins: "Where did I come from?" "How did I get out of there?" and "How did I get in there in the first place?" (see Chapter 3). This approach worked well with my second son, Adam, when he was about four. One day, having noticed a box of tampons in my bathroom, he asked what they were for. When I explained that older girls and women used them when they were grown up, he asked why boys couldn't use them, too. It turned out to be a great opening for talking about openings—which ones boys and girls have and don't have, and where they are located. Sometime later, as a result, answering his questions about origins followed much more easily, and in fact, with the help of additional information and some diagrams, he gradually pretty much figured out the whole thing all by himself.

**Genital Touching.**   As concrete thinkers, young children learn best by what they take in with their senses. Looking and touching, especially, are essential to understanding, and the issue of sexuality is no different. Even infants, once they have developed the requisite motor ability, delight in finding and touching their genitals, and recognizing and enjoying the sensations they can produce. Parents may continue to notice this kind of sporadic and spontaneous genital touching throughout toddlerhood. By the time the child reaches the age of four or five, rubbing on the genitals, or rubbing them against a handy object, may become something the child chooses to do more and more frequently and consciously, because it feels pleasurable, relaxing, and soothing.

As Debra Haffer points out in her fine parenting guide, *From Diapers to Dating,* it's important not to confuse these explorations with preadolescent, adolescent, or adult masturbation, which is most often motivated by developmental changes, peer influence, or sex drive. The young child is simply "being with" and enjoying his or her body in a way that fits his or her unique developmental stage. Eventually, as the child's intellect is able to comprehend the concept of privacy, parents (and teachers) will want to set limits around this behavior when it occurs in the presence of others. They'll want to be careful, though, to do so in a way that affirms the naturalness and normality of the child's curiosity and enjoyment of his or her body: "I can see that you really like touching yourself in that way, but remember that those are private parts of our body that we don't show or draw attention to when we're with other people. That's a fine thing to do when you are alone in your room, but not here in the family room or at Grandpa's or in school." It may take a few of these gentle reminders for the child to comply (remember that the behavior is most often reflexive, not consciously motivated), but eventually he or she will get it.

The desire to look at or touch other people's bodies is also very common at this stage, and adults may need to remind themselves to interpret this request from the perspective of a small child, not a grown-up: The child is asking out of simple curiosity, not sexual interest. As we have said, children learn best by seeing and doing; they simply don't have the intellectual machinery just yet to form a mental image from a verbal explanation. Some parents may feel comfortable allowing the child to observe their body directly, although others will prefer to set limits around the request: "Those parts of my body are private, but I can understand how you might be curious about what grown-up bodies or the other gender's body looks like. Let's go to the library and see if we can find some picture books to help." Again, the child's normal curiosity is affirmed, within the parent's acceptable limits.

**"Sex Play" with Other Children.**   Playing "doctor" is also a common way that children this age and somewhat older attempt to satisfy their normal curiosity about body parts and differences. Parents who stumble onto children examining one another in various states of undress are sometimes very unnerved, especially living in a society where child sexual abuse has become so publicized and where children are exposed to so many adult-oriented references and conversations about sex. They are apt to misinterpret this thoroughly age-appropriate childhood "game" and worry unnecessarily that their children's (or their playmates') "precocious sexual behavior" may be an indication of unhealthy development, or even worse, sexual abuse. (For some general guidelines about detecting and preventing sexual abuse, see the end of Chapter 12.)

Parents need to remind themselves that children have engaged in this "show me yours, I'll show you mine" behavior for generations long before any possible kind of media influence. The context of this behavior is curiosity, not sex. Although playing "doctor" may sometimes be cause for alarm (see Chapter 12), the best response is usually to calmly assert that "when we play with other children, we keep our clothes on," and then to encourage them to get dressed and move on to another activity. Some parents might find they are totally comfortable with this type of play, and choose to react by simply excusing themselves and allowing the game to continue undisturbed, especially if they know that the other children's parents would be in agreement. (Writer and radio humorist Garrison Keillor tells a funny joke about this on the radio: A parent angrily calls another parent to say that he just caught their children playing "doctor." The second parent says, "What are you getting so excited about? This is a harmless way that children explore their sexuality." "Harmless?!" said the man. "Your child just took out my child's appendix!") Whether parents prefer to discourage the game gently or let it continue, they might want to affirm their child's natural curiosity directly or provide an alternate way of satisfying it by suggesting a trip to the library to find books on the subject.

**Gender Messages.**   The preschool years are also a crucial time for parents to think deeply about the messages they wish to give their children about gender, especially gender roles. The gender myths examined at length in Chapter 6 are pervasive in our culture, and even young children are exposed to them constantly through media images as well as everyday experiences with friends, family members, and acquaintances. Teachers and parents with whom I work across the country report in increasing numbers how disturbed they are by the very narrow and stereotypical gender ideals their children emulate, even in early elementary school. In a meeting with second-grade parents just the other week, mothers expressed concern about their daughters who are afraid to come to school unless outfitted in the latest Gap fashions, and their sons who enjoy athletics but are afraid to try out for certain sports because they're not as skilled or aggressive as other boys they may have to play against, or even with.

That children in our culture as young as seven are already worried about the dangerous prospect of "failing" at gender is a dramatic wake-up call for those of us who teach and parent preschool-aged children. Anticipatory guidance about the social pressures associated with gender—or in Mary Pipher's terms, the teaching of skills for intelligent resistance—must begin early on (see the end of Chapter 6 for specific suggestions). It's also a topic you may want to bring up with your child's day care provider or preschool, along with other issues of sexual development, such as learning about body differences and names for sexual parts, genital touching, sexual curiosity and play, and answering questions about origins.

**Nudity in the Family.**   As children approach school age, parents sometimes begin to wonder about the issue of nudity in the family. When is the right time to stop bathing siblings together, or for parents to stop allowing children to see them nude? Professionals and others have a wide range of beliefs about this issue. On the one hand, some psychiatrists and psychologists say that parents and even young children should be fully clothed in each other's presence whenever possible. Others think it's a matter of individual comfort. Many families take a very modest approach, and others are very free and easy about it. Some families go together en masse to nudist colonies!

My own approach tends to be very practical and individualistic: Whenever either a parent or a child begins to feel some discomfort with nudity in each other's presence, it's time for setting a new limit. If not before, children tend to develop a strong sense of modesty as they experience—or even as they begin to anticipate—pubescence. Parents, too, may develop sudden inhibitions at a certain point when they sense that their child may be touching, looking at, or thinking about their bodies in a more self-conscious way. What's important is that parents communicate changes in a positive context: "Now that you're growing up, it's time for us all to have private time to shower." And be careful not to instill a sense of shame either about nude bodies or about the child's curiosity about them.

Equally important is for parents to recognize that affectionate hugs, kisses, and snuggles are *always* OK, even when nudity in each others' presence starts to feel uncomfortable. Too many fathers, especially, begin to pull away physically from both sons and daughters when pubescent body changes start to become apparent. There is absolutely no need for this sudden distance, and it is often a source of sadness and confusion for their children.

Parents worry, too, about what to do if a child comes upon them while they are engaged in sexual activity. There is no harm in having children understand that parents share a special way of being physically intimate with one another. Although such an experience may be disconcerting or embarrassing, for both parents and children, the best approach is to try to remain calm and matter-of-fact. Parents can say that they are having some private time together and would like the child to leave the room and be sure to close the door (and to please knock when it is closed in the future). Then, it's probably best for one of the adults to go to the child to ask what the child saw or thought he or she saw (younger children, especially, may interpret the behavior as angry or aggressive) and to invite questions or offer reassurance about what has happened.

## Ages Six to Nine

Six- to nine-year-olds are increasingly out and about in the world beyond the protective environs of home and family, day care, or preschool. Though still very much children, they have nonetheless become rational beings. Within the confines of certain very well defined limits, they are capable of logical ideas, independent thinking, and responsible action. Life is no longer all play or focused entirely on their immediate needs and desires, and they are put to the task of beginning to acquire the ever-expanding knowledge and skills they will need in adulthood.

Much of what they require from us in regard to their developing sexuality is an extension of what has come before. Their questions—about how babies are made, how they grow, and how they are born—will continue, and they may need to hear the same information again and again before they can get it all straight in their minds. (Books that you pick out together from the library can really help.) They may also want more pointed information about sexual intercourse and how it happens, and they might even ask if they can watch you sometime (a request that has much more to do with their concrete learning style than budding voyeurism).

**Input from Peers.**   By second grade at the latest, they'll be overhearing sexual terms on the playground, around the neighborhood, or from older siblings or cousins. You'll probably overhear some of these conversations yourself, and you can always choose to follow up with a teachable moment: "I heard you and Lynn talking about 'sex' the other day, and I'm wondering what that word means to you." Or, at other times, they may come to you directly and ask for information about what they've heard. Those are always golden opportunities for you to solidify your role as a trusted adult guide and mentor and to ensure that your child will continue to recruit and include your grown-up voice and perspective about sexuality among the many to which he or she increasingly will become exposed. What's important is that you try to train yourself to become shock-proof, at least on the outside. Once children have to start worrying more about your reactions than their questions, they'll hesitate to ask them. It helps to remember that these days, kids of almost any age are likely to ask about almost any topic. All it means is that they've overheard something that's caught their attention. How fortunate that they bring it to you, so that they can get your spin on the topic before they get someone else's.

Remember, too, that you might want to talk to the child about *how* sexual information is being shared among peers and classmates, not just *what* is being discussed. Are their friends silly or giggly when this topic comes up? Do they act as if they're doing something secretive or naughty? Are there teachers around? If not, why not? If so, what do they say or do? What kind of language is used, slang or "proper"? Are the genders uncomfortable with one another or disrespectful of one another? Are the kids teasing one another about what they know and don't know? Asking these kinds of questions—not all of them at once, of course—will encourage your child to be aware of the unspoken and often unhealthy attitudes peers typically communicate to one another during these early conversations about sex. It will also give you an opportunity to reinforce your own values.

**Gender Constancy.**   Even if the topic of sex hasn't quite hit the playground in a big way by second grade, the issue of gender roles usually has. As parents and teachers will testify, many children are suddenly more aware of gender-typed clothing, toys, and interests. Friendship patterns often shift dramatically as well, as boys and girls begin to take off in different directions—on the playground, in the cafeteria, and on the weekends—once cut loose from more structured, adult-controlled activities. Interestingly, the impetus for these changes is probably more intellectual than social, since the emergence of important new cognitive skills enables seven-year-olds to understand gender and its ramifications with much greater sophistication.

For example, if you were to show a younger child a pair of anatomically correct male and female dolls, then dress them in front of the child in stereotypical boy or girl clothing, they would correctly identify each according to gender. However, if you then switched the clothing, again in front of the child, and asked the gender of each doll, the child would incorrectly switch her or his answers. The child's level of mental capacity simply cannot take into account two variables—the image of the doll's genitals *and* the image of the gender-typed clothing—at the same time. Giving the correct response requires the intellectual ability to hold one of the variables constant while manipulating the other. A handy way to assess if children have acquired this mental capacity is to ask the following question: "Are there more boys in your class, or children?" If they attempt an answer, they haven't yet acquired this intellectual ability. If they look confused or refuse to respond because the question makes no logical sense, they probably have.

The average seven-year-old, on the other hand, can manage this mental task quite handily. As a result, the concept of *gender constancy*—the notion that one's biological gender is independent of the gender roles or behavior that one adopts—becomes firmly integrated. The child can now understand that regardless of present or future circumstances, he or she is, always has been, and always will be irreversibly male or female. (The small minority of children who will eventually self-identity as transgender or transsexual may experience this developmental juncture as extremely confusing and even painful.) As teachers and casual observers have long noted, this age is also when, especially at school, boys and girls begin to gravitate more and more to same-gender activities and relationships. Although sociologists propose many psychological and practical explanations for this shift, I am convinced that culturally defined gender myths play a significant role. By this stage, the child has also learned that males and females are supposed to be "opposite," and that being just the "right" kind of "real" boy or girl is vitally important in American society. It makes sense that they would tend to form tighter gender-based associations at precisely this age in order to solidify their gender roles and learn from one another how to become the "best" little boys and girls they can be.

Clearly, powerful developmental, social, and cultural forces are at work here. Parents and teachers attuned to these dynamics can do their best to encourage girls and boys to maintain good friendships and positive, relaxed interactions with one another throughout the elementary school years. They can try to ameliorate or at least soften the gender myths that help fuel this tendency toward strict, self-imposed gender segregation. In my view, it is one of adults' most important roles as anticipatory guides during these years. After all, children ultimately will live out their lives in a coed world, and for most of them, the intimate relationships they will form with the other gender will be central to a healthy and satisfying life. It truly does not serve them to think of themselves as opposite sexes or as an entirely different species ("ooh, cooties!").

**The Concept of Homosexuality.**    It is often during the second grade that the words *fag* and *gay* surface in children's conversations. (They may have used them before, but not necessarily with any specific understanding of the terms.) As discussed in Chapter 6, these words are commonly used—even at this age—to put boys down for doing "girly" things. Unless adults intervene, the words become powerful social weapons for teaching the basics of homophobia and sexism and cementing the implicit connection between them. Moreover, the children's use of these words helps spread the mistaken belief that sexual orientation, gender role behavior, and perhaps even gender identity are one and the same.

Adults who want to short-circuit this confusion before it takes hold will need to be proactive. Tough as it may seem, adults must bring up the subject of homosexuality *before* their children hear about it from someone else, and in an accurate context that reflects *their* belief system and values. (We'll discuss how to bring up this and other seemingly tricky subjects in Chapter 10.) Many will also want to keep tabs on what their children are hearing from other sources, so that they can provide correct information and counter negative and hurtful stereotypes.

**Sex and Culture.**    As I often tell parents and teachers, second grade is an important year in sexual development, and one of the most important reasons is that it's the year before third grade! Playground banter about sex seems to increase exponentially among eight-year-olds, and it's important to remember that this is nothing new. Although it's tempting to blame their heightened—almost obsessive—interest in sex on the escalating media hype over the past decade, third grade has always been a significant developmental juncture, sexually. When my older son was in the third grade, in the early 1980s, he came home from school one day and asked about five new words he'd overheard in one afternoon: *azho* (asshole, I presumed), *pemp* (for pimp?), *prostitute* (all syllables pronounced so perfectly, I'll bet he could have spelled it), *bases* (see Chapter 3!), and *blow up* (blow job?). That was a tough day, even for me. I must admit, however, that when it came to "blow up," I took the easy way out. "Josh," I said, "I don't know about that one. Maybe it has something to do with photography. See if you can get some more information." I figured that until he got it right, I wasn't officially obligated.

Again, it's important to understand sexual issues in the context of over-all development. As discussed in Chapter 3, middle to late elementary students are newly able to conceptualize the notion of society in terms beyond their own immediate social world. Figuring out how this larger social, economic, and political universe works is one of the central developmental challenges—or psychosocial tasks—of the age and a capability that will enable them to navigate adolescence.

As many a savvy fourth-, fifth-, and even third-grader already understands, sex is one of the linchpins of American culture. For many children at this age, random but constant exposures to sexual content and innuendo—through media, advertising, friends, peers, and adults—abruptly coalesce into new interest in sex. Given the developmental imperative of the age, figuring out how society works sexually becomes a sudden and pressing priority. Keep in mind, too, that this level of interest is far removed from the mechanistically oriented concerns about origins and reproduction that engage younger children. The focus here is on sex per se, that is, on sexual behavior and those things connected to it. Children this age are becoming very aware that people "do it," and it is the "doing" part that has them fascinated (and disgusted all at the same time, which, of course, for most children, only heightens the interest).

In their role as anticipatory guides, parents of children younger than third grade are wise to know that this shifting interest and focus is coming—if not for their child directly, certainly for many of the children with whom they will interact on a daily basis. It's another reason that parents will want to try to open up the subject of sexuality (or whatever issues happen to interest their particular child) by the second-grade year. This way, they'll be seen as "askable" and approachable whenever the subject kicks into high gear later on. Ideally, parents should also become advocates for realistic and responsive education at their children's school, so that teachers can be encouraged and trained to be aware of the ever-present sexual banter and bring it back into the classroom for discussion.

In most schools, especially elementary schools, children know that "sex talk" is taboo, and they confine it to when and where they think they will not be overheard. (Sometimes, I have to reassure my students repeatedly that they won't get into trouble if they ask a certain question or say a certain word—even in sexuality class!) What a terrible message. Again, adult evasion and ignorance of real developmental need abandons children to peers and media as their only guides. In-the-know parents are the best hope for change—and schools need their input and support.

## Anticipating Puberty and Adolescence

For years, teachers have told me that fourth-grade students are especially interested in learning about fetal development. As mentioned, children's interests in sexual topics mirrors the larger developmental issues in their lives. Thus, fourth-graders' fascination with growth and development in utero reflects the anticipation of their own coming "gestational" period. In Chapter 10, we'll explore some useful ways to help children understand these dramatic, life-altering changes that they will experience.

It's clear as well that many fourth-graders are the product of years of missed opportunities for age-appropriate sex and reproduction education. Consider the following questions, gathered recently from fourth-grade students: Why do men have penises and girls have vaginas? If you were born a boy, can you turn into a girl? Why do kids sometimes talk about things they want to know with kids, but never with a grown-up? Why does sex (I don't know what it is) cause children? What does reproduction mean? Where do babies come out of? Why do people's bodies change? What do babies' private parts look like?

Other questions from the same group of fourth-graders also make clear what they have learned about sexual attitudes and values and that they've been noticing and storing up questions about sexual issues for quite a while: Why is it assumed that *sex* is a bad word? Why are people scared to say *penis* and *vagina*? Why do kids sing and make up rhymes that talk about private parts? Why do people make such a big deal about "doing it?" How come you never really are allowed to talk about it freely? Why does it get so important when you become a teenager? What does it mean to "blow someone"? Why do men find rape and harassment "nice"? Why do kids and adults make fun of gay people and lesbians? Who invented *fuck, shit, damn, hell, bitch,* and *bullshit*? How come people like seeing and making "sexy" movies? Why do they talk about your private life on talk shows?

Fourth-graders are also clearheaded and fair-minded on issues about which older students sometimes have blind spots. They have a keen sense of fairness about demeaning and disrespectful behavior and are uncommonly receptive to conversations about sexual labeling and bullying. They are just beginning to test the power of sexist language with one another—*bitch, 'ho, slut, wimp*—and they have the brainpower to really understand an adult's explanation of why and how it is unfair and hurtful. With continual reinforcement at home and at school, I'm convinced they would be less prone to carry this language—and the attitudes it coveys—into middle school social life.

Many at this stage are also beginning to emulate adolescent culture—in their dress, hair styles, make-up, accessories, language, and music. Dubbed "tweens" by the media moguls, they have become the youngest and latest target of advertisers and merchandisers hoping to create a new and very large market of style-conscious consumers. Just as teenagers have been recast in the image of young adults, and preteens as little teenagers, late elementary aged children are being encouraged to look and act like little grown-ups and to want the things that grown-ups (supposedly) want. The pressures on children and their parents can be enormous. Parents must remain conscious of who the *real* grown-ups are. Teenagers, let alone children, are not simply small adults and should not be encouraged to think that they are. The real danger is that by the age of fourteen or fifteen, many young people increasingly have come to think of themselves as capable of, and even entitled to, free agency regarding their personal and social lives. Ask them. They will readily tell you that adults really should have no say over what they and their friends do with their time, their bodies, their money, and their values.

Late elementary school is the time for parents to take this not-yet-raging bull by the horns. Children not yet in the throes of adolescence still accept and expect that their parents will set limits around their behavior. Even if they don't like it, they know they are obliged to defer to adult authority. And the truth is, limits make them feel safe and cared for, despite the temper tantrums they may throw. Now is the time to set the stage for the adolescent years, not by laying down the law or establishing who's boss, but by making it clear that as a parent you have certain responsibilities that you take, and that you will continue to take, very seriously. The message should be this: "As the adult in our relationship, I must make certain decisions when it comes to your physical, social, and emotional well-being. You may not always like them, and in fact, sometimes I'll even make mistakes and either underestimate or overestimate your ability to safely make your own decisions. But I will always try to be fair and realistic, I will always give you my reasons, and I will always ask for your input."

Parents would be wise, too, to set up a supportive network with other parents, whether through grade-level meetings at their children's school or, more informally, by actively getting to know the parents of their children's friends. Together they can decide on appropriate limits for socializing and other activities. (Remember that the exact limits set are not as important as the strong message that it is appropriate and necessary for parents to be involved in limit setting.) Communication between parents can also reduce the chance that parents will be pitted against one another: "But Sally's mom lets *her* do that!" Movies, videos, TV programs, phone time, e-mail, Internet use, curfews, sleep-overs, bedtime, allowances, supervision, clothing, shoes, makeup, and so forth are all important and helpful topics for conversation. Although parents cannot present a unified front on all issues (that would be impossible and far too heavy-handed), their dialogue with one another helps clarify important developmental issues and highlights and reinforces the parental role of limit setting.

## The Middle School Years

I don't admit this to everybody, but middle school is my absolute favorite age to teach. A teacher I know likes to say that children at this age are a cross between an automobile mechanic, a newspaper reporter, and a sponge: They want to know everything about everything, and they want to know it *now*. Obsessively fact- and detail-oriented, they insist on understanding how everything works, including their own bodies. Although they can be pretty embarrassed and giggly, their feelings of discomfort are usually right on the surface and fairly easy to allay (see Chapter 10 for specifics). Also, since they're gradually but steadily developing the brain power required to think in abstract terms, they're eagerly drawn into— and terrifically excited by—discussions of complex ideas, controversies, and moral dilemmas. What wonderful opportunities these attributes create for cultivating strong, clear values and critical thinking skills.

Also, from a cognitive, social, and psychological perspective, ten- to fourteen-year-olds are increasingly able to step outside themselves and think about their lives and their relationships with a much more grown-up point of view. They are ripe for looking at formal decision-making and problem-solving strategies. Moreover, even though sooner or later they will all be up to their knees in adolescent struggles over identity and separation issues, most are not yet even ankle deep; they are quite willing—even publicly—to seek out adult input and guidance. The majority are also still clear-headed about risk taking. They can tell you exactly what is good for you and bad, and through seventh grade at least, they're willing to make socially conservative statements about topics like sex and drugs, even in front of their peers. In short, if you can get them to sit still long enough and to trust you and each other genuinely enough, they're a sexuality educator's dream.

**Double-Digit Status.**   I've included fifth-graders among middle schoolers, because in some schools, that's when middle school begins. Although in many ways fifth-graders are still much more like children than early adolescents, their double-digit status can make them feel a cut above their younger schoolmates, as if they've crossed an important developmental threshold. Many of them have also begun to notice pubescent body changes in themselves or others, and they're consequently aware of both boys and girls as different in new ways. A lot of girls, in particular, become excruciatingly self-conscious at this age and are prone to overpersonalize any mention of puberty or body changes. Boys generally are not seeing changes just yet and don't have any new body parts or attributes to feel self-conscious about.

I encountered this reaction in a very dramatic way years ago, the first time I held up a nondescript line drawing of a uterus and fallopian tubes in front of a group of fifth-grade girls. At least five of them, spontaneously mortified en masse, immediately covered their faces with books or notebooks. To them, those were *their own personal fallopian tubes* I was showing the entire class, and they simply couldn't bear to look at them, or to be seen.

Parents, moms especially, are often quite taken aback by their fifth-grade (or slightly older) daughters' reticence, if not outright refusal to talk about sexuality. Especially if mothers have enjoyed a pleasant history of easygoing and comfortable chats up to this point, they may feel mystified and even hurt or rejected by what is sometimes a very abrupt change.

They might worry they've done something wrong or that there's something they're not doing right. Most likely, the sudden distance has nothing to do with them at all and everything to do with normal, predictable physical and emotional changes. The solution is for the adult to separate his or her own reaction—real and understandable as it is—from the child's needs. Parents can then refocus on the child, in this case on her need for space and time enough to adjust and gain a renewed sense of developmental equilibrium. A parent can best help by affirming directly what the child is obviously feeling ("I can see that you're really not comfortable or interested in talking about this right now") and letting her know that you'll be glad to talk again whenever she wants. She'll appreciate your attentiveness to *her* feelings and *her* needs, and she'll be much more likely to reconnect later on because she knows that her agenda, not yours, comes first.

Despite this sudden discomfort, it's not at all unusual for a few boys and girls at this age to start pairing up as "couples," and for the question of "Who likes who?" to become the hottest gossip of the entire grade. (Boys and girls in earlier grades sometimes pair up, too, but those kids are pretending they're growing up, whereas these kids know they really are.) These liaisons are typically short-lived and are a harmless kind of preparation and rehearsal for teenage life. Most commonly, the "couple" are content to confine their interaction to school time, to the telephone, and e-mail.

Parents may react with great surprise or even alarm that sometimes a girl or boy at this age may want to ask someone out on a "date." They should know, however, that to make a large issue of the idea would be an overreaction (children don't really conceptualize dating in the same way that teenagers or adults). Instead, parents can use the situation to calmly initiate many opportunities (not all at once, of course) for affirmation, information giving, limit setting, and anticipatory guidance: What does it mean to you to go on a date? What kind of relationship should there be between people who date? What kind of dates—if any—are OK at your age? How about for older preteens? Older teens? How can you tell if someone is old enough or mature enough to go on a date? What is appropriate behavior on a date? These kinds of questions can be revisited time and again as dating takes on different meanings at different ages.

It will be important for parents to think through their own views in advance of these conversations and take care not to reinforce precocious behaviors by subtly ("Oh, isn't this cute!") or directly ("Great! Let's go buy you something fantastic to wear!") encouraging "real" dating at this age. Parents would be well within the range of age-appropriate guidance to set and explain why they've decided on a "no-dating" policy at this age. An alternative would be a time-limited, parent-orchestrated outing to the movies or another structured activity. They might also insist that other friends be included. In this way, parents have become involved in a way that affirms the children's yearning to be regarded and treated as more grown up, but without anybody's losing sight of who the real grown-ups are.

**Entering Adolescence.**   A friend tells a very funny and revealing story about the day he learned that his sixth-grade son had became an adolescent. The two of them were listening to the car radio, when a news story came on about the "morning-after pill." The father glanced over at his son a few times and noticed that every time the phrase "morning-after pill" was mentioned, the boy seemed more and more confused. "But, Dad," he finally said, looking very earnest, "what do they use if they *do it* in the morning?"

The story didn't surprise me one bit when I heard it. Sixth grade is another one of those years—like third grade—when the antennae on top of a child's head abruptly shoot up two full notches. Overheard words, phrases, facts, concepts, news items, snippets of conversation, which previously would have simply whizzed by, suddenly begin to materialize on the child's radar screen. In fact, information is penetrating so rapidly at this age, I always joke that each sixth-grader really needs his or her own personal sexuality tutor!

In my experience, you can always spot a group of twelve-year-olds by the phrase that nearly always begin their questions, in class or in the hallway: "Is it true that . . . ?" Having overheard some brand new nugget of information *this minute*, they just can't wait to check it out. To teach them, I seldom have to lecture or even have to prepare so much as a tentative lesson plan: They will ask every question necessary for me to give them every piece of information that I wanted to get across in the first place. And, invariably, should we happen to leave something out, a student or two will catch me on the way out the door. They instinctively know there's a great big puzzle out there that they must assemble in their minds and that they need all the pieces to get it right.

Their interests at this age extend way beyond reproductive facts and information about sexual behavior, since the issue of sexuality has become, suddenly, less academic and much more personal. Given the opportunity for freewheeling discussion, they will want to spend time talking about a large variety of topics. Changing bodies and the new feelings of privacy, modesty, and self-consciousness they provoke—especially for very early or very late developers—are hot topics. So are changing feelings and relationships with friends, family, and same- and other-gender peers. As the school year proceeds, cliques, popularity, and the need to fit in begin increasingly to drive the social dynamic. Peer cruelty as a means of social control and dominance rears its ugly head in powerful new ways. Conversations around these issues are essential, especially for kids who don't easily fit the stereotypic mold of what's "in." As more boys and girls start to eye one another as potential romantic interests, and "getting" a boyfriend or girlfriend becomes a more widespread priority, navigating this new social terrain provides more grist for the rumor (and class discussion) mill. They'll also want to talk about the crude and sexist language that the genders use against one another and that the girls, especially, are bothered by. And of course, they're more than anxious to chat and ask questions about all the sexual content they've seen in movies and TV or on the Internet, and the sexual (mis)information they're hearing constantly from one another.

Although later many of these same topics will be kept away from adult ears, at this stage, trusted parents and teachers are often truly welcomed as listeners, affirmers, and anticipatory guides. And in schools, where groups of kids can talk together, teachers can help them help one another, by normalizing common experiences ("Well, if others feel this way, maybe I am normal!") and boosting self-esteem. These are opportunities not to be missed.

**The Safety—and Tyranny—of Peers.** Seventh grade is the perfect year for a formal, comprehensive, semester-long course in school on the broad topic of humanity sexuality. I've taught one for twenty-five years, and it's absolutely the most rewarding work I do. A tad more comfortable and at home with their bodies (many have been experiencing changes for quite a while), they're still fairly close to and dependent on adults in their lives for guidance and support. Moreover, many are developing or refining fledgling abilities as abstract thinkers, and I'm hard-pressed to think of any sexual- or gender-based topic they can't be helped to understand and critically analyze. It's simply a wonderful age for shaping attitudes and for building in an exceptionally broad base of knowledge and important thinking, decision-making, and interpersonal skills. It's also a wonderful time for doing so before they fully enter adolescence.

For children, seventh grade is a very tough age socially and emotionally. Parents often describe these newly crowned teenagers as unbelievably self-centered. Most days, they are so focused on their own needs, feelings, looks, insecurities, and perceived imperfections, that they're almost impossible to please if not downright unfit to live with. They may become suddenly hypersensitive to the way adults, especially parents, speak to them. They'll react with fury if they feel babied, snap shut like clams if we pry, and may stop sharing things altogether if they're afraid we'll overreact or "catastrophize" their problems. It's also the age when peer approval and acceptance are probably never more important to achieve and never harder to come by. Just think, I tell parents, how hard it is for you to please them. Now imagine what it must be like for them to come to school every day, desperately needing to please a room or grade full of kids who are all just as hard to please and to live with as they are!

For young adolescents, this difficult stretch of time requires nerves of steel; for us, it requires patience and the knowledge and acceptance that this trial by fire is an unfortunate but necessary part of their entering adolescence and beginning to leave us. As those of us who have watched our children live through this period remember well, there's painfully very little parents can do directly to help, though there's plenty to do indirectly, in the way of listening, affirming, and helping them anticipate and problem-solve specific situations. In fact, our helplessness is actually the point. It's one of the first signs that they are growing up and having to take unequivocal charge of their own lives.

As children become teenagers, they and their peers become the absolute creators of their own social world, and in large measure, their social world becomes their real world. Doing well in school, being accomplished in sports or the arts or hobbies, and pleasing parents and other adults may all remain important, but their deepest satisfaction—and deepest wounds—emanate from relationships with friends and peers. From this point on, their peers' views will carry infinitely more weight than ours about many things, since they are now compelled to look to each other—not to us—to affirm their basic acceptability and worth. No wonder that the need for conformity, popularity, and loyalty to peers (sometimes at grave cost) peaks at this age; it speaks volumes about how desperate they are to find and create safe ground as they take their first precarious leap away from us and our unyielding and unconditional love.

Young teens will have increasing opportunities to test this growing independence, as they begin to take all kinds of new risks, including sexual ones. They may experience their first serious crush and their first real sexual experiences. Holding hands, kissing, cuddling, and touching may become an occasional but important part of their social lives, and the experience of getting and giving sexual pleasure a new and powerful reality. From now on, their interest in sex will be prompted no longer by simple curiosity or external stimuli, but also by internally based needs and desires. Masturbation—now most often to the point of orgasm—increases and typically becomes the topic of playful banter (especially among the boys). In short, they become sexual beings in profound new ways.

**Discovering Their Identity.**   By the end of the eighth-grade year, virtually everyone has entered full-fledged adolescence and has engaged in the hard psychological work of discovering his or her own unique identity. I always say that you can see it in their eyes one day. There's a sudden wariness or distance, or maybe just the slightest of veils, but it's unmistakable. They have pulled themselves inward and away from the surface. In part they're in hiding, and in part they've simply got so much internal work to do that they have little extra energy to reach out and connect. Being cool sets in with a vengeance, and they wear it like armor: "If I'm cool—not warm—I'm invulnerable. If I act like nothing bothers me, then maybe nobody will. If I seem to have everything together, maybe no one will guess I'm barely holding anything together." And it will be harder and harder for them to ask for help—even from trusted adults—since showing they need it would both blow their cover and defeat the purpose of proving they can do it on their own. Parents may find they are suddenly at arm's length.

## Fifteen- to Eighteen-Year-Olds

Adults can help most through these years by keeping a loving distance—by being interested but not overly involved, caring but not smothering—π
208
and by recognizing that their high-school-aged children may need ever-increasing independence, but not total autonomy. There is still much for parents to do because there is much for adolescents to accomplish: completing their academics, cultivating unique talents, earning and learning to manage money, planning for their future, and fulfilling their personal, family, religious, and community obligations on increasingly adult levels.

As teens take on more and more adult responsibilities and characteristics, their needs for affirmation, information, values clarification, limit setting, and anticipatory guidance take on multifaceted and complex new dimensions. If they (and we) adjust well to these new demands, by the latter high school years, by which time their adolescent angst and search for separate identity are in large measure resolved, they often reemerge as refreshingly real, approachable, and thoroughly appealing young adults. If we've done our jobs, just when we are enjoying them the most, we know we have to give them over to themselves.

Socially and sexually, during the high school years, our roles as parents and teachers also remain crucial. It is self-serving and irresponsible just to say, "Oh well, I guess they know it all already." (Often, we will have to convince them of the folly of that belief as well.) They will need a broad base of very practical sexual health information, as well as some remedial work in working through any residual embarrassment or discomfort that may keep them from using it as needed. Moreover, although their expanding brainpower will enable them to comprehend, ultimately, the huge concept of human sexuality in all its breadth, they won't "get it" unless they are deliberately trained to see through the narrow cultural blinders in their way.

As they become more sophisticated thinkers, older teens must rethink their sexual values and hear their peers think out loud as they do the same; most of them will need an adult guide to facilitate this process effectively. Their independent social life will become increasingly active, but they will continue to need the watchful eyes and skillful limit setting of adults, especially as alcohol (and other drugs) and driving become an escalating part of the picture. They will date (although the exact form will vary greatly from teenager to teenager, community to community, and even school to school), many will fall in love, and most will experience the awful and awesome pain of rejection and unrequited feelings. They'll need us to listen to, or at least respect, their anguish.

As they change developmental course—usually sometime in junior year—from an intense and totally self-absorbed focus on *self and identity*, to the twin developmental concept of *other and intimacy*, they'll need help in grappling with a whole host of new relationship issues. They will struggle to differentiate infatuation from love, closeness from ownership, good sex from good relationships, intimacy from lust, conflict from battle.

Through it all, we can help by enabling them to understand the meaning of adulthood in realistic and honest terms. Too often, in their eyes and in society's depiction, an adult is someone who does "adult" things—driving, drinking, spending money, having sexual intercourse. We can help them see that being an adult involves *how* we do things, not *what* we do. They will inevitably make some very good decisions and some very bad ones, and we may never know about many of them. But if we keep encouraging them to stay connected to us as anticipatory guides, we'll maximize the chance that they'll put off making major decisions—the ones that can most affect their health and their future—until they're secure and mature enough to make the right ones. The next few chapters will provide many practical suggestions for guiding them successfully.

## More To Come

This description of eighteen long and complex years of development has been overgeneralized, of necessity, but it's touched upon most of the central themes and issues that parents and teachers will need to recognize and affirm in their role as nurturers. As we turn to more detailed discussion of information giving, values clarification, limit setting, and anticipatory guidance in the next four chapters, we'll refine and apply these major themes.

# 10

# Information Giving: Empowering Children Through Knowledge

An incident many years ago tested to the nines my mettle as a sexuality educator. My two boys and I were on our way home from the supermarket (the car as classroom again!), when completely out of the blue, my older son, then about eight, piped up from the back seat, "Hey, Mom. Are you and *my father* [I knew I was in trouble already] planning on having sexual intercourse anytime soon?"

Yes, he really said that, word for word. (I wrote it down.) And there was real urgency in his voice, too. I must admit, my first inclination was to say something definitively unprofessional. I don't remember exactly what, but the gist of it was probably "Why, Josh? Planning on selling tickets or something?"

Actually, that's not true. My *first* inclination was to drive off the side of the road.

Then, thankfully, I remembered what I do for a living. "He's probably not asking me about my sex life, even though it certainly sounds like—and worse yet feels like—he is," I told myself. "You must be reading something into his question, because obviously you're feeling so shocked and uncomfortable that you've lost your good common sense. Take a deep breath, remind yourself who the adult is here, and then try to figure out what his question is really about." (This advice and the emotional distance I needed to muster it required every ounce of my training over the previous dozen years.)

And, of course, it was right. We adults, especially when feeling threatened, tend to attribute our own adult interpretation or worst projections onto children's questions and concerns about sexuality. To understand Josh, I had to put myself in his place. And at that moment, his place was right next to a very rambunctious three-year-old younger sibling who was driving him bonkers.

Piecing it together, I realized later that his eight-year-old thought process, immediately prior to submitting this now-infamous question to the annals of our family history, probably ran something like this:

> *This kid is a complete pain. Life was so much better before this little monster was plopped down into it. Why did they have to bring him into this family, anyway? Things were going so well those first six years. The three of us were doing just fine, thank you. Boy, I sure hope they don't decide to do it to me again, especially if it's a boy. Just my luck, I'll never get that cute little baby sister I always wanted. Hey, wait a minute! Maybe they're already planning on it! Oh, no! Maybe they're even going to do that intercourse thing again really soon,* maybe even tonight! *I've got to stop them . . . before it's too late!*

I've probably told this story hundreds of times since, it was such a marvelous object lesson—for me—in separating out adult "stuff" in order to better see a child's needs. It demonstrates, too, the essential need to focus on the *context* of a child's question, sometimes even to the exclusion of its *content*. In Josh's case, doing so revealed that he was not really asking a question at all, but rather wanting to make a very strong statement about his current state of misery and exasperation with his little brother. Solving that problem, by the way, became the entire extent of our conversation on the way home. He truthfully had no interest whatsoever in talking about my sex life.

The bottom line: *Listen first* before assuming you know the child's wavelength, take the time to *reflect back* the question or the feelings behind it, and see what ideas the child has about the subject. That last step almost always brings a comment or new question that reveals to you the real question (or statement) behind the given one. In the case of Josh's question, a simple "This seems awfully important to you, Josh," probably would have elicited the real concern.

A mother once told me how her nine-year-old daughter asked if she would get "hair," too. The woman, deciding immediately that her daughter meant pubic hair, launched into a lengthy treatise about puberty and body changes. She welcomed the opportunity, having waited for just such an opening. When she was finished, the daughter said, no, she'd really wanted to know if she was going to get yucky hair sticking out of her nose and ears like her Great Uncle Joe.

## Eight Universal Questions

Tuning in to what your child is really asking can be a tricky business. But just as there are only five universal developmental needs (affirmation, information, values clarification, limit setting, and anticipatory guidance), it's comforting to know that there are only eight basic questions that a child or an adolescent will ever ask you about sexuality. From decades of experience listening to thousands of kids, I've realized that all their questions fall into eight fundamental questions about their sexuality or other aspects of themselves. I'll share them here, with examples from my own classroom "question box" (the ones below are from middle schoolers) and with pointers for responding in developmentally helpful ways.

The idea is similar to the approach in Chapter 8: Knowing that there are only eight basic question categories, you'll immediately feel more prepared, I hope, to deal with individual questions that may come your way. Then, once you've learned to figure out the real question behind the question, you'll be able to draw on the suggestions offered below to know how to respond effectively.

### What's True?

What is an STI, really?

How long are rubbers?

What is "making out"?

What is the most effective way of birth control?

When you change sexes, what happens to the man's penis?

As evidenced by the stormy history of sexuality education in the United States, when the subject is sex, answering the simple question "What's true?" can be anything but a simple matter. The misplaced fears that sexual knowledge is dangerous and that "knowing leads to doing" are the culprits. These anxieties make us doubt ourselves and the process of sexual learning itself. When our children ask us for information about sex, remembering to pause and internally restate the request as "What's true?" makes the right answer obvious: We simply tell the truth. After all, isn't that the same question we so effortlessly and confidently respond to thousands and thousands of other times as parents and teachers?

Most questions concerning sexuality, and almost all of them asked by children younger than ten, are fundamentally what's-true? questions, in one form or another. All we really need do is check out our understanding of the question and remind ourselves that if the child can ask it, we can answer it. We don't need to give enormous detail, or in the case of a young child, even tie the answer specifically to sex, but we do need to give a direct and accurate response. For example, a seven-year-old asks, "Why do ladies use tampons?" Answer: "Teenage girls and women use tampons because they have something called menstrual periods." For a beginning conversation, that might be quite sufficient, and if not, more questions will follow. Another example: A six-year-old is listening to the radio and asks, "What does the word *rape* mean?" Answer: "Rape is a legal term used when one person forces another person to do certain things they don't want to do."

Children older than nine or ten are intellectually and emotionally ready for more detailed information, even about very sensitive subjects, and we should proceed slowly, but confidently, by following their lead. By the time children are middle school age, we should not hesitate to respond with—and even volunteer—as much detail as they want to know, or we want to tell. And as children become adolescents and their questions become more and more pointed, we'll need to keep our own reactions increasingly in check. Most especially we'll need to resist the strong temptation to ask, "And just *what* do you want to know *that* for?" In the same way that knowing doesn't lead to doing, just because they want to know something doesn't mean they are doing it or want to do it. If we fall into this trap of believing that wanting to know means wanting to do, we'll scare them off; according to my students, this is the number one rea-son they stop going to their parents for information. It is much better to answer the question and then calmly add, "I'm really curious about what made you ask that. Can you tell me?"

## Can You Please Help Me Figure This Out?

How does the boy's penis get in the girl's hole, because the hole is rel-atively small?

I'm pretty sure that most parents have sex every so often. What if they don't want more kids? Isn't that risky?

What is 64?

How do women have orgasms?

How can girls get pregnant if they are virgins?

Exactly what is an STI? I know it's a disease of making love too much.

The questions above, different forms of the generic question "Can you please help me figure this out?" are actually a subset of "What's true?" with an interesting twist. Just beneath the surface of many what's-true? questions is an excruciating sense of confusion. Because of large gaps in their formal learning over the years and because of their relative inexperi-ence, children and adolescents typically acquire relatively disjointed bits and pieces of information along the way. Often, half of their information is totally correct, and the other half totally wrong ("What is 64?" being a truly classic example!). In these kinds of questions, children are thinking out their confusions aloud. Other times, they've got two pieces of correct information, but they're missing an important connector, like, for exam-ple, the existence of a whole concept—contraception!—in the second question above. Or they're struggling mightily to put together two pieces of seemingly contradictory information, as in a relatively big object and a relatively small "hole"!

We need to treat these kinds of questions exactly as what's true? ques-tions, but try really hard not to laugh out loud because they often sound so funny or cute. We simply fill in the missing pieces and acknowledge that this can be a tricky and confusing subject for everyone.

## How Do People Go About Doing That?

What happens when you give a guy a blow job? How do you go about it?

What do you do during foreplay?

What do you consider the difference between making out and kissing?

What is making out? Exactly what does happen?

Questions about explicit sexual behaviors are typically those about which young people are most fascinated and often most giggly, embarrassed, and unsure. Not coincidentally at all, they are also the ones that adults most commonly are reluctant to talk about. Those words—they're just so hard to say!—and there's that underlying (and totally irrational) fear that our willingness to explain will be acted upon or misinterpreted as endorsement or permission. Also, if the question happens to have the word "you" in it, we may think they're asking about us personally, which they rarely are.

Again, these questions are best treated exactly as we might any other what's-true questions, except that we'll probably have to practice—a whole lot. We can always begin with a very general answer, starting with what the child already knows and is fairly comfortable talking about, and then adding new, less comfortable information. For example, a nine-year-old asks, "What's a blow job?" Answer: "'Blow job' is a slang term, and you should know that some people find it a very offensive expression. It means the same thing as 'oral sex' or 'oral-genital sex.'" New question: "What does that mean?" Answer: "Remember when we said that sexual intercourse means when genitals—the penis and the vagina—come together? Well, oral sex means when one person's mouth comes together with another person's genitals." You can always follow up with your own views about the subject, or solicit the child's (which will probably be something like, "Ooh, gross, disgusting"), but first just answer the question! By the way, if a child of five or six should ask about a topic like oral sex, he or she will probably be very satisfied with "That's a private behavior that some grown-ups do." The rule of thumb is this: The more unsure you are or the younger the child, start with a response that's as general as possible.

## Am I Normal?

Do you think there is an age limit for masturbation? Between ten and
. . . ?

Whenever I read a book that has sex in it, I get a funny twitch in my
privates. What is that?

To me having sex sounds disgusting, but it's supposed to be fun. Why
is it queer to me?

At what age do you think a girl should have a date?

Is masturbation wrong? Does this mean you're a fag?

Young people, especially early adolescents, worry about their adequacy
and normalcy along many dimensions—physical, social, emotional, and
intellectual. Moreover, the constant changes that they experience make it
especially difficult for them to establish a baseline against which they can
measure and feel good about themselves. Additional performance pressures are created constantly by society's narrow definitions of sexual normalcy and physical attractiveness. What young people need is a great deal
of reassurance, which can best come from peers who help each other understand that they are not alone with their worries and inadequacies. It
can also be provided by adults, who with the perspective of knowledge,
time, and maturity can help them define normalcy in as broad and accepting a way as possible.

"Am I normal?" questions often sound very much like what's-true?
questions. Adults who train themselves to listen to young people with
their "third ear" intently tuned in to the emotion behind a question usually detect the hidden "Am I normal?" plea. It's a signal that the adult
should tread carefully and be as reassuring as possible. Unless there is a
clear indication that something is undeniably wrong, an adult's answer to
a child or an adolescent's "Am I normal?" query should always be a resounding *yes!*

## Can I Trust You? Can I Get to You?
## Will You Set and Stick to Clear Boundaries?

Why do we have to have this course?

Were you a virgin when you got married?

What method of birth control do you use?

When you are screwing, how do you really turn a guy on?

These kinds of questions are not really questions about sexuality at all, but about the relationship between the questioner and the person being questioned. Trust between adolescents and adults is a variable commodity. Adolescent struggles with issues of identity, autonomy, separation, and independence require them to challenge authority and test limits. Adults are ambivalent, too, about holding on and letting go. Add the topic of sex to the mix, throw in a culture that can't decide if sex is the very worst thing in the world or the very best, and you have a situation ripe for testing and manipulation. Being able to identify and respond appropriately when questions are being asked for the purpose of testing ("Can I trust you?") rather than acquiring information ("What's true?") is an acquired skill.

Adults learn to judge if they're being tested by paying attention to hints like the language the child chooses (often very explicit), how he or she looks (you can usually detect a sly, telltale glint in the eye, or slight curl of the lip), and how the person sounds (very giggly or surly) while asking. You can also tell that it's a testing question by how the question itself makes you feel: crummy! You may feel backed into a corner, embarrassed, on the spot (especially if the question is very personal), unsure, intimidated, or all of the above. Experienced teachers can also tell by what happens to the rest of the class, since there will be instant pandemonium or, perhaps, deafening silence.

Don't expect to handle or even be able to detect these questions easily at first; children and adolescents are very good at manipulation. Eventually you'll be able to identify the clear symptoms and signals that you're being "had," and you'll learn to respond to the *real* question being asked, which is, "What will you do if I test your limits?" You'll want the answer to be "I'll set them again, even more clearly this time!" You'll learn to respond to their *indirectness* with your *directness*. "You know," you might say, "that's a good and serious question, but you didn't look or sound serious when you said it. Can you ask it again more respectfully?" Or, "That question (because of the language or its very personal nature) made me really uncomfortable. Are you trying to put me on the spot for some reason?"

Keep in mind that many personal questions are not testing questions at all, but a sincere expression of curiosity. In other words, they're just another kind of what's-true? question. Don't ever hesitate to refuse to answer a question that feels too personal; that is your right, and you also will model how to set appropriate boundaries around sexual curiosity and personal sharing. With careful listening, however, you might be able to respond helpfully in a more indirect way—by *changing the question* to a question you are comfortable answering. If asked, for example, "Were you a virgin when you got married?" you might say, "That feels too personal, but would it help to talk about why people choose to wait—or not wait—until they are married before having intercourse?"

## Could This Hurt Me?

Does an abortion hurt?
Is it safe to swallow sperm?
How safe are rubbers?
My mother told me that when she was in the eighth grade a girl got pregnant in her class. Is that happening commonly today?

As much as they might favorably anticipate it, growing up can look scary and forbidding to children and adolescents. In the sexual realm, young people have very real fears about the dangers of pregnancy and disease, which the media play up with dramatic and often sensationalized coverage, or play down with endless portrayals of consequence-free scenarios. Young minds lack the cognitive sophistication required to sort out these kinds of extreme messages, and unhealthy misconceptions and distortions can result.

The key concept for adults to remember whenever they present scary information is *balance*. It may seem very tempting, and even logical, to use fright as a means to control or inhibit behavior. However, fear tactics can just as readily backfire, causing teenagers, especially, to become more reckless, not less. There is always the danger that they will become overwhelmed by an overdose of negativity and respond by retreating into denial or its flip-side reaction, paranoia, as a way of coping: "Why bother to even think about it, since there's nothing I can do anyway?" Adults should always tell the truth, but also make sure that a teen leaves such a conversation feeling at least a little more reassured than scared. Follow this rule of thumb: Always give the bad or scary news first, quickly followed by a slightly larger dose of good news. For example, "Yes, AIDS is really scary for the following reasons. But, it's also almost totally preventable, and here's how." In talking about scary subjects like AIDS with young children, too, be sure to tell the truth, but remember that your reassurance is what they need most: "Yes, AIDS is a very dangerous and scary disease, but adults know all about how to protect themselves from it, and when you're older, we'll be able to tell you everything you'll need to know, too."

## What Should I Do?

How do you act toward a girl on a date?

What should you do when a boy asks you to sleep with him? How should you react?

When my mother asks me about having sex with a boy and I tell her I let a boy touch my breasts, she gets shocked. I feel that this is my business and unless I get pregnant, she should leave me alone. What are your feelings about this?

Could a boy get hard at any time?

Young people continually find themselves in new and challenging situations. Because of their longing for independence, adolescents particularly have a growing need to be seen as effective people. Also, their craving for peer acceptance and approval creates the constant need to look good and prove themselves worthy—all the while staying cool. In the midst of these acute performance pressures, sexual and social situations can become especially intimidating, because the vulnerabilities involved are potentially so very intense and complex.

Resisting the temptation to give advice and learning instead to guide young people through the steps of problem solving, from problem definition to identification and evaluation of alternatives to choice making and follow-through is a vital skill for adults to develop. If we learn to do it well, even as our children approach adulthood, they'll continue to call upon us as trusted consultants when they face a hard-to-solve problem. Chapter 11 discusses values and decision making in detail.

## What's Right?

How far should people go at parties?

What do you think is the right age for intercourse?

How about living together before marriage? Do you agree?
Is abortion our best choice?

Only in adolescence do we acquire even the rudimentary capacity to think in the abstract terms necessary to make moral judgments. Questions of sexual morality, although among the earliest moral issues young people face—often on their own—are also among the hardest. Moreover, many situations that require these sensitive judgment calls are completely unplanned and highly pressured. And, in the midst of a society highly ambivalent about sexual morality, it is hard to discern clear values to emulate or even to rebel against.

Discussions with our children about sexual values challenge us to clarify our own deeply cherished beliefs and help them to formulate theirs. If our talks go well, we'll continue to have an influence on many of their decisions. In Chapter 11, we'll explore many communication skills, such as active listening, open-ended questioning, and open-minded sharing of beliefs and values, that are essential to productive and trust-enhancing dialogue.

## What to Say and How to Say It

Once adults have communicated that they are "askable," and once they have learned how to correctly interpret the questions that children and adolescents typically ask, what remains, of course, is to teach. To do so effectively, all teachers and parents should be aware of the *what* (the content) and the *how* (the process, method, and context) of good teaching. In fact, the *what* of teaching and learning and the *how* are inseparable. No matter how valid or important the content, unless the medium for teaching it is effective, learning will be compromised. Conversely, if we use all the best teaching methods, but the material is not what the children need to learn, then we have also failed our children.

As discussed, our children's learning about sexuality is often compromised in terms of content *and* process. It is sad and scary, but by the time most children are eight or nine years old, they have absorbed much misinformation—factually and attitudinally—under many adverse learning conditions.

Much of our children's sexual miseducation comes indirectly through peers and culture, but much comes directly from the adults in their immediate lives as well. We simply pass on what we ourselves learned and how we learned it as children and adolescents. I've listed below some of the more common examples of "under-education" and miseducation that I encounter almost universally. These are followed by several important teaching pointers. All adults—in families and in schools—should know this information, so that by working together, we might gradually interrupt this ongoing cycle of impoverished sexual learning.

## Organs, Systems, and Openings

I am constantly amazed at how little children and adolescents know about the bodies they inhabit. As soon as children learn to talk, it's crucially important to start teaching them about their bodies and how they work. I've made this point earlier with the suggestion that adults take care to label sexual body parts, just as they do all others, with correct, matter-of-fact terminology. As children approach three or four years old, we can also begin to teach them that bodies have an inside and an outside, and that many of our parts, or organs, are located where we can't see them. An easy way to teach this concept is to help them understand what happens to their food after they swallow it and can't see it anymore. (There are many clever and engaging big picture books available in stores and public libraries that show and educate about the internal parts of the body.)

Gradually, we'll also explain that each organ inside our body is connected to other organs, and that together certain groups of organs make up each of our body systems. We have many different body systems, and in each a group of different organs works together to do a particular job that helps keep our body alive and healthy. Once children have grasped this concept, we'll be in a good position eventually to fit the reproductive system right into the body along with all the others—making it ever so much easier to talk and learn about. The conversation won't be about *SEX!* but will simply be a continuation of many earlier low-key and matter-of-fact discussions about how our bodies work.

Another handy concept to teach young children concerns their *body openings:* We have several places on the outside of our body that lead to certain organs on the inside, and it is through these openings (please don't say *holes!*) that things from the outside go in, and other important things from the inside go out. With very little effort, adults can use many different everyday experiences to reinforce this idea. This basic anatomical concept makes it much easier to explain the mechanics of intercourse and birth later on. Be sure to explain as well that girls and women have *three* openings in the area between their legs—the *urinary, vaginal,* and *anal* openings—and that these openings are connected to tubes and organs and systems (the *urinary, digestive,* and *reproductive),* which are not connected either structurally or functionally. It pains me to think of how many high school students and even adults whom I taught did not understand this basic fact about female bodies and how much further confusion that has caused them.

## Stomachs, Abdomens, and Uteruses

Food and stomachs are very real to children and easy for them to understand. Unless we are careful in how we speak to them when they are young, they will grow up thinking that their stomach, their belly or abdomen (which is nothing but a space or cavity), and their abdominal wall (the wall of muscle, fat, and skin in front of the abdomen) are one and the same. This sloppy terminology—especially if we also tell them at some point that babies grow in stomachs or bellies—sets them up for untold confusion later on.

By late elementary school, most of my students have no conception of their abdomen as a space in which many organs and parts of different body systems are located. As a result, they have various parts of the reproductive, urinary, and digestive systems hopelessly intertwined. Since what they learn the earliest is often what they remember the longest, what I try to reteach them may or may not stick. Not surprisingly, when I see them in the classroom again two or three years later, their understanding has often reverted to their earlier learning. When it comes time to discuss fetal development, it becomes clear that many even think the umbilical cord is connected directly from the baby's stomach to the mother's!

## Vaginas and Vulvas

An even more fundamental confusion exists in the minds of most girls and boys, and probably many adult men and women: the vagina, contrary to popular opinion, is *not* located on the outside of the female anatomy. The vagina is an internal pouch—really a potential space, located just inside the vaginal opening. The *vulva* is the collective name for all the external female genitalia, which include the inner and outer labia, the clitoris, and the mons (the mound of skin on top of the pubic bone, where pubic hair eventually grows). Thinking that the vagina is located somewhere on the outside or that it is both inside *and* outside, as many people do, is tantamount to not knowing the difference between your face and your throat!

Many girls and women have never even heard the word *vulva* and can barely name any organs that make up this part of a woman's or girl's anatomy. This ignorance of girls' and women's bodies and the names that describe them harkens back to the days when women's organs were considered dirty and shameful. And since the function of these organs is primarily sexual and not reproductive, it also reflects a time in our history when "good" and "normal" girls and women were considered incapable of sexual feelings—*ever*. Is it any wonder that many young girls and teenagers even today act as if these parts of their bodies are foreign objects and seem disgusted by their very existence? If we don't want our girls to have nineteenth-century attitudes about their bodies, we have to raise them as if they and their bodies live in the twenty-first.

## Males Have Reproductive Parts, Too

For the thirty-odd years that I've been teaching, it's been clear that neither males nor females know much at all about the internal male parts. This lack of information probably derives from a time when most "sex education" was really "menstrual period education"; as a result, many adults have never really been required to formally learn about the male reproductive system. Even today, the young people whom I teach—both girls and boys—are often incredibly confused about such basic concepts as the difference between sperm and semen, or erections and ejaculations. And terms such as vas deferens, seminal vesicle, and prostate gland (an organ mentioned frequently in the news today) are not even in their memory bank. It's quite revealing that many of us know the most about internal female organs (which are about reproduction) and external male organs (which are about sexual pleasure), and the least about female external organs (which are about pleasure) and male internal organs (which are about reproduction). Clearly, we need to be doing a better job of educating everybody about everything.

## The Reproduction and Sexual Response Systems

The reproductive system is unique among all other body systems. First, each person only has half of a system. Second, the half of the system we do have is totally nonfunctional for the first several years of our lives, as well as the last (at least for women). And finally, even during the years that our reproductive system is working, we can survive quite well (as individuals) if we never use it! These three features are a great opening for discussing myriad sexual and reproductive facts—intercourse, conception, puberty, menopause, and sexual and reproductive decision making, to name a few.

A related system, the sexual response system, is much more straightforward. Like the reproductive system, the sexual response system is not necessary for individual survival. Unlike the reproductive system, however, it is fully present and functional at birth. It greatly surprises most adults and young people to learn this basic biological fact. Perhaps it would help us better integrate and talk about the sexual parts of our lives if we came to accept our sexual system as simply another one our body's basic functions. In truth, babies' bodies are quite capable of sexual feelings, even to the point of orgasm. Baby boys experience frequent erections, and in baby girls, sexual lubrication regularly passes through the walls of the vagina. Indeed, both of these reactions occur involuntarily every ninety minutes during sleep throughout our entire lives. And although only males ejaculate, both male and female bodies, when sexually aroused, experience roughly the same sequence of physiological events and body sensations (referred to in the sexology literature as *excitement, plateau, orgasm,* and *resolution*) known as the sexual response cycle.

## Puberty, Pubescence, and Adolescence

Imagine how much we would hamper our children's understanding of the concept of time if we were not clear with them about the difference between a second, a minute, and an hour, or if we were to use the same word, *minute*, to describe all three. Yet, when it comes to explaining their own development, we are precisely that imprecise.

The concepts of puberty, pubescence, and adolescence are related, but they are not at all the interchangeable terms we commonly make them out to be. Although most people have probably never even heard of the term *pubescence,* they frequently use the terms *puberty* or *adolescence* when pubescence is the concept they really mean to talk about.

First of all, puberty is best thought of as an *event,* whereas pubescence and adolescence are *processes.* Puberty is a precise term that refers to the exact point in time when a boy or a girl becomes reproductively capable. For a girl, this event occurs at the moment she experiences her first period. (She may well have been technically fertile two weeks before her first period—when ovulation occurred for the first time—but she was probably not aware of it at the time.) For a boy, puberty occurs at the moment he experiences his first ejaculation (again, more technically when his body began manufacturing sufficient quantities of sperm and semen). The experience of first ejaculation commonly happens during a wet dream, or nocturnal emission, but it might take place while a boy is masturbating or engaged in sexual behavior with another person. Most adults are not aware that boys do reach puberty on an exact day in time, just as girls do, and this lack of knowledge hampers their ability to prepare boys adequately for the developmental processes they will experience.

Pubescence, unlike puberty, happens over a very long period. It begins with the release of small quantities of sex hormones (testosterone or estrogen) from the gonads (testicles or ovaries) at roughly the age of eight. These hormones enter the bloodstream and begin to give the body a series of chemical instructions that will set in motion the development of a boy or girl's *secondary sex characteristics,* such as breast enlargement and hip widening for girls; chest and facial hair growth and muscle development for boys; and growth spurts, voice changes, skin changes, and the appearance of pubic and underarm hair for both. The presence of testosterone or estrogen will also gradually cause the *primary sex characteristics,* namely, the reproductive organs present from birth, to enlarge and develop their full adult capacities and functions. Although these changes may not be apparent for several months or even years (it may take the body quite a while to respond overtly to the new hormonal messages), sooner or later all the expected changes will occur.

Pubescence ends when each girl or boy is fully grown and the body has been completely transformed from girl to woman, or boy to man. Since pubescence can begin when a child is eight and end as late as eighteen, the entire process can take up to ten years. In contrast, although it may have been several years in the making, the actual event called *puberty* takes only about ten seconds, that is, the time it takes to go from being a person who's never experienced a period or an ejaculation to being a person who has.

Besides avoiding unnecessary confusion about the developmental processes, I find this distinction between puberty and pubescence essential for helping children and adolescents understand and feel good—or at least better—about their own individual growth. A girl, for example, might experience her first period anywhere between the ages of eight and eighteen. (The average of puberty is twelve and a half for a girl and thirteen and a half for a boy, but a large range is possible.) At a time in her life when if feels so important to be "in" and the same, an early or a late developer will likely feel excruciatingly different. However, if we can learn to differentiate and emphasize the several-year process of pubescence—rather than the highly variable event of puberty—we can help young people understand that they are all much more alike than different. "Sitting there in that chair," I like to tell my middle school students, "you are all pubescing right along, and you will continue to do so at your own rate and pace over the next several years. And on one of those 3,650 or so days, according to your own particular timetable, you will reach puberty."

A final word of caution in explaining puberty to boys: Although wet dreams are definitely wet, they're not necessarily about dreaming. The common explanation typically includes something about how a boy is having a dream about sex and how this causes his penis to become erect and eventually ejaculate. Though that may often be true, it isn't always. In any case, parents may wisely de-emphasize the "sex dream" part. Many boys who might want to ask questions or confide in their parents about their first nocturnal emission hesitate to do so because they think it amounts to an admission that they are having thoughts, desires, or dreams about sex. On top of other intense feelings of confusion, discomfort, or embarrassment that this event might provoke, the sexual implications may be overwhelming. *Puberty is essentially a reproductive—not sexual—milestone,* which would be easier for everyone to talk about if it were defined in that way. Just as a girl cyclically releases the lining of her uterus because it is no longer needed by the body, boys have nocturnal emissions because periodically there is excess sperm and semen that the body needs to release.

*Adolescence* includes the concepts of puberty and pubescence, but is infinitely more complex. It involves not only physical development, but also myriad emotional, social, intellectual, and spiritual changes that young people undergo as they make the arduous transition from child-hood to adulthood. Its beginning and ending—in contrast to puberty and pubescence—is marked by subjective experience, not measurable physical change. As I tell my students, adolescence begins at that point in life when you stop thinking of yourself as being totally a child (most kids say around ten) and ends when you start thinking of yourself as more or less an adult, whenever that might be. Answers from adults whom I've polled range wildly, depending on life circumstances, from before ten to mid-thirties! With this definition as a starting place, my students are in a good position to talk about the true meaning of being an adult, the vari-ous characteristics it entails, and the developmental learning and experi-ences it requires.

## Menstrual Periods and Menstrual Cycles

Another example of how we tend to mix up reproductive events and processes involves the menstrual cycle. Understanding the menstrual cycle is the key to understanding almost everything that occurs in the repro-ductive life of girls and women. And yet, many people cannot clearly dis-tinguish the concepts of periods and cycles, much less identify accurately the correct series of events that take place.

The menstrual cycle is best described as a series of reproductive events, of approximately twenty-eight days in length, that repeats itself in the female body (except during pregnancy and early breast-feeding) from puberty to menopause. Each menstrual *cycle* begins anew on the first day of each menstrual *period.* In other words, day one of each new cycle coincides with day one of each new period. Once the menstrual bleeding has stopped, the other events in the cycle proceed in order. These include the rebuilding of the uterine lining, the release of an egg from one of the ovaries (ovulation), the death and disintegration of the egg in the fallopian tube (unless it is fertilized), and, finally, a message to the uterus that the egg has died. Upon receiving this hormonal mes-sage, the uterus prepares to shed its lining, and the cycle begins anew on day one of bleeding.

Although everyone need not know this sequence precisely, all adults should be able to reinforce the following three concepts: First, the begin-ning of each cycle coincides with the beginning of each period; this day, which a girl or woman should always mark on her calendar, is called the LMP, or the "first day of the last menstrual period." Second, ovulation and menstruation are two distinct events, separated by two weeks; the egg does not "die and come out" during the woman's menstrual period. Third, although the risk of pregnancy varies greatly throughout the menstrual cycle, *pregnancy is always a possibility*; therefore, if a couple does not desire pregnancy, they must abstain from sexual intercourse or make sure to always use an effective method of pregnancy prevention.

## Hormones

Because hormones are invisible chemicals in the blood that communicate silent messages to the body, children and adolescents often have difficulty understanding how they function. Yet, hormones are crucial to every aspect of the male and female reproductive systems. Parents and teachers can help by introducing the concept of hormones as early as possible, as soon as children can understand that some things are so tiny they can't be seen but still can do very powerful things. Besides the sex hormones, there are many hormones in the human body. All hormones can be likened to messengers that travel from one place to another and deliver important instructions. Eventually, we can give children the whole picture: Hormones are chemical messengers that are produced by one organ of the body, travel through the bloodstream to another organ, and tell it what to do.

One more thing about hormones: I absolutely cringe whenever I hear someone say that teenagers are driven by their "raging" hormones. This is an inaccurate, totally misleading, and even dangerous remark. Although hormone changes may affect mood, and moods may affect some behavior, *normal, healthy teenagers are capable of controlling their own behavior at all times.* Just when we are attempting to teach them about the importance of assuming personal responsibility for their actions, why would we even suggest that they're fundamentally incapable of doing so? Are we perhaps simply projecting our own feelings of being out of control, in relation to their growing freedom and independence? What's more, and equally as alarming, I have heard over the years many teenagers and preteens claim that the high incidence of rape and date rape in our society is attributable to the "fact" that boys and some men simply cannot control themselves sexually.

## The Basics of Communicable Disease

Another way that parents and elementary and middle school teachers can set the stage for important learning is by explaining and reinforcing basic information about the communicable disease process. Just as hormones are invisible and therefore hard for young minds to understand, so are the microorganisms that cause sexually transmitted disease and other serious infections. As early as possible, we can begin gradually but deliberately to teach the following concepts:

1. There is a difference between being sick and being well.
2. Sometimes people become sick because they have come into contact with tiny, invisible objects called germs.
3. There are two different kinds of germs: bacteria and viruses.
4. Being infected means that you have come near certain germs in your environment, through contact with another person or an object, and those germs are now living in your body.
5. There are many things that people can do to keep from coming into contact with germs that can make them sick and to help themselves get better if they do become infected.

How much easier later sexual health education would be if all youngsters began their formal sexual education with a firm understanding of these concepts!

## The Basics of Pregnancy Prevention

Almost all teens and preteens today know, of course, that sexually transmitted infections and unwanted pregnancy are potentially negative consequences of sexual intercourse. However, many are amazingly underinformed or terribly confused about the important differences between disease prevention and pregnancy prevention. In Chapter 13, we'll spell out these distinctions and suggest ways to explain them clearly.

# Some Final Pointers

The following paragraphs present some quick but important suggestions about how to make discussions about sexual knowledge and information go smoothly.

## Checking In, Checking Out, and Checking Up

Keep in mind that even though the need for age-appropriate information is ongoing throughout childhood and adolescence, just as the specific contents shifts over time, so does our role. Although young children need for us to be available so that they can "check in" when their internally based timetable of questions surfaces, older elementary and middle school children need us nearby so that they can "check out" all the new information they are suddenly absorbing from their increasingly larger world. Older teens, who typically are not nearly as forthcoming and who tend to overestimate greatly their level of basic knowledge, sometimes need for us to insist they get a "checkup"—either from us or in a school-, religious-, or community-based educational program—to make sure that they know what they think they know.

## Keep It Conversational

The stereotypical image of the "big talk," with the obligatory sweaty palms and throat clearing, is a far cry from the fun, easygoing, everyday conversations that make for healthy family communication about sexuality. It will help if you remember to stay calm, trust in the process, and welcome your children's questions—all of them—as unique and precious opportunities.

## Everybody Can Talk to Everybody

Parents often ask if it's better for the same-gender parent to do most of the talking to an individual child. Certainly, that approach is sometimes a good one, depending on the topic and circumstance. As a general rule, however, there is no reason why mothers or fathers should restrict themselves to particular topics (or offspring). Single parents, too, worry if there is no same-gender parent in the home to do the educating. I always tell them that my personal experience of single parents is that they often do a better job at many things than many co-parents do, because they seem to take their parenting role doubly seriously. In any case, what kids need most is to witness as many different combinations of people speaking openly and respectfully about sexuality as possible, so that conversations of all kinds become normalized.

## Don't Ignore Embarrassment

Embarrassment—yours or your child's—is something you can expect to surface from time to time. It will show up in various forms: giggling, joking around, fidgeting, tension, silence, or out-and-out blushing. Remember that embarrassment connected with talking about sex is not natural, but *learned*, which means that it can be *unlearned*. Encourage your child to verbalize his or her feelings instead of acting them out indirectly, especially through nervous laughter. (Laughing and enjoying yourself during conversations about sex is perfectly OK, as long as the fun is about something really funny.) The message to get across is that sexuality is a fundamentally serious subject and that it's therefore important to act, look, and sound fundamentally serious when we speak about it. Before you know it, with practice and a few reminders, the embarrassment will begin to dissipate. If you try to talk over it and don't deal with it directly, your child will likely remain stuck with her or his embarrassment. The embarrassment may continue indefinitely as an unnecessary and potentially dangerous communication and learning barrier.

## There Is No "Bad" Language

Everybody knows that "dirty" words are dirty because they're about sex; therefore the expression itself not only perpetuates negative attitudes toward sex, but also toward talking about it. Words are just words; they can be used in a bad way, but they're not intrinsically bad. (Some words—like *nigger* and *faggot*—are considered intrinsically bad because they're almost always used in a way that is horribly pejorative and nasty; however, members of certain minority groups actually choose to use and "own" some of these very words, as a deliberate strategy for diminishing their meaning and punch.) Adults should always try to teach and encourage proper terminology about sexual parts and functions, but shouldn't hesitate to talk about slang terms—whatever they might be—with young people. Explaining slang terms and why many people find various words and expressions so offensive is a great way to raise consciousness about (and even help change) the many sexist and demeaning sexual attitudes that abound in our culture and to teach about the appropriateness or inappropriateness of using certain words in certain settings. When we talk about slang terms and the context behind them, it also takes the power out of using these terms to shock or hurt others, since they are no longer taboo and, therefore, not as enticing.

## Start with What the Child Already Knows

Many times when we say, "You're not old enough to know that," what we really mean is that we can't figure out how to explain it, especially to someone so young. Often a topic seems so totally out of the context of a child's life that we just can't come up with a proper starting place.

The topic of homosexuality is a great example. Sometimes, often because they have close family members or friends who are gay, parents want to inform their children but can't imagine how or when that might be appropriate. Usually their stumbling block is that they're thinking of being gay or lesbian as a purely sexual concept and therefore one that is totally foreign to the child's world. Here's the key in situations like this: Think of a related issue with which the child is already familiar, and start there. In this case, the concept of coupling, which children as young as five or six can certainly understand, is a perfect one. The parent can say something like: "I know you've noticed that when people get older they become attracted to and want to become a romantic couple with someone who is very special to them—like me and Mommy, and Aunt Jane and Uncle Bill, and Joey and his girlfriend Sara. And I'm sure you've also noticed that all the couples you've met so far are male and female. Well, what you may not know, is that some people are attracted to and want to become a couple with someone of the same gender, and that's called being 'gay.' In fact, Mom's friend Sally is gay, and we wanted you to know what that means."

## Stay Concrete

Children and even many adolescents are basically concrete thinkers: If they can't see something, feel it, taste it, smell it, or hear it, then they have a hard time learning about it. Keep in mind that most sexual and reproductive organs and processes are invisible; they happen on or in bodies that aren't built like your own or inside your own body, where they can't be seen. Moreover, many reproductive concepts—like the all-important female menstrual cycle—are total abstractions. No one alive has ever seen a menstrual cycle! (I've always said that the best way to teach about the menstrual cycle is to line twenty-eight kids up against the wall, put bright red hats on the first five and a yellow hat with green stars and pink polka dots further down the line to represent ovulation. *Then* maybe they'd remember!) Pictures, diagrams, videos, and active learning techniques that involve visualization, analogies, repetition, interaction, doing, and imagining are essential. There is one precaution, however: Make sure they don't take you too literally. I once told a group of eighth-graders that there are so many sperm in one ejaculation (300 million to 400 million) that if you could stretch all of them all out in a row from head to tail, the line would extend for about eight miles. One girl in the class promptly went home and informed her mother that a man could ejaculate and make it go for eight miles!

## Think Small

As I'll discuss in Chapter 13, health educators, unlike most instructors, try to teach their middle and high school students as little as possible, not as much as possible, so that the material is easy to remember. Don't worry excessively about how much your children know. Concern yourself with how well they know the important stuff, how easily they can talk about it, and whether they know how to acquire the additional knowledge they may need in the future. With younger children, the same rule especially applies: Give a simple, general answer to most questions, see if the child seems satisfied, and if not, keep giving a little more.

## Reframe the Issue in a Nonsexual Context

When my younger son, Adam, was about four, he asked if he could play with some of the tampons in the bathroom. He wanted to put them in the sink, watch them fill up with water, and pull them around like boats. I had a ridiculously hard time with this request and obsessed over it for days; I just didn't know if this was a "proper" game for a four-year-old boy. Finally, I remember asking myself: If there were another object in the house that was this harmless, this inexpensive, this disposable, and this much fun to play with—and could at the same time teach a lesson about Archimedes' principle—would I even hesitate? I went out and bought him his own box.

## Try Not To . . .

When children ask questions, it is always best to avoid saying, "You're not old enough to know that," or asking, "What do you want to know that for?" Also, try hard not to overreact to a particular question or choice of language, to pressure yourself to be some kind of sex expert, or think that you have to wait until you or your child are totally comfortable. You can always say: "Give me some time, that's a hard one!" or "I don't know, but let's look it up together," or "Boy, that's embarrassing, but let's talk anyway." All these responses build trust, model honesty, and reinforce open communication.

## Parenting Is Almost Always a Do-Over

The good news (and sometimes the bad news!) about family is that we're stuck with each other. *You can't really blow it.* There's always tomorrow, and there's almost always the chance to say, "You know, I didn't really like the way that last conversation went. Can we try it again?" Remember that it's your willingness to "hang in there," especially when the going gets tough, that really matters.

# Values Clarification:
# Highlighting "Right" Thinking

Try this values-clarification activity with your middle or high school age children at the dinner table some night. Read the following story, and then ask for responses to the question at the end (having paper and pencil handy might be a good idea):

### Who Is Responsible?

Brenda and Robert had been going together for several weeks. Although Brenda liked Robert a lot, more than any other boys she'd ever gone with, she wasn't sure she was ready to have intercourse with him or with anyone else, for that matter. As time passed, though, and their relationship grew stronger, finally one night, "it just happened."

Since they had not used any type of birth control, Brenda worried for the next several weeks about whether she might be pregnant. When her period arrived, she was grateful and very relieved. She vowed never again to go through another experience like that, and decided to get some protection for herself.

She started by asking her teacher at school for help. "Sorry," the teacher said, "the school board has ruled that we are not allowed to discuss subjects like birth control with the students."

Embarrassed, but still determined, she gathered her courage and called for an appointment at a clinic located at a nearby hospital. But when she arrived at the hospital the day of her appointment, the doctor told her she would have to come back with a permission slip from her mother before she could be seen.

Brenda was beside herself. She just didn't know how she could possibly tell her mother, and decided to confide in her older sister instead.

"What?" her sister said. "You don't need to know about birth control, because I don't want you to see him or do that again!"

Brenda was crushed. She decided that in the morning she would talk to the only person left who could help her—her mother. She and her mother had not talked much about sex, but her mother did love her after all and would surely want to help. But the next morning, as she was trying to find the right words, the lump in her throat was so big that she just sprang up from the breakfast table and ran up the stairs.

Two months later, she had a positive pregnancy test at a clinic in the next town.

Question: Who is responsible for Brenda's pregnancy? Rank the six characters in the story—Brenda, Robert, teacher, doctor, sister, mother—in order from 1 to 6, according to the character you think is most responsible, to the character you think is least responsible. No ties are permitted!

## Thinking About Values

The educational technique known as values clarification is just as its name implies—an opportunity for individuals to look inward and clarify their attitudes, feelings, beliefs, and values about important life issues. Participating in values-clarification exercises similar to the Brenda and Robert story is like taking your "affective temperature": it's a window into yourself.

The characters in the story, of course, are not real people. Each is presented in an intentionally vague manner, so that listeners will project onto him or her their own unique constellation of attitudes, feelings, beliefs, and values. To most people, the characters Brenda and Robert represent the value of *personal responsibility;* the teacher and doctor, *professional responsibility;* and the sister and mother, *family responsibility.* How listeners decide to rank the six characters will depend on how they personally come to prioritize those values in this particular situation. Those decisions will be colored by their own unique set of related attitudes, feelings, and beliefs—all of which have been shaped by their individual experiences with their own mother, sister, doctors, teachers, and the teenage boys and girls in their own lives. As a result, even people whose rankings are identical will have somewhat, or even entirely, different reasons for selecting them. That's because their affective life is specific to them; it's like an internalized fingerprint of who they are.

Some people contend that the values-clarifications approach is values-free, because it implies that there is *no one right answer* to complex values dilemmas, but they are mistaken. What is implied clearly in the values clarification process is that complex questions call for thoughtful answers, that moral issues require sophisticated and careful attention, and that certain core human values—such as the value of responsibility in the Brenda and Robert story—are givens.

I wrote the Brenda and Robert scenario about a quarter century ago (it's remarkable how relevant it remains today!) to nudge the thinking of a group of high school students who had concluded that anyone who "got herself pregnant" as a teenager was just plain stupid. Later, I began to share it with adult groups to help them to consider the exquisite complexities of adolescent decision making—and teenage pregnancy prevention—in American society. We'll use it here, not so much for its content, but to learn how to facilitate productive discussions about values and decision making with children and especially adolescents.

## Talking About Values

Adolescence is sometimes described as a return to the "terrible twos," when it seems as if, almost overnight, our pliant and relatively easy-to-please infants suddenly turn stubborn, truculent, and hell-bent on resistance, just for the sake of it. Toddlers are driven to toddle and to *explore* on their own. Just try to put one in your lap and keep her or him still for any extended period! In the same way, adolescents are driven to *think* on their own. Their central developmental imperative—to establish a sepa-

rate and unique identity—compels them to want to draw their own conclusions about what is right and wrong, just and unjust, appropriate and
inappropriate. That's why moralizing is almost always guaranteed to push
them away from us or may well backfire and lead to excessive rebellion or
defiance. When we moralize, the message conveyed in our tone of voice,
if not our words, is "Now, you listen to me! I will tell you what to think
and do, because you can't be counted on, or allowed, to figure this out on
you own!" This is a message they will resist and want to push against
every time, *because they must*. They know instinctively that it is contrary
to their developmental best interests.

Although all adolescents may from time to time take a position simply
because it's different from ours, it's a mistake to assume that they automatically want or need to be contrary. What they do want and need, always, is to be taken seriously. When adults speak and listen respectfully to
a young person's views, especially when they strongly disagree with those
views, they will invite much less adolescent angst and unnecessary con-
tentiousness. They will also increase the likelihood that young people will
continue to seek out their counsel. As the title of Adele Faber and Elaine
Mazlish's book captures so well, the key to effective communication and
ultimately to effective parenting is to know "how to talk so kids will listen, and listen so kids will talk."

## Open-Ended Questions

As children move into adolescence, they increasingly require more private
emotional and physical space, both as a buffer against the external stresses
and demands of growing up and as a safety zone for tending to their internal emotional needs. Indeed, attending to themselves during this time
can take on a spiritual-like quality: "Alone time" becomes their salvation,
their room a sanctuary, and their belongings sacrosanct. What's more, as
my young adolescent students tell me, they often feel a sudden compul-
sion to draw a tight circle around what they tell their parents and other
adults about their lives. Many times this change comes as a great surprise,
even to them; they themselves can't find rhyme or reason to explain the
parts of them they now choose to keep more private. Adults, too, are often taken off guard by this development. If they don't recognize it as a
necessary, normal, and predictable part of growing up, they can react with

understandable but unwarranted fear, suspicion, or deeply hurt feelings that their child is pulling away or rejecting them.

As with so many characteristic adolescent behaviors, adults must learn not to take this one personally. It signals change, not trouble or rejection, and that simply means we have to change with it by developing a different style of communicating. To keep the channels open, we'll need to adapt with new ways of responding, listening, and sharing that signify our respect for their newfound and more grown-up sense of self. And we'll want to look for opportunities to talk about personal issues without getting "too personal." Let's use the Brenda and Robert story to demonstrate some of these skills.

The art of "open-ended" questioning is a wonderful skill for parents and others who nurture or work with young people. Open-ended questions are intended to accomplish just what the phrase implies: to encourage open-minded thinking and to generate many possible answers all at once. *Its hallmark is the attitude and intention of the questioner.* To pose open-ended questions effectively, the questioner must have minimal vested interest in the particular answers he or she receives. The emphasis is on discovery and exploration and on teaching young people *how* to think about a particular issue or problem, not *what* to think.

Here's why the skill of asking open-ended questions is so important when talking with adolescents about sensitive or values-laden issues. As we have observed, adolescents experience an acute need to protect their personal boundaries, and that can make them hypersensitive to any line of questioning they construe to be a potential violation of self. They'll dread or avoid conversations with us if they find our questions to be "closed-ended." Closed-ended questions come in three types: prying, pointed, and manipulative. Our questions will come across as *prying* if it seems that we're trying to get or pry personal information out of them to meet our own needs, interests, or agenda. *Pointed* questions usually result when we have a particular answer in mind, and that's really what we want them to say or agree with. And, questions will feel *manipulative* if our questioning is designed to get them to think a certain way and to reach a particular conclusion that will please us.

Here are some examples of prying, pointed, and manipulative questions that an adult might be tempted to ask in response to the Brenda and Robert scenario:

- *Prying:* Would you or your friends ever do something like this? Have you? Would you ever go to a doctor or clinic without asking my permission?
- *Pointed:* Don't you think Brenda should have learned her lesson the first time? Brenda's mother was pretty clueless, wasn't she?
- *Manipulative:* Well, you've said you thought Robert was really irresponsible. Does that mean, I hope, that you won't get involved with boys until you're much older?

Questions such as these might provoke heated discussion, but if the adult is using the opportunity to "smoke out" information or is only interested in being "right" or in leading others to the "correct" answer, the prospect for real dialogue will be slim. Real dialogue requires that all participants be open to hearing different points of view. Adolescents will be much more receptive to open and honest dialogue if that and that alone is truly our goal.

Here are some examples of the kind of open-ended questions, again based on the Brenda and Robert story, that are great discussion starters because they keep the focus on thinking and problem solving skills:

The story implies that Brenda was not sure she was ready for intercourse. What do you think changed her mind? How would a person know he or she is "ready"? Are there different considerations for boys and girls? It's pretty typical that first intercourse for teenage couples in unplanned, and many don't use protection against pregnancy or disease. Why does this happen so often? Why do you think Brenda continued to put herself in harm's way? The story is written pretty stereotypically from Brenda's perspective, and we don't know much about Robert. What do you think he's like? How would the story be different if written from his perspective?

If you were Brenda's sister, how would you have reacted? If Brenda had spoken to her mother, what do you think her mother would have said? What should she have said? Some schools think talking to kids about birth control *and* abstinence gives a mixed message about whether it's OK for teenagers to have intercourse. What do you think about that line of logic? What would you say to the doctor about the clinic policy? What do you think Brenda will do now? What do you think you might do in the same situation? Suppose the story ended with Brenda having a positive HIV test. How would you rank the characters then? Why? How old did you assume Brenda and Robert to be? How did those assumptions affect your rankings?

## Active Listening

Probably the most worthwhile course I've ever taken, personally or professionally, was called Parent Effectiveness Training. Based on concepts and skills developed by psychologist Thomas Gordon in a book of the same title, it was taught by a brilliant local instructor who used virtually every moment of the course—and thereby taught us how to use virtually every moment of life—as an opportunity to learn about effective communication. One skill that I use constantly in my own life and work is *active listening.*

Most people think of *speaking* as the active component of any conversation and *listening* as passive. In fact, in any speaking and listening situation, speaking is usually considered the more favored, powerful, and difficult role. President Ronald Reagan, for example, was often called the "great communicator," because he was an extremely gifted speaker. As I have learned, however, both in the classroom and in virtually all of my relationships, *skilled listening* is uniquely active, powerful, and every bit as difficult. Done well, it embodies and employs the three most important building blocks in any relationship: understanding, trust, and acceptance.

There are three components of active listening, one verbal and two nonverbal. The verbal component conveys to the speaker that he or she has been *understood.* The listener basically paraphrases what the speaker has said, not by parroting the exact words (that would just be annoying!), but by distilling the central meaning of the message and saying it back to the person in an abbreviated form.

> SPEAKER: We really don't know what the mother would have done if Brenda had reached out to her, so I ranked her last. She might have been terrifically supportive, but Brenda never gave her the chance to help.
>
> LISTENER: So you weren't as hard on the mother as the other characters, because you gave her the benefit of the doubt.

If the listener has heard correctly, the speaker will likely say something like, "Yes, that's right," and if not, "No, that's not what I meant. What I meant was . . . " A follow-up paraphrase will provide a check on understanding and leave the speaker feeling heard, acknowledged, and probably wanting to talk some more.

The second and third components of active listening demonstrate that a skillful listener communicates—and doesn't simply receive—important information. The information he or she communicates is a powerful and visceral message of trust and acceptance; it is delivered not by words but by the listener's body language and his or her tone of voice. An open body posture, that is, uncrossed arms, direct eye contact, head nodding, and an inviting and responsive facial expression, speaks volumes about the listener's trustworthiness and receptiveness to what the speaker has to say. The third component, voice tone, is at least as important to the listener's credibility and effectiveness. Try saying the sentence, "So you weren't so hard on the mother as the other characters, because you gave her the benefit of the doubt," first with an accepting tone and then with dripping sarcasm. Add a question mark to the end, and despite the spoken words, the real message becomes "I can't believe you could be so stupid as to let the mother off the hook that easily!"

To be an effective listener, it's crucial to realize the difference between acceptance and agreement. Active listening is absolutely not about agreement or disagreement; on the contrary, its whole tenor is fundamentally nonjudgmental. While in the active listening role, the listener must very consciously put her or his own opinions on hold, shift to a neutral mindset, and get ready to suspend personal judgment. Although the point is not to show agreement, it is about projecting acceptance—not about *what* the person says, but about his or her absolute right to think and say it. That's the most important message that the active listener delivers: "I want to hear exactly what you think about this issue, and I have no need to judge or change your opinion in any way. Whatever position you hold is going to be OK with me, so please just be honest."

What I'm proposing is a mighty tall order: listening nonjudgmentally to our own children about sensitive and values-laden issues! But like anything else hard and worth doing, it can be mastered with time and practice. *And it is worth it.* It's the most effective way I know to build the kind of trusting relationships with our adolescents that will encourage them to continue to talk and to listen.

I'm in and out of school buildings all the time, asking children and adolescents to talk with me, someone they may have just met, about sensitive and personal issues. I've learned time and again that if I can just get them to talk with me about *anything* of substance, and if I can demonstrate by the way I listen how much I genuinely value and want to hear what they are thinking, we're well on the road to a trusting and open relationship. You can prove this to yourself, too. Try out this skill on everyone around you all the time—at home, at work, even in the supermarket or on elevators—and see if it doesn't change the quality of your interactions. You'll find endless opportunities to practice.

One last set of examples to cement the skill: You'll know you've mastered it when you can listen nonjudgmentally to two completely opposing points of view (especially if you strongly disagree with both of them!).

SPEAKER: I put Robert first because guys are out for one thing and I'm sure he pressured Brenda into the whole thing.

LISTENER: Sounds like you wouldn't trust most guys as far as you could throw them!

SPEAKER: I put Robert last because, obviously, it's her body and her business if she gets pregnant.

LISTENER: So it's very clear to you that birth control is first and foremost the girl or woman's responsibility. The guy has little or nothing to say about it.

And finally, the other side of the mother's character:

SPEAKER: I put the mother first, and it was no contest. Parents have a responsibility to know what is going on with their own children. She should have seen how upset Brenda was at breakfast and asked her what was wrong.

LISTENER: So as far as you're concerned, the situation could have and should have been prevented by better parenting.

## "I" Messages

Of course, dialogue with your children is not a one-sided affair. Just as you'll want to work hard to listen so that they will talk, you'll want to talk in ways that will encourage them to listen and to think. Ideally, any conversation with young people about values will involve an even blend of listening, questioning, and sharing on everyone's part.

The flip-side skill to active listening is the art of the "I" message. Thomas Gordon, who coined the phrase *"I" message* in the 1960s, originally developed this skill to help parents confront their children's unacceptable behavior while still encouraging a positive and cooperative response. I'll present it here in a modified form intended to help adults share their views with young people in a way that facilitates open-ended discussion. (I've also somewhat modified his original concept of active listening; his ultimate intention was to help parents "hear" the deeper emotional feelings embedded in children's conversation, not simply the verbal content of the message.)

An "I" message is a way of giving voice to your own deeply held beliefs and values that communicates clearly your passion and commitment to those ideals, but without imposing or pushing them on the listener. Instead of making global statements about right and wrong or inferring, "Here's what I believe and you should believe it, too" (what Gordon calls a "you" message), you simply state your point of view as convincingly as possible and invite a response. As with active listening, the art of delivering an effective "I" message lies in the tone of voice. The message embedded in your inflection should be the opposite of the moralizing message described several paragraphs above. The tone should convey this message: "These are opinions I've thought long and hard about. I share them with you because I want you to know what I think—and why—and because I hope you will give my ideas serious consideration. But I will not attempt to impose them on you, and I'm going to insist that you figure out what you personally think about these issues, too."

For most parents, this is a hard, even scary tone to muster. On some deep, visceral level, what many of us really want is to be able to pour our ideas into our children's heads, wholly intact, as a kind of sheltering and all-protective brew. Indeed, it feels counter-intuitive to so demonstratively "allow" our adolescents freedom of thought about issues and decisions that we know may hurt them (I've put "allow" in quotes, because, of course, we have no direct control over their thinking, but merely influence, if we work at it). Yet, it is one of the most important developmental transitions we need to make as they make theirs. Remember also that we are talking about the freedom to think on their own, not act on their own. Acknowledging adolescents' drive for intellectual independence does not at all diminish their continuing need for limit setting and anticipatory guidance.

As with active listening, delivering an effective "I" message is a challenging skill that requires rehearsal. Ironically, a good approach is to practice stating out loud some strong opinions that you *don't* agree with! Pick a controversial topic, and write out a list of six or eight possible opinions across a continuum from most conservative to most liberal. Then read each of the statements out loud—with conviction—even the ones with which you disagree. For example, I'll pick the highly volatile subject of abortion:

1. In my view, abortion is the taking of human life and is never acceptable.
2. In my view, abortion is acceptable only under the extreme circumstance in which the mother's life is in danger.
3. In my view, abortion is acceptable only when the mother's life is in danger or when the pregnancy is the result of rape or incest.
4. In my view, abortion should only be permitted when the mother's life is in danger, when the pregnancy is the result of rape or incest, or when there is severe fetal illness or abnormality.
5. In my view, abortion is a highly personal decision, and with some exceptions, should be left exclusively to the conscience of the individual woman.
6. In my view, abortion should be left to the woman's conscience, but should be discouraged or prohibited for the purpose of gender selection and after a certain point in fetal development.
7. In my view, an abortion decision should be left to the woman's conscience for any reason, but not past a certain point in fetal development.
8. In my view, an abortion decision is completely a woman's choice, for any reason and at any point in fetal development.

As you read through these statements, notice the quality in your voice as you say the ones with which you least agree or most disagree. That's probably just the right tone you'll want to effect in sharing your view: firm and compelling, but not insistent. (You might try out this exercise with another adult and give one another feedback about voice tone.) It's the insistent part, remember, that might feel like moralizing and as we've said, may be where you'll lose your credibility. Being careful not to overstate your opinion (i.e., making it sound as if yours is the only possible correct one) makes good sense not only developmentally, but culturally as well. Unless you're prepared to raise your child in a near culture-proof bubble, you can fully expect that in an open and highly pluralistic society, she or he will eventually become exposed to compelling viewpoints—spoken by decent, ethical, caring, and responsible people—that are in direct opposition to yours. Although the child might be so totally imbued with your particular view that exposure to others won't matter, it's probably still safer to say, "Here is what I believe absolutely, and why. Others may disagree, but here's why I think their conclusions, though perhaps well intentioned, are misguided."

## Other Ways to Get Your Point on the Table

Sometimes I just know I'll get farther with a group of students or with one in particular (or with my own children, for that matter) if I refrain from directly giving an opinion on an issue, at least initially. If I want to stretch their thinking, but I'm getting or expecting resistance simply because their adolescent ego or my adult ego is in the way, I'll say something like "Let's step back and take a look at the big picture here. There are a lot of different viewpoints about that particular issue. Some people think this, many people think that, and others think such and such. What do you think about those ideas?" Or, I'll say, "I thought of [or heard] a new and interesting point of view the other day about that very topic. I'd love to know what you think about it." Or, if I'm really frustrated, I usually say, "Look, you're only seeing one side of the issue here. There are some really smart people who would probably totally disagree with you. Can you be thoughtful enough to stop and figure out what their arguments would be?" Many times, framing the issues in this more intellectual and less personal way provides just the right amount of challenge and intellectual and emotional distance for people to make some headway. Everyone can save face, and no one needs to be at loggerheads, because they're simply thinking about or attempting to solve an interesting problem together, not trying to win a power struggle.

## What to Do When You Simply Can't Be Nonjudgmental

Often it's simply asking too much for parents to remain separate and open-minded in a freewheeling values discussion with their children.

Sometimes children touch a nerve that's just too irritating, personal, or scary. Maybe they're totally disregarding relevant information or simply don't have it at their disposal. Or perhaps, simply because you're older and more experienced, you know they really don't have a clue what they're talking about. It's really OK to step back squarely into your adult role, where all things aren't equal and your voice isn't just one among many. I've learned, though, that the best way to assert your adult role so that eventually you can get back to a more egalitarian plane, is to do it in a very exaggerated fashion. "Cut, hold, stop!" I'll say loudly. "I have to interrupt here and get up onto my soapbox for a minute, because I have something that has to be said. You'll need to stop talking and indulge me." It usually works, because I've acknowledged I'm aware that what I'm doing is very close to moralizing or at least sermonizing. Since I'm overtly identifying and taking responsibility for it, setting an obvious time limit, and showing my respect by not thoughtlessly imposing my authority, they're usually remarkably amenable!

## *The More You Give Them Permission to Disagree . . .*

Two maxims hold true when an adult is talking with adolescents about values: "It is easier to ride a horse in the direction in which it is going," and "The more you give an adolescent permission to *disagree* with your point of view, the greater the likelihood she or he will end up *agreeing* with it." The first maxim reminds us, first and foremost, that we must respect who they are. The second suggests that if we want to remain influential in our children's lives, even as we are losing much of our power, we must be smart about it. Then, if we consciously model commitment to our own values, add a sufficient dose of humility, and remain open, fair, and reasonable, we'll have an excellent chance of playing a continuing role as their evolving moral compass takes shape.

## Applying Values

In Chapter 4, we noted that in our language the word *value* may be used in three different ways: as a verb, a noun, and an abstract concept or ideal. So far in this chapter, we've focused primarily on ways to facilitate open-ended conversations about abstract values and controversial, values-laden issues. We'll turn our attention now to the more practical topic of instrumental values.

As explained earlier, in everyday conversation, the concept of values is most often used in reference to specific objects, people, activities, experiences, ideas, or ideals that are important or have worth to a particular individual. Because these serve as practical guides to our actions, they are sometimes referred to as instrumental values; we express them moment by moment through what we say and, most significantly, what we do. In fact, every time we make a choice of any kind, we are in effect making a very personal and practical statement about ourselves and our instrumental values. At the end of the day, it is our instrumental values that tell us who we are.

Although the overt choices we make in life are obvious and concrete, the values they represent are most often invisible and a matter of subjective interpretation. We'll use the Brenda and Robert scenario to make the point. Although we have only incomplete information about what truly transpired, if we take the behavior of the characters at face value, we can attempt some educated guesses about the instrumental values that played into their decision making. On the surface, each time Brenda faced a decision-making juncture, for example, she clearly chose one course of action over another. But, each of her actions also represented a choice between competing values: In deciding to participate in unprotected intercourse, she perhaps chose relationship over responsibility; in choosing to talk to her teacher and sister, information over face saving; in choosing not to speak to her mother, avoidance over confrontation. We could make similar kinds of inferences about the other characters as well: the sister, perhaps righteousness over support; the teacher, bureaucracy over empathy; the doctor, self-preservation over service; the mother, denial over protection.

As challenging as these interpretation skills may be for adults—and in my experience they require a great deal of reflection and practice—they are nearly impossible for concrete-minded children and adolescents to accomplish. Without adult guidance and training, they'll tend to focus on the visible actions. But if we want our children to base their decisions on "good values," we need to help them understand the values at the base of each of their choices.

Because values exercises like "Who Is Responsible?" entail making hard choices (like life itself), they also nudge people to discover what they really believe and value, as opposed to what they may think and say they do.

For example, although most people have a very hard time deciding where to rank Brenda and Robert (they usually want to place the two in a dead heat), when told they *must* make a choice, almost every one of the thousands of people I've ever asked has ranked Brenda higher than Robert. If the choice is truly such an even struggle, why haven't their answers panned out at fifty-fifty, not ninety-nine to one? Although it's easy—and politically correct—to say that pregnancy prevention absolutely should be shared equally between males and females, when push comes to shove, the potential consequences of this act are *not equal.* Suddenly, an abstract absolute must be reframed to accommodate a very concrete reality. (There may well be some blatant or latent sexism at work, too, which is also important grist for the mill!)

## Values and Decision Making

Many school-based programs aim to teach students "good decision-making skills." This is the wrong premise: No one really needs to teach anyone how to make good decisions. By the time children reach middle school, for example, they will have made thousands and thousands of good decisions—and quite a few bad ones as well. Our job as adults is to hold up the mirror of life to those decisions and help young people abstract and apply for themselves what they already know about good and bad decision making. Without our help, they may not come to realize what they already know.

Even though they are making decisions every single moment (as I tell them, in many ways decision making is life itself), children and many adolescents cannot usually see themselves making them; the steps occur spontaneously and invisibly—and most often instantaneously—*inside* their minds, where they can't be seen or experienced directly through the senses. Our job is to make them very visible, in very slow motion. I'm always looking for fun, simple, and interesting ways to make that happen. For example, I might stand before my students and say, "I need a volunteer to demonstrate some things to the class about decision making. Please raise your hand if you want to help." (This works really well with adults, too.) In less than five seconds, a few hands will go up. "Thank you for volunteering," I say. "That was the demonstration." Then we spend the next fifteen minutes or so identifying all the invisible mental steps each person in the group went through in deciding whether to volunteer.

Years ago, I came across an easy acronym for the steps in decision making or problem solving: IDEAL. First, you *identify* the decision to be made or the problem to be solved. Next, you *decide* on a list of alternative solutions, which you then *evaluate*. You then *act*, that is, you choose among the alternatives and implement your selection. Finally, you see what there is to *learn* about the choice you made. Each time we face a decision—which almost always happens quickly and unconsciously—our mind is biologically programmed to take us through these steps. That's why we never have to teach anyone how to make decisions, only how to make better ones, since we don't always proceed through the steps methodically enough. Although, many people's lives have certainly been altered forever by split-second decisions that they or others did not recognize as important, it's only for the important ones—for which a lot is at stake or costly mistakes are easily made—that we need to be extra-conscious of making good decisions.

Good decisions are usually preceded by a careful, deliberate process, in which each step is completed with a great deal of thought. Indeed, when we look back on our bad decisions, we'll probably discover that our process was lacking in relation to one or more steps. (The only exception is when we couldn't have anticipated certain factors or outcomes.) Perhaps we failed to recognize that there was an important decision to be made, or didn't take the time to define the problem accurately. Maybe we didn't think creatively or do enough research to identify all our best options. Did we systematically evaluate the possible short- and long-term outcomes of each alternative and take the time to interpret each in light of the values most important to us? Did we develop a good plan for implementing the option or options we selected, and did we follow through carefully? Finally, did we remember to reflect on how it all turned out, and discover what we could learn that might be useful in the future? (Or did we just beat ourselves up for being "stupid," if things didn't go as hoped or planned?) Virtually any decision-making process or follow-up, whether ours or our children's, can be enhanced by consciously using these steps and considerations as a guide. You might want to revisit the actions of the characters in "Who Is Responsible?" for practice.

Another gift we can give our children is to help them understand that some of the most powerful decisions we make are not those that translate directly into action, but the invisible "microdecisions" embedded deeply in our internal thought processes. As we go about living our lives, our minds are constantly sizing up people, situations, events, and options with lightning-fast frequency. Without ever realizing it, we quickly and unconsciously turn many of these fleeting conclusions into hard and fast beliefs that in turn will inform many of our later decisions. These assumptions (what I mean by the term "microdecisions") may be inaccurate, but we nevertheless act upon them as if they were correct. It's only when one of our faulty assumptions jumps out and smacks us in the face one day that we realize our error. Sensitizing young people to catch themselves making unconscious and unquestioned assumptions—especially in their relationships—can help save costly missteps and painful heartache.

It's fun and interesting to use a scenario like the Brenda and Robert story to help people realize the (false) assumptions we so easily make. Did you assume, as most people do, for example, that the doctor was a man, and the teacher a woman? That Brenda was a virgin and Robert wasn't? Suppose I told you that Brenda, six months before meeting Robert, had had an abortion? Or that Robert had carried a condom in his hip pocket, but was embarrassed to use it because he wasn't sure how? How about if you found out that Brenda's mother was a pregnancy counselor, or that her sister was quite a bit older and a single parent with three teenage daughters of her own? How many of those pieces of information fit your original assumptions?

The art of catching our children making both good and not-so-good decisions—and helping them learn to catch themselves—is a perfect role for parents and teacher. With younger children, whose decisions are not so weighty, it can become a fun and challenging game. With older ones, it can enable us to remain in the decision-making loop, even as they strive for increasing independence. We can continue to be there by letting them know that although more and more of their decisions will be entirely theirs to make as they grow up, we are always available to them as "process" consultants. To the extent that we and they are comfortable, that goes for their sexual decisions as well. (Remember to keep a broad definition of sexuality in mind; we're not just talking about sexual intercourse here, but all decisions connected to sex, gender, health, and other complex aspects of our sexuality.) We need to communicate also that although we hope they will make "good" decisions, we realize (and even hope) that they will probably make some "bad" ones as well. In fact, in my classroom, I almost always thank my students whenever they make a mistake. Permission to make mistakes will help take some of the sting and the unnecessary, counterproductive guilt or blame out of those inevitable moments, so that we can all focus on what there is to learn for the next time. All the while, we'll be helping young people to heighten their awareness, hone their skills, and reinforce their sense of personal responsibility.

## Highlighting "Right" Values

If life itself is decision making, and if values are at the base of all decisions, parents have literally a lifetime of opportunities to teach about values and how they work in our lives. Moreover, the good news—and the bad—is that American popular culture provides endless opportunities for adults to teach values lessons about sexuality. Here are some final suggestions on how to make good use of those ubiquitous opportunities:

### First, Do Your Homework

If we want to provide clear guidance about sexual attitudes and values, we must be able to clearly identify and explain our own opinions and ideas. We'll need to examine in an ongoing way not only *what* we think about a variety of specific issues, but also *how* we think about sexual values in general. Reviewing the questions at the end of Chapter 4 periodically can help. You should also take the time to think out loud with another adult—or even better, a group of adults in a parent education setting—who are struggling with similar topics and age groups. Since much of this territory is brand new for adults living at *any* time in history, we shouldn't expect to be able to sort it all out on our own.

Also keep in mind the reasoning capacity of children at different ages and stages of development. A young child conceives of right and wrong very concretely: good behavior is behavior that brings positive and enjoyable consequences; bad behavior leads to unpleasant or harmful consequences. If asked, he or she will offer an explanation of right and wrong choices that focuses on *tangible outcomes*. For example, copying an answer from someone else's paper at school is wrong because you might get in trouble. Older elementary and middle school students, too, think primarily in concrete terms, but they can also comprehend a more sophisticated notion of morality and justice based on *formal rules, laws, and fairness for all*. For example, copying from someone's paper is wrong because he or she did the work and you did not. Only in adolescence can children begin to reason utilizing *abstract principles* of right and wrong (e.g., cheating is wrong because it is immoral to be dishonest). We'll address some specific sexual examples in Chapter 12.

## Embrace Your Role as Cultural Interpreter

Earlier we imagined a child growing up in the United States as a little transplanted Martian, surrounded suddenly by an array of misleading, out-of-context messages about the meaning of sex and sexuality. It is folly to assume that children will be able to extract a coherent, healthy, and humane understanding of sexuality, absent adult intervention. Just as parents and teachers know to be on guard constantly about other safety and health issues, they need to very consciously sensitize their adult radar screen to the ubiquitous, unsafe, and unhealthy sexual influences in popular culture. They'll want to point out advertisements, for example, that cheapen and exploit sex by using it to sell everything from shampoo to garden equipment; story lines and song lyrics that glorify casual, impersonal, and seemingly unprotected sexual encounters; and suggestions throughout the media that alcohol and sex are great companions and that "beauty" (as defined by artificially confined gender-typed standards) is the most important determinant of a person's happiness and worth. They'll also want to carry an invisible highlighter that they can pull out at any time to underscore "right" and healthy messages as well: "Now there's an honest, positive, and realistic portrayal of sex and relationships."

Parents of younger children will want to shield them as long as possible from unhealthy media messages by restricting and supervising their exposure to television, the Internet, music, and film. However, some exposure is inevitable—we can't screen billboards, magazine covers, and product packaging—and some is accidental. (I remember encouraging my eight-year-old son to watch a rerun of the movie *First Monday in October,* about a fictional first woman Supreme Court justice, only to discover later to my horror that I had forgotten about a scene in which the justices preview a porno flick!) Sooner or later, parents must face the fact that even partial censorship is utterly hopeless; by the time students are in late elementary school, many will have seen adult-rated movies, so that even if yours haven't, they will inevitably hear the buzz at school. In middle school, parents can ask the right questions, but can't always make sure that their child won't be exposed to objectionable media when at the homes of friends.

At some point, there is ultimately only one sound strategy: If you can't beat 'em (and you can't!), join 'em. When you realize that you are no longer in a position of control, shift to *influence.*

Acknowledge to your children that you will gradually permit them to view and listen to previously proscribed material, but not until you've taught them how to interpret what they'll be seeing. Allow them to pick out two movies, for example, that you will watch together. After the first, interpret for them the messages in the film that you find objectionable, and why. After the second, ask them to tell you what you probably found objectionable, and why. Repeat this tactic until you're sure they have the media literacy skills they'll need to be a discriminating viewer. You can take the same approach to song lyrics. (If your children balk at this strategy, tell them that's fine, but that you absolutely won't change your rules until they agree to participate in this kind of interchange. That way, you'll at least score points by asserting your parental prerogative and role.) Remember, you absolutely cannot change the media, but you absolutely can change how your child processes the media.

One final caveat: Make sure that your child understands your underlying concern. It's not the sex in this material that's the problem, but the context, or absence of context, in which the sex occurs. Otherwise, the child may receive a message that is antisexual, rather than anti-exploitational.

## Put a Human Context Around Factual Issues

Virtually any factual question or issue our children ask us about can be turned into a teachable moment about values. All we need do is take a moment to think of a connecting concept: If boys ask about periods, we can raise the issues of how girls feel about their changing bodies; a question about the "morning-after" pill can lead to discussing the importance of forethought; a child who asks, "What does it mean 'to make out'?" can be asked, in turn, to consider the attitude that the phrase connotes or the kinds of sexual behaviors he or she thinks are appropriate at certain ages. If children know that we will always answer whatever questions they bring to us first—in an inviting, nonjudgmental, and matter-of-fact manner—they'll likely be very receptive to a friendly, open-ended exploration of the general topic.

## Help Your Children De-Construct the Sexual Language They Hear and Use

Children usually avoid slang or sexual terminology in the presence of adults, for fear they will get into trouble. We need to invite them to do just the opposite—to bring that language to us—so that we can explain not only the factual meaning but the destructive, demeaning values and beliefs that may be embedded in its use. We should be prepared to do this early on, as soon as they're exposed, and before certain words and phrases become an intractable and sacrosanct part of their communication with and about peers. One of my least favorite examples is the word *slut*. There is no more damning or sexist word in our language, except perhaps *fag* or *wimp*, and its use epitomizes and perpetuates the sexual double standard. (*Fag* and *wimp* both epitomize a gender *and* sexual double standard.) With help, late elementary students will recognize this injustice immediately, whereas older boys and girls will often insist that there truly are people their age (read: girls) who are "sluts," as if being so represented an immutable aspect of identity. Even while acknowledging how subjectively the word is defined and how easily and maliciously rumors can be spread, teens will often insist that these girls deserve what they get. For some, it will be impossible to get them to see it any other way.

## Define Your Terms, and Insist That Others Define Theirs

Conversations about sensitive and subjective topics like sexuality can be especially contentious or frustrating when people do not take the time to clarify their terminology. Fuzzy words and concepts—such as *promiscuity, abstinence, morality, morals, premarital, responsibility, readiness, maturity,* even the term *values* itself—may be tossed back and forth with little clarification or even a simple acknowledgment of the vastly different ways they may be interpreted.

Once debate about sexuality turns to topics that are hot buttons in the public or political arena, the communication problems only intensify. Buzz words and pop phrases—*pro-life, pro-choice, sex education, absti-*

*nence, values clarification, traditional values, ultra-liberal, religious values, homophobia, homosexual agenda,* etc.—become battle cries and rallying calls producing much more heat and noise than light. People or groups of people may appear to be communicating about the same issues, but actually may not be on the same wavelength at all—much like two television sets facing each other, but tuned to different channels. I am always amazed that when people take the time to speak in precise and direct terms, it is much easier for them to find common ground or at least respectful disagreement.

## Make Good Use of Sexuality in the News

I mentioned earlier that in the high school classes I teach, we use the newspaper as our text (usually the *New York Times* and our local paper, the *Baltimore Sun*). When I tell other adults about this approach, many assume it means we read about rape and harassment cases and an occasional scandal. In reality, during any given three- or four-month period, we'll read about every topic I want my students to think and learn about and many more. (We net about fifteen to twenty articles, features, letters, or editorial pieces a week!) For families, too, the daily paper and TV and radio news provide limitless opportunities for conversation. Here's a smattering of stories from a recent course: "partial-birth" abortion and the political process, gays and the Boy Scouts, ethical issues concerning frozen embryos, approaches to teenage pregnancy prevention in France, AIDS in Africa and Asia, teens and contraception, the gay marriage debate, HIV treatments and research, alcohol use and risky sexual behavior, male attitudes toward seeking health care, the "new" feminism, religious views of homosexuality, abortion in Canada, treatment of women in Afghanistan.

In "bashing" the media for its exploitation of sex, let's be careful not to lump the entertainment and advertising industries together with the news media. The increasingly open coverage of sexual topics in the news is a marvelous development for our children—not only as a vehicle for disseminating information, but also for normalizing and highlighting the topic of sexuality as a serious, important, and everyday topic for learning and discussion. *There is no better way to parents and schools to encourage our children's sexual literacy.*

Keep in mind, however, that in your local public school, this excellent strategy may be impossible to implement under current policy; any materials used in Family Life classes generally must be approved months in advance, and teachers cannot deviate. Moreover, many specific topics themselves are likely prohibited by curriculum guidelines. What a disservice, and what an unfortunate message we are giving to young people about the willingness of schools—the primary educational institution in their lives—to deal with the topic of sexuality in an honest, authentic, and timely manner!

# 12

# Limit Setting: Keeping Our Children Safe and Healthy

As parents, our most practical role—and our most visceral—is that of protector. From their first few hours in our care, until we finally launch them into young adulthood, seeing to our children's needs will tug at our heart and challenge our character and resources in ways we could never have fathomed. Indeed, it's not until that miraculous moment when we cradle them in our first protective embrace that we even begin to know what this role is about.

Whether we consciously think in these terms or not, our primary means of parental protection is limit setting. Limits are those brackets that we place around our children's lives and range of options in order to keep them safe and healthy. A baby's crib is actually a wonderful metaphor for the practice of limit setting: When they are infants, we deliberately reduce their sphere to a tidy three-by-five terrain whenever we're not immediately nearby to keep them safe. From then on, to a very large degree the art of parenting will be in knowing how and when to move the limits outward, when to hold them firm, and when to draw them closer again.

Although the fundamental need for limits remains constant from birth through adolescence, the content bounded by those limits shifts continually, in tandem with our children's unique developmental timetable. Sooner or later, for example, we allow our young children free roam of their room, then other select areas, and then an entire floor of the house without immediate supervision. Then they may play by themselves in the fenced backyard, but not the open front lawn. We continue to move and then eventually remove every new set of brackets, but we always replace them with the next new set as our children continue to expand their world.

And so it is in relation to their sexual development. As discussed in earlier chapters, when our children are young, we'll want to set limits around their sexual curiosity and related issues of privacy and appropriateness: "Let's go find a book to learn about girls' and women's bodies, because Mom's body parts are private." "When we go to the bathroom to urinate or have a bowel movement, we close the door." "Touching your genitals gives you pleasurable feelings, and that's fun to do as long as you're in your room or some other private place." "I can see you kids are having a fine time playing doctor, but when we're with other people, we keep our clothes on." "You like to walk in a 'sexy' way like women in advertisements, but that behavior is only for grown-ups." "Most parents like to tell their own children about intercourse and how babies are made, so we want you to keep this information in the family for now."

As children grow older, we'll need to shift our focus to influences and experiences outside the immediate family. We'll want to monitor and restrict their exposure to media, make sure their various social activities are adequately supervised when they're in the care of others, and keep on top of sexual information and attitudes they may be picking up from—or sharing with—peers and other children. We'll also want to provide guidance about sexual language and about how, when, where, and why certain language may or may not be appropriate.

Remember, too, that the all-important messages we send about gender roles also constitute a powerful form of limit setting. Children come into the world open to all kinds of experiences and only much later begin consciously to divide traits, toys, clothing, colors, behaviors, interests, talents, and personal styles into mutually exclusive "boy" and "girl" categories. Although much of this learning is unconscious or culturally imposed and beyond the direct control of individual adults, as discussed in Chapter 6, parents can exert early and lasting influence on how broadly or narrowly their children come to view their options with respect to gender.

In American culture, the late elementary and middle school years are a critical period for adults attempting to accommodate their children's growing independence, yet maintain an active and effective presence as limit setters. As discussed earlier, many youngsters at this age begin to imitate adolescent culture—in their dress, hair styles, makeup, accessories, language, and music. Just as the media have recast teenagers in the image of young adults, and preteens as little teenagers, late elementary children are now being encouraged to look and act like little grown-ups. In the midst of these powerful pressures, it is parents who must remain ever conscious of who the real grown-ups are. Teenagers, let alone children, are not simply small adults, even though there are insidious forces trying to convince them and us otherwise. Parents will need to be vigilant in saying no to purchases and activities that are truly appropriate only for adults and perhaps older teens, despite protestations from their younger children to the contrary.

Absent the assertion of sufficient parental limits when children are younger, it should not surprise us that by the age of fourteen or fifteen, many young people think of themselves as capable of, and even entitled to, free agency regarding their personal and social lives. *If we don't know the difference between the adult and nonadult world—and we don't know how to communicate about and draw clear lines between them—how can we expect our children to do so?*

Late in the fourth-grade year is about the ideal age for parents to begin proactively to head off this dangerous possibility. Children on the verge, but not yet in the throes, of adolescence still readily accept and expect that their parents will set limits around their behavior (even if they don't like it). It is an expeditious time to make explicit that as a parent you have certain responsibilities that you take—and will continue to take—very seriously, even as they get older. The message suggested in Chapter 8 bears repeating: "As the adult in our relationship, I will need to make certain decisions when it comes to your physical, social, and emotional well-being. You may not always like them, and in fact, sometimes I'll even make mistakes and either underestimate or overestimate your ability to safely make your own decisions. But I will always try to be fair and realistic, I will always give you my reasons, and I will always ask for your input."

We've also said that parents would be wise, too, to set up a supportive network with other parents, whether through grade level meetings at their children's school or, more informally, by actively getting to know and routinely checking in with the parents of their children's friends. Together they can decide on appropriate limits for socializing and other activities and reduce the chance that their children will successfully pit them against one another. This unified front becomes even more important during the middle school years, when limits become all the more confusing—half the time our children won't know where they want them, and the other half we won't be sure where to put them!—and our confidence as limit setters can really plummet.

As our children mature, many aspects of their social life will rightly become the province of the youngsters themselves, whereas others will persist as areas of parental concern. It will be extremely important for parents to acknowledge that just as soon as possible, and in whatever ways possible, teens will be expected to regulate themselves and not rely on parental limits. Routine communication among groups of parents cannot be perceived as snooping or policing; if so, it will eliminate any hope of trust and will simply engender rebellion and underground activity. Parents need to reassure their children—and truly believe themselves—that the ultimate goal of regular communication among families is not control but age-appropriate guidance and support, for both parents and children. The school counselor or other community resource person can help parents make sure that their developmental expectations are fair and realistic, in other words, that they're setting down the "brackets" in the right range and in the right way.

Some issues will become even more pressing as the years go by. Once driving and weekend parties and gatherings become the norm, especially as the presence of alcohol becomes more and more likely, safe limits will take on renewed and critical significance. Parents will need to be persistent and vigilant about adequate supervision and clearly enforced house rules whenever and wherever young people socialize. How much easier it will be to insist on *those* limits with older teens—who in some respects *are* in fact free agents—if shared limit setting and ongoing family-to-family communication have been an integral and accepted part of the social landscape for years. Although this kind of sustained, collective history is beneficial, it isn't totally essential. Parents can decide to initiate grade-level support groups at *any* age, using ongoing developmental issues as a logical context, such as transition to high school, safe driving, alcohol and drug education, prom safety, or preparation for college or independent living.

Our lives are incredibly hectic and overscheduled. What's more, many communities are neither close-knit nor geographically set up for the kind of interfamily communication and shared parental responsibility that our children need. As difficult as this strategy might seem, however, I am convinced that it is the single most important thing parents can do to create safe, healthy, and enforceable. The winds of culture, the developmental pressures to be popular and "in," and the escalating sense of entitlement among American children are simply too powerful for individual families to battle successfully; only a collective voice can effectively deliver the message that it is absolutely necessary and appropriate for parents to be involved in setting limits around their children's social lives. Finding just the right limits or presenting a united front on all issues is not the point. The process itself is the point—the process of clarifying important developmental issues, of inviting and encouraging parents to check in with one another whenever it seems prudent, of highlighting and reinforcing the limit-setting role.

## Sexual Limit Setting

Quite ironically, most of what is called "sex education" is rarely about "sex." Topics like sexual arousal, pleasure and pleasuring, and orgasm are rarely discussed in school-based programs and are often too "touchy" for conversations at home.

When these topics are left out of the educational picture, children receive the definitive message that adults are not available for guidance about physical, emotional, and romantic intimacy. Children are then left entirely on their own to sort out the difficult questions of how to set safe and comfortable sexual boundaries and how to decide which behaviors and what kinds of relationships are right or wrong, appropriate or inappropriate. Moreover, on a less conscious level, they may also interpret adult silence to mean that there is something wrong, bad, or "dirty" about sexual pleasuring—or at least about discussing it.

I always find it quite telling that whenever I ask my junior and senior students to identify the characteristics of a sexually healthy adult, the one word that is conspicuously missing from their answers is *pleasure*. They are quickest to point out the issue of responsibility—that healthy sexual people are free of disease and unwanted pregnancy—and this response is certainly positive, admirable, and reassuring. But it's also a reflection of adult emphasis, especially today, on the dangerous aspects of sexual behavior. When the emphasis on danger is combined with adult silence on pleasure, we are clearly presenting a dreadfully skewed and incomplete understanding of sexual relating. Ubiquitous media depictions of instant physical and emotional intimacy between near total strangers only compound the problem. After all, our children will spend most of their lives in relationships in which unwanted pregnancy and disease will not be ongoing concerns, but issues of communication, longevity, intimacy, and reciprocal pleasure will be paramount. How are we preparing them for that?

## The "Oral Sex Phenomenon"

As society becomes more and more fast-paced, our shared cultural memory becomes shorter and shorter. We "forget" that aspects of our lives we take for granted today might have been considered patently outrageous twenty, ten, or even five years ago. The common use of explicit sexual terms in public dialogue and in the communications media—let alone in "polite" conversation—is a clear example. How many of us recall that a word like *condom,* for example, today so ordinary, was neither seen nor heard anywhere a "short" fifteen years ago. Just as the AIDS epidemic catapulted prophylactics from behind the pharmacy counter and the word *condom* onto the airwaves, many other taboo sexual terms have been brought out of the media closet by a series of high-profile news stories. I will never forget the looks on the faces of all those desperate anchorpersons, working so hard to remain cool and professional when pronouncing "pubic hair" on the evening news during the Clarence Thomas hearings or nonchalantly trying to enunciate the word *penis* while explaining what had happened to the unfortunate Mr. Bobbitt. With the first breaking news about Viagra, catchy sound bites like erectile dysfunction and penile stimulation made seasoned sexuality educators of them all.

The Clinton-Lewinsky scandal, of course, shattered most of any remaining journalistic taboos. (Interestingly, though, an article I wrote at the time for a national newspaper, directed at parents of teenagers on how to use the scandal as a teachable moment, was put on hold until I agreed to remove the words *ejaculating* and *vagina* from the text. The terms were deemed inappropriate and offensive because the publication, which only weeks before had printed the Starr Report in its entirety, was, after all, a family newspaper.) Overnight, it seemed, the phrase *oral sex* was everywhere. Reporting about it, talking about it, writing about it, and publicly joking about it had been instantaneously transformed from nowhere to the norm.

Less than six months after the final gavel had fallen in the president's impeachment trial, the first of several stories about oral sex among American teenagers—middle schoolers, no less—appeared in the national press. Anecdotal evidence was being reported about sex "rings" of sorts, in which groups of boys and girls were meeting clandestinely in out-of-the-way places like parks or were "hooking up" with people they had just met at weekend parties, individually or even in groups, to perform a variety of sexual acts, including oral sex. There were also reports of oral sex happening within schools or during school activities—in bathrooms, on bus rides, in study halls, and in stairwells. And the kicker: These youngsters were high-achieving kids from middle- to upper-class families, with all the advantages and proprieties a "good" upbringing supposedly affords. Parents everywhere freaked; the prospect of middle school children engaging in oral sex wasn't even in their worst nightmares, let alone on their parental radar screen.

Predictably, the knee-jerk reaction of some observers was to blame the phenomenon directly on the president's conduct, even though most of the anecdotes were collected at least several months before the scandal. (What we probably can "blame" on President Clinton or Kenneth Starr, or perhaps both, is the newfound permission in the media to talk about oral sex, and to therefore learn about, investigate, discover, and report about it.) Confirmation that this is a deep-rooted Western culture dynamic, not merely Clinton/Lewinsky fallout, came soon after the first U.S. article on the subject appeared on the front page of the *Washington Post* in July 1999. An eerily similar but totally unrelated story was printed in the *Dublin Times* only days later. It told of middle school boys and girls meeting for oral sex at a park adjacent to the grounds of a convent in an affluent community outside of Dublin. Absent the obvious foreign locations, spellings, and idioms, anyone reading the text would assume that it came straight out of an American newspaper article written about American teenagers.

What on earth is going on here? Is this journalistic sensationalism, or first warning of a widespread and growing trend?

In terms of hard scientific data, the jury is still out. All the available information on the subject is purely anecdotal, most of it gathered by journalists in interviews with health officials, parents, school personnel, therapists, and the youths themselves. This absence of objective research data on the sexual experiences of young teens and preteens is a highly charged political issue. Full-scale national surveys of teenage sexual behavior and other health risks typically focus only on high school students, and questions about ultrasensitive behaviors like oral sex are deliberately excluded from research involving younger adolescents—for fear of congressional (or parental) ire and diminished funding. We don't know what's really going on statistically with this age group, because the powers that be don't want to know or are unwilling to ask.

Frankly, what grabs my attention about this phenomenon, no matter how widespread, is not just that it is happening, but *how* it is happening. The real wake-up call for adults isn't only in the details of the specific sex acts involved, but in the context—or absence of context—that these anecdotal reports consistently reveal.

First of all, consider the ways young teens portray these so-called hook-ups. (That's the current lingo for spontaneous trysts between couples who barely know one another; in the Irish account they're called "meetings.") "It's no big deal, . . . it's safe and fun," they say with a detached shrug. "Everybody does it; it's just the thing to do." Indeed, worried therapists and educators, having listened to many of these accounts with a well-trained ear, describe them as alarmingly mechanical, dehumanized, and devoid of warmth or even minimal emotional connection. Sometimes, reportedly, the participants don't look at each other or even seek out privacy. It's "body part-sex," as psychologist Wayne Warren put it in a *New York Times* report in April 2000. To some of these youngsters, acts like oral sex—considered by older generations as perhaps the ultimate in physical and emotional intimacy and certainly *not* a prelude to sexual intercourse but more likely the reverse—have apparently become as common, meaningless, and expected as a good night kiss.

If anyone doubts that these young teens are way out of their league, consider their given explanations for the popularity of oral sex: It's a way of having sex without having sex, and besides, you're still a virgin; it can lead to an immediate "in" with the popular crowd (especially if it's with a cute guy or girl) and uncommon respect from your friends for being daring and experienced; since there's no worry about pregnancy or disease, it's consequence-free. (If asked, they'll tell you that the prospect of disease is nil, since the rule is you "do it" only with people you "know," and isn't that, after all, what all those AIDS prevention messages tell you to do?)

For girls, there's yet another great "bargain," a package deal, really: You can give a guy oral sex as a way of getting him to stop pressuring you for intercourse. Plus, since this is something the girl does to him, it gives her the upper hand for once, as well as something that she can finally brag about. (Although there is again no hard data, anecdotal evidence suggests that girls were much more often in the servicing role of giving than receiving oral sex.)

With the grand simplicity of their early adolescent thought process, these misguided kids have raised the tired old oxymorons *casual sex* and *free love* to the level of cult ethic. Or as one mother quoted in the *Washington Post* article summed it up, "They would [probably] argue that they were acting responsibly." And that in a nutshell is the great danger in allowing young adolescents to act, and to think they are capable of acting, as independent agents: Their mental processing can only go so far, and no further. In other words, if they believe they have even one good reason for doing—or not doing—something, it's easily deemed sufficient. *They simply do not have the mental facility to handle complex behaviors and grown-up situations all by themselves.*

According to these published accounts, the aftermath for many youngsters has been tragically predictable: sexually transmitted infections, ruined and ugly reputations that follow them well into their high school years, strained and damaged relationships with parents and other adults who may have learned of their behavior. Especially for some of the girls involved, who have eventually wised up the hard way about the incomparable brutality of the sexual double standard when stoked by an early adolescent rumor mill, the emotional and social consequences have been profoundly difficult. Therapists worry, however, about the long-term effects for both boys and girls, even and especially those who aren't "caught" by adults or who don't suffer immediate consequences.

Many young teens on the fast track sexually, counselors say, become jaded and hardened. They may have trouble developing intimate relationships later on, either because very little feels new or exciting to them or because there has been so little trust and mutual caring in their earlier formative experiences. All the emphasis has been on "getting," as if a sexual act is some thing or service granted to you or that you coax, pressure, or "get" someone to provide. The coarse expressions they use—*getting a blow job, getting eaten out, getting laid*—pretty much say it all. It's all about *me, and what's in it for me.* There is no *us.*

Some of this dynamic is predictable and normal. Early adolescents are by definition self-centered experimenters; their life is supposed to be about *me*—about pushing limits, about trying out all kinds of new things in order to see *who and what I am and what I want to become.* Ironically, although it is this very process of identity formation that will enable a healthy capacity for intimacy later on (a clear sense of *me* is fundamental to establishing a healthy sense of *us*), the requisite preoccupation of the age with self will preclude real intimacy for the time being. One of the dangers for young adolescents who become caught up in a pattern of pre-cocious sexual behavior is the false and misleading emphasis on *getting*, or on *giving only to get.* Instead of growing naturally into a healthy under-standing of intimacy, in which giving and getting are the natural conse-quences of a loving relationship, they will need first to unlearn a history of self-centered preoccupation and sometimes outright exploitation.

On the other end of the spectrum are those younger adolescents who become involved prematurely in intense, long-term couple relationships. For them the danger may lie in compromising the vital process of individ-uation: They may lose themselves in each other before finding themselves as individuals. It makes sense, then, from a developmental perspective, to discourage young adolescents, at least until the age of sixteen, from in-tense physical or romantic intimacy; it is simply not the right fit for the age.

Unfortunately, the national trend has been moving steadily in the wrong direction for years. From the early 1970s to the late 1990s, the in-cidence of sexual intercourse among fifteen-year-old girls and boys more than *doubled* for boys and increased more than *sevenfold* for girls. (As dis-cussed, statistics on oral sex and other behaviors are not available for this age group.) Even more disturbingly, this downward trend in the age of first intercourse persists at a time when the figures for older teens seem to be taking a decidedly different turn: Among high school students of all ages, rates of intercourse began to *decline* by the late 1990s.

Why the precipitous drop among younger adolescents and the discrep-ancy when compared to older teens? Nobody knows exactly why "slow-down" messages are taking hold so disparately, but I'd put my money on "grow-up-faster" media messages being targeted at younger and younger children, who are much less experienced and sophisticated at deciphering the ever-increasing sexualization of our society. (According to the Parents Television Council, the sexual content on television alone *tripled* from

1989 to 1999!) Add to the mix the "same old, same old" watered-down and restrictive school-based education, throw in ambivalence or downright ignorance about the kind of consistent adult presence that early adolescents need and want as well as parental discomfort about giving explicit sexual guidance, and the pressures and opportunities for earlier sexual experimentation begin to accelerate. Should we really be all that surprised that some kids have reached the conclusion that there are no boundaries (probably the most dangerous message of all for any early adolescent) and that they have no clear sense at all of how far is too far? And though these kids are in the minority and hopefully will stay so, their cavalier attitudes and behaviors are increasingly a part of the social landscape for all kids. If adults aren't aware of this dynamic and aren't pointing out its dangers in explicit terms, how are other kids going to know that these attitudes and behaviors aren't the right ones?

## Redefining Sex as Intimacy

Ask any inexperienced substitute teacher what happens when adolescents sense that no one is really in charge: bedlam. The class is "out of control" because there are no clear limits to tell them how they are expected to conduct themselves. It's an open invitation to test adults and themselves and to find out how far they can go before someone, anyone, will step in and say, "Enough!"

For kids, American culture, with its keep-pushing-the-envelope-at-all-costs ethic, is like a great big sex education classroom with no responsible adult in charge. Like the assistant principal who comes in to set the class and substitute straight, the immediate adults in children's lives need to stand up boldly in front of them and say, "Now, now class. All of this distraction has certainly seemed fun and interesting, but it's time to give your undivided attention to us. We are the adults you need to heed, because our job is to teach you what's really so, and what you really need to know about sex." Unless and until we deliver this message, the bedlam will continue; if our tone is from the heart and not critical but matter-of-fact, they'll stop and listen.

First, we have to figure out what we want to say. My own response to American culture over the years—an antidote, really—has been to take every opportunity possible to help young people recast sexual behavior within the concept of emotional and physical intimacy. "The question to ask yourself about sex," I constantly tell my students, "is not 'How far should I go?' or 'How far can I get?' because that makes sex into a selfish game, and other human beings into sexual objects. The real—and right— issue to consider is 'How close do I want to be, or should I be, with this other person?'"

More specifically, as I first explained in Chapter 3, I like to offer the concept of an *intimacy continuum,* an imaginary line of behaviors that involve increasingly close physical contact. The behaviors at the least physically intimate end of the continuum—like hand holding, kissing, and hugging—involve embracing, connecting with, or touching body parts that we think of as public, such as the hands, lips, and shoulders. Behaviors at the other end—such as sexual intercourse in its various forms—involve connections between what are considered to be the most private and personal parts of our bodies. In the middle are behaviors that involve increasingly intimate contact, such as touching the breasts, penis, or vulva, first through clothing, then skin to skin.

In given situations, a couple's or an individual's comfort level with these different kinds of touch—both when receiving and when giving—will vary. To identify the point past which further intimacy becomes uncomfortable, we need only tune in to those same internal cues and feelings that tell us when we are being asked to share ourselves emotionally in a way that is too advanced for a particular situation or relationship.

To make the point, I like to explain the concept of a parallel emotional intimacy continuum, along which lie increasingly personal and private parts of our emotional selves. We might tell almost any stranger, for example, our first name, the city where we live, and our favorite book or movie, but only more trusted acquaintances our e-mail address, our telephone number, and our honest opinion about a certain teacher or classmate. For our good friends, we'll reserve deeper thoughts, feelings, experiences, and opinions, and we'll probably tell only our most sensitive and guarded secrets to a best friend, close sibling, or parent. In other words, most of the time we'll be most comfortable matching our level of personal disclosure with our level of mutual trust. Moving beyond that point with a particular individual will require an emotional risk on our part that we may or may not feel ready to take. If we do take it, depending on how we feel afterward (which will probably rest on how sensitively the other person responds to this new and more intimate piece of information about us), our relationship with that person will likely move in one direction or the other along our emotional intimacy line.

Whenever we are tempted or pressured to share personal information about ourselves before we feel emotionally ready, we usually experience an automatic, internal warning bell—an "oh-oh" feeling—that puts us on alert. Imagine a co-worker, for example, who asks out of the blue exactly how much money you make or what your favorite sexual position is, and note your immediate emotional and physical response; that's the reaction I'm referring to. That's exactly the feeling we want to teach our children to recognize and respect whenever they find themselves in any kind of pressure situation, sexual or otherwise, peer or self-imposed, because it means they're being asked to consider violating their deepest and truest sense of self.

When this alarm sounds in a sexual situation, we'll want them to understand, it means they're being asked to give away a piece of their private selves that's not yet trusting, and whatever the reason for that hesitation, it's a good and right one that deserves their heed. We'll need to train them to recognize their discomfort, to respect it absolutely, and to say proudly in whatever words they choose, "No thanks, but my feelings tell me that our relationship is not ready for that kind of closeness." In this way, we'll be teaching them important lessons not only about the concepts of emotional and sexual intimacy, but also about the relationship between them.

Of course, as behaviors intensify along the sexual continuum, the issue of intimacy is not the only one to consider. Other issues and questions, which we've addressed in depth in other chapters, also become paramount, and we must prepare our children to recognize and deal forthrightly with these as well:

- Integrity: Do I think that this kind of intimacy with this person at this time is morally right or wrong?
- Physical safety: What are the physical risks, and are we adequately protected?
- Maturity: Am I emotionally, intellectually, and socially ready for this experience?
- Mutuality: What are the needs, desires, motivations, and expectations of the other person involved, and how do they relate to mine?

I especially like the continuum approach because it equips parents and teachers to give information and guidance that is both practical and conceptual. It communicates unequivocally that all sexual behaviors between people are to be considered real, meaningful, and significant. All involve real feelings, real decisions, and real accountability. Although some sexual behaviors may be more powerful than others and require considerably more maturity, commitment, and thoughtful consideration, all involve unique and special powers. There are no ethically or emotionally free spaces when it comes to being sexually active, no matter what the activity.

The continuum approach is also terrifically challenging for many adults. First of all, it means that we have to figure out what we really think about the idea of teens and preteens engaging in the range of possible sexual behaviors. We'll need to lay out the continuum before us and think hard about which behaviors we think are appropriate and inappropriate, and at what ages and stages of development. And then we'll need to share our conclusions and our thought process: "At your age, I think kissing and hugging are fine, but that's all, because . . . "; "I think that by the time teenagers are sixteen or so, they may be ready to consider . . . and here's why." Clearly, we'll also have to develop comfort—or at least the ability to be uncomfortable and communicate anyway—in speaking about specific sexual activities in very direct terms. To do less is to fool ourselves that we are adequately preparing our children for centrally important and potentially life-altering decisions. It would be like saying, "Now listen, there's this very long, very wide thing outside, with lots of big, dangerous objects going up and down it very fast, so be careful out there," and expecting we've prepared them adequately to cross a busy street.

And we'll need to do more than talk. Just as we don't allow little children to cross busy streets without us, our teens and preteens should not be allowed to socialize in unsupervised settings. We certainly don't have to be there every minute, but our adult presence must be felt. Otherwise, it is inevitable that they will wind up in situations requiring limit setting beyond their developmental reach. *Only clearly stated rules and a consistent adult presence will ensure that will not be the case.* I am constantly amazed at the stories I hear: party situations for up to fifty or sixty fifth-graders with only an older teenage sibling to "chaperone"; coed sleep-overs in totally unsupervised basements; roaming parties, with free access to alcohol and an open invitation list, that move from house to house where the adults are out of town; gatherings in which parents take the car keys away and turn a blind eye to dangerous use of illegal substances in their own homes.

Most often I hear about these situations from parents who are trying their best to face down the social tidal wave they and their children are confronting. Their biggest challenges are adults who don't get it, and their own children, who whine and stomp and cajole: "Why don't you trust me! Everybody else's parents let them! I'll never speak to you if you call the parents and ask your dumb questions! I'll never be invited anywhere again! I might as well just die right here and now!" As thorny as it might be, we have to be willing to risk asking the hard questions, making the hard phone calls, and standing our ground even when we fear that other adults, kids, or our own children won't like us very much or won't think we're cool. We must be willing to parent.

Even if we do, our children won't keep all our limits and won't take all of our advice, but they'll be much less likely to go too far out of bounds. And if we don't, we run the risk that they may not learn—except the hard way—that there are boundaries to be kept at all.

## Gender and Intimacy

So far in this chapter and most of the entire book, I've attempted to keep the focus most often on *children and adolescents*, not on *boys and girls*. That's because I think we do best when we try to think about boys and girls as people first and as subcategories of people second. In reality, of course, boys and girls are targeted with very different messages about sex in this culture, and these messages can exert a profound influence on their social and sexual values, beliefs, decisions, and experiences. Moreover, basic male and female differences—hormonally, anatomically, and physiologically—cannot be discounted. Males and females may be predisposed biologically as well as culturally to approach sexual encounters with somewhat different agendas, needs, and expectations. Maybe deep in their genes, men are programmed more to sow their seeds, and women to tend the hearth.

Whatever innate differences there might be, American culture certainly highlights and distorts them in grossly unhealthy (and anachronistic) ways. We talk about boys and their "raging hormones," stereotype them as being "only out for sex," and expect that they won't stick around in case of pregnancy. We overhear them talking about girls and their bodies—and gays—in the most demeaning and disgusting terms, and chalk it up to "boys being boys." We understand and even expect that they'll say yes to sex whenever it's available, and we perpetuate concepts like "scoring" that make them out to be some kind of conquering sexual heroes when they do. (Consider the names for some of the most popular brands of condoms: Trojan, Ramses, and Magnum.) We tell them that boys don't show emotions or other "weakness," and then when they do, we permit them to challenge and sometimes brutalize each other until "masculinity" indeed begins to look like heartlessness. We need desperately to ask ourselves, Why do we expect so little from boys—and for them? And how exactly do we expect them to turn around and become loving, sensitive, monogamous, "new-age" husbands and fathers just because they're grown?

Girls, on the other hand, are the only gender still eligible for the label *slut*. In fact, the term is defined so subjectively today, almost any girl is eligible at the whim or discretion of almost anybody else (especially via e-mail). At the same time, they're told that their fundamental worth still depends on being attractive, desirable, and sexual, but that to succeed, they'll have to play and win a dating game in which they have little or no control over the rules. We tell them that boys care about sex and that girls care about love, then shake our heads when they try to use sex to get it.

We don't show them or teach them the names for the most sexually arousable parts of their anatomy, and then we declare that by their nature, boys and men need sex, but girls don't. (That's why they have to be the ones to say no and the ones who'll be blamed if they don't.) We terrify them with the fear of pregnancy and disease and lead them to believe that "losing their virginity" is gory and painful. We make god-awful-looking female condoms brand-named Reality and teach boys little or nothing about how to *give* sexual pleasure. Just when do we begin to worry about the potential effects of these cumulative messages on our girls' diminished capacity for sexual fulfillment? Indeed, as they grow into young adulthood, is their potential for sexual fulfillment even on our list of concerns for their health and well-being?

To get out from under this destructive cultural baggage, as I've said time and again, we must go back and start over. We must begin anew with a gender-blind emphasis on basic human needs and values: trust, decency, fairness, caring, authenticity, self-fulfillment, reciprocity, responsibility. These are the kinds of values we try to teach our kids about every-thing else in life, regardless of their gender. Why not sex, too?

## But What About Abstinence?

Then again, wouldn't it be simpler if we just said, "Just say no!"? It most certainly would, and that should tell us immediately that the abstinence-only approach is, at its core, self-serving. It makes *us* feel good, because we feel we're giving a simple, clean, unequivocal message. The problem is that the culture that we adults have created and in which we choose to live and raise our children is anything but simple, clean, and unequivocal. Therefore, we (families and schools) have to take responsibility for raising our children to cope with culture as it is, not as we wish it to be.

This is not to say that abstinence messages aren't a meaningful and im-portant part of the package. It's all in how we deliver them. We shoot our-selves in the foot when we present them moralistically ("Do as I say!") and hypocritically ("but not necessarily as I do or did"). What truly works is to engage young people in the dialogue and actively draw upon their own good common sense. In my classes, I often ask, "A lot of adults think that abstinence from sexual intercourse at your age, especially in today's world, is your best approach. What do you think are some of their reasons?" The students will then thoughtfully and respectfully identify all the best rea-sons that adults can identify and some new and interesting ones of their own.

We also weaken our message when we present abstinence as simply an alternate means of pregnancy and disease prevention or as a synonym for "choosing not to have intercourse before you are married." When I ask my students to list the reasons why a person might choose to abstain from sexual intercourse, after they've identified fear of pregnancy, fear of disease, and religious belief, they think they're done. What escapes them are the multitude of other reasons—physical, emotional, social, moral, interpersonal, developmental, familial, legal—that are just as real and just as important to acknowledge and understand. We should be present-ing abstinence (and its opposite) as an ongoing life option, not as a birth control method. People of all ages—even married people—make contin-uous choices throughout their lives about whether to participate in a particular sexual act. Figuring out when and how to say yes or no is a lifelong matter.

Nor do we do the subject of abstinence justice when we fail to specifi-cally identify our context. The word *abstinence* by itself is an empty con-cept. If we intend to give advice about it, we need to be clear about what we mean: abstinence from what, with whom, and under what circum-stances? Abstinence from intercourse, oral sex, genital touching, kissing on the first date? With someone they just met, a steady boyfriend or girl-friend, a fiancé? Until they're in high school, while they're still living at home, when they're away at college, when they're married? To leave things open-ended is much too abstract; if we think there are important parame-ters, we need to say specifically what they are.

And we also have to be prepared to clearly explain why. There are many valid reasons to encourage young people as a group to abstain from cer-tain sexual experiences—religious, moral, developmental, and safety-re-lated concerns, among others. In clarifying the messages we most want to impart, we need to prioritize these general areas of concern, since they may overlap but are not the same. If developmental, moral, and safety is-sues are paramount to us, we need to be honest and say so. "Sexual inter-course (or other forms of sexual intimacy) when you are not married is acceptable to me, but only under the following very well-defined circum-stances." If at our bottom line is a deeply held religious conviction (in this case we should probably emphasize the word *chastity,* not abstinence), we could say, "Although I hope you would take steps to protect yourself, since I certainly would not want you to suffer an unwanted pregnancy or STI or be deeply hurt from a premature intimate relationship, I want you to know that according to our religion, there is no such thing as *spiritually* "safe sex" when you are not married." By lining up the issues separately, we can avoid giving messages that are mixed or confused, and can ensure that the ones we do give are straight. "Wait!" and "Protect yourself!" are not necessarily contradictory statements: "The best decision, which will protect you in all possible ways, is to wait until you are [married, older, etc.]. The next best way to protect yourself and others is by doing every-thing you can to ensure your physical, social, and emotional safety. Here's how."

## Beware the Illusion of Control

One reason that our children's sexual life terrifies us is that, by definition, we can't be there to protect them. Experimenting with sexual behavior and making important sexual decisions are among the first grown-up choices they'll need to make totally on their own. Try as we might to influence those decisions, it's unlikely they'll be made either because of us, in spite of us, or even to spite us. Our children will ultimately make whatever decisions they need and want to make for themselves, not us. And isn't that the way it should be?

If we've done a good job as limit setters, however, they'll be less likely to have to decide until they're ready. And if we've also taught them how to set their own safe and healthy limits whenever the time comes, we'll probably feel proud of the way they've made their decisions—even when we don't always agree with their exact choices.

## Some Final Comments on Sexual Harassment and Abuse

Not long after the highly publicized nomination proceedings for Clarence Thomas doubled as a nationwide in-service session on the problem of sexual harassment in the workplace, I surveyed several hundred of my own students, thirteen through seventeen, about the topic. The results were stunning and incredibly depressing. Nearly every girl (and some boys as well) had their own story to tell. It was clear that for young girls growing into womanhood in our culture, being the target of sexual harassment is every bit as much a rite of passage as getting their first periods or buying their first brassieres.

What I learned most from their stories is that girls in our society are targeted for harassment everywhere—and by everyone—imaginable: at school, at work, in church, on the street, in stores, in bowling alleys, in their own homes, at camp, on vacations. It is perpetrated by strangers, relatives, friends, friends of friends, friends of the family, shop clerks, bosses, and boyfriends. The harassment is sometimes verbal, sometimes by look or gesture, sometimes in writing, sometimes by touching, grabbing, and cornering. Much of it is relatively mild, none of it is provoked, and some of it incredibly disgusting and violating. Whatever the degree, sexual harassment is clearly pervasive and almost all of it damaging.

Girls are by no means the only victims. Boys target other boys in supposedly friendly horseplay or as part of institutionalized hazing rituals that can become vicious and even violent. For boys who are even *considered* gay, life at school, in the neighborhood, or even in the family can easily become a living hell. And there are certainly boys who are sexually taunted, touched, and pressured by girls whose attention is unwanted, uninvited, and unwelcome.

The pervasiveness of sexual harassment in our society tells us that this is not a problem for our children to solve. We can certainly help them understand the social and psychological dynamics of sexual harassment and how to deal positively with the aftermath of having been a target or a bystander. We can also raise them with respectful and egalitarian attitudes toward sex and gender to minimize the chance that they themselves will ever become perpetrators, and we can require them to own up to their misbehavior if and when it occurs. But we can't help them avoid it or expect them to prevent it. It's too big, too pervasive, and too powerful.

Sexual harassment is an adult problem, rooted deeply in our adult cultural landscape. It is not, as some people contend, a natural, expected, and harmless part of adolescence. When it spills over into our children's lives, especially when it happens repeatedly and pervasively in school— where children must go every day, where there is absolutely no escape, and where they have a moral and legal right to a physically and emotionally safe environment—adults must make certain that the institution's policies are sufficiently clear and its practices sufficiently firm. Moreover, it's a parent's job to make sure that proper supports and limits are in place.

I would suggest a similar approach to child sexual abuse. I have long worried about "good touch/bad touch" programs, which subtly (and unintentionally, I am sure) place too much of the onus for sexual abuse prevention on children and not adults. There is a fine line in a very young child's mind, I fear, between "I can make this stop if I don't like it," and "I'm responsible for fixing this, and if I don't, I'm responsible for its happening." I also worry about the antisexual undertones communicated within a program whose fundamental context is abuse, not healthy sexuality, especially when sexual parts ("privates") are often not even called directly by name. Moreover, can we really expect young children to distinguish the idea that "having people touch my sexual parts is bad," from the notion that, therefore, "my sexual parts must be bad."

There are certainly helpful and important instructions that we can and should give to young children, including messages about appropriate and inappropriate touch. Along with many other safety rules, children should know that they should always tell a parent if someone wants to touch their genitals (except when bathing or wiping them or examining them in a doctor's office), even if the person tells them to keep it a secret. However, there is no reason to separate those messages from the general topic of safety by treating sexual safety in a special program. The larger the context we can create around the topic of sexual abuse, the less we will highlight or tinge the topic of sexuality in a negative or an alarmist fashion.

Our most important job is to train ourselves, not our children, so that we avoid placing them in harm's way (by very careful screening and supervision) and can detect quickly if, despite our precautions, abuse has occurred. Parents should be alert to possible warning signs of abuse and should seek immediate advice from a pediatrician or trained specialist if they notice evidence of the following in a preschool or elementary-aged child: unusual discharge from the genitals; compulsive masturbation in public (after the child is old enough to understand the concept of privacy); excessive interest in touching or drawing genitals; a preoccupation with sex that interferes with friendships or school life; a child's engaging in atypical sex play (such as oral, anal, or vaginal intercourse, or penetration with fingers or objects) with an age-mate; involvement in sex play *of any kind* with a child more than three years older; or when a youngster appears fearful, angry, or withdrawn in the presence of a suspected abuser. Any of these activities *might* indicate that a child has been exposed to sexually explicit materials or has been sexually abused.

## Turning Our Children Over to Themselves

The parenting skills we have addressed so far—affirmation, information giving, values clarification, and limit setting—will gradually give way to anticipatory guidance as our children approach maturity. As we'll discover in Chapter 13, anticipatory guidance aims to impart the kind of self-awareness, knowledge, personal values, and decision-making skills that our young adult children will need in order to affirm, educate, understand, and take care of themselves.

# Anticipatory Guidance: Making Ourselves Dispensable

When my older son graduated from high school, one of the first gifts I picked out was H. Jackson Brown's *Life's Little Instruction Book*. I'm a major list person, so its simple format of 511 pithy and practical pointers had immediate appeal. Also, I especially liked that number 511 counseled, "Call your mother." In fact, I couldn't resist adding the following inscription: "Number 512. If your mother is not at home, see numbers 1, 16, 20, 41, 97, 156, 190, 296, 375 and/or 481. They'll probably help you solve whatever problem you were calling her about in the first place!"

Then I had a good laugh at myself. The panic of sending my firstborn into the world and off to college was just taking hold, and I was trying to head it off by extending my parental reach from Maryland to Massachusetts. Already I needed a more dependable connection to my son than mere telephone wire could supply; I wanted a veritable berth inside his head, or at least on his bookshelf, which he could always turn to in a pinch.

As Brown says in the introduction to his book (he wrote it as a parting gift for his own son as he was leaving for college), it's not the responsibility of parents to pave the way for their children in life but to provide a road map. Little by little, as they begin to take charge of their own lives, we'll need to exchange aspects of our limit setting role with our best anticipatory guidance, so that they can find their own way.

The role of anticipatory guide is just as its name implies. As adults, we are expected to remain at least one step ahead of our children—practically and developmentally—so that we can anticipate and help guide them through the next set of challenges and demands they will face. When they are very young, we do so easily, almost instinctively, as soon as they take their first steps toward independence. We call out to them as they run off into the preschool building: "Hey, do you remember where we put your milk money?" or, "Don't forget, I might be a little late picking you up today because of traffic. It's always bad on Fridays. But don't worry, OK?" We take them to buy school supplies every August and help them think through all the things they might need the very first day and what can wait until the teacher gives more detailed instructions later. We remind them that everyone is nervous the first day of school, or camp, or middle school, or high school, and help them think of strategies for making new friends or finding their niche. We prepare them in advance for the body changes they can expect during pubescence and what to do if they happen to get their period in school or have a spontaneous erection while doing a math problem on the board in front of the whole class! We send them to driver's ed and spend hours in the passenger seat teaching them the rigors of road safety.

The role of anticipatory guide—the last of the five core parenting skills—takes on crucial and renewed significance as we shepherd our children through the adolescent years. As they gain increasing independence and freedom of movement and association, we begin to lose more and more direct control over their lives and their personal decisions. To retain our influence and to be there for them even as we are losing our power, our role is to be aware of and help prepare them for the kinds of decisions they may confront.

Some of the first independent decisions our adolescent children will make will involve what they do with their bodies—what they put on them and in them, what they do to them, and how they choose to share them with another person sexually. Those decisions, many of which can have direct and profound effects on their health and well-being, are among the ones that worry us the most, precisely because they will likely occur away from our watchful eyes. That's why we'll need to be vigilant in our role as limit setters when they are younger—to lower the chance they'll even encounter situations in which they'll be called on to make these decisions. And, when we're not there to protect them, or when they're old enough to be on their own and make their own independent choices, our best shot at ensuring that our children will set their own safe and healthy limits is skillful anticipatory guidance.

The focus of this chapter will be on preparing adolescents for independent sexual decision making by nurturing the self-awareness, knowledge, values clarification, and internalized limit setting they'll need to draw upon to make healthy choices and to avoid dangerous risk taking. In other words, we'll want to make ourselves dispensable, by enabling them to acquire the same skills we've been cultivating within ourselves. That's the essence of anticipatory guidance.

## The Challenge of Health Education

A not-so-funny but instructive joke began circulating among AIDS educators in the early days of the epidemic:

Two IV drug users are standing on a street corner, about to share a syringe. A passerby remarks, "Aren't you afraid of passing AIDS?"

"No, no, it's OK," one of them replies. "We're wearing condoms!"

Even about much less onerous subjects than HIV infection, health education is an ambitious enterprise. Unlike more traditional and academic disciplines, it intends not only to teach information and thinking skills but also to directly influence attitudes and behavior. When the issue at hand is as intensely personal and value-laden as human sexuality and the cultural context as muddled as ours in the United States, delivering preventive health messages effectively—as the two men on the street corner remind us—becomes tremendously challenging.

One long, rainy summer afternoon, my eleven-year-old son was so bored that he actually filled his time watching a tape in my video cabinet about gonorrhea. After finishing, he walked into the kitchen and exclaimed, "Guess what!" with obvious shock—even relief—in his voice. "With gonorrhea, all you get is sterile!"

After regaining my composure (I was momentarily overcome by visions of my potential grandparenthood quite literally going down the tubes), we had a long talk. Later, reflecting back on his pronouncement and my upset, I "got it." Well, of course! Why not? I thought. Why would an eleven-year-old boy have seen things any other way?

At his age, the concept of fertility was a total abstraction; for one thing, he didn't have any as yet, and for another, anything having to do with the future to him meant next year, at the latest. What's more, having been barraged incessantly for the past two years of his short life (the year was 1985) with terrifying accounts and images of an awful disease called AIDS, he, like many others his age, had been drawn in by the drama and sensationalism and had begun to feel personally at risk in some distant, but real way. No wonder that when stacked up against a disease that to him meant sure death, gonorrhea seemed a veritable bargain!

My son's story reminds us as parents and educators that we must always bear in mind an old axiom: There may be a huge difference between what we intend to teach, what we actually teach, and what ultimately is learned. The "educational" message Josh had received was certainly not intentional, but it was powerfully delivered—and received—nonetheless.

## Getting the Message Across to an Adolescent Audience

Communicating successfully with adolescents about important health risks requires the understanding that what may seem reasonable, useful, and clear to us from our adult perspective is frequently heard and processed quite differently from theirs. As explained in Chapter 9, for example, providing too much scary information without adequate balance can just as easily cause teenagers to become less cautious, not more, because the high level of anxiety it creates—absent other coping strategies—may simply induce denial and avoidance.

Whenever adults are significantly off the mark in the health messages they deliver to adolescents, there are usually one or two predictable causes: Either we're motivated too much by our own needs, or we're simply ignorant of or blind to theirs.

### Whose Needs Are We Meeting, Anyway?

As sexuality educators, most adults admit to feeling nervous and apprehensive. Inexperienced and insecure in our role, we are also deeply worried for our children. These powerful and combined anxieties make us vulnerable to responding to children out of our own intense feelings and needs rather than to theirs. The pressing need to allay our own feelings of panic and to feel more in control may cause us to embrace approaches designed not to educate young people but rather to contain their behaviors. In reality, rather than diminishing risky or unwanted behaviors, our attempts at control will likely cause adolescents simply to go "underground" with their actions, as they attempt either to avoid adult scrutiny or disapproval or to simply challenge adult authority. Meanwhile, deprived of critical information, and cut off from adult input and support, they will do so at greatly increased risk. To avoid alienating our children in this way, the solution is to remember the first developmental skill we've identified, the ability to see our children as they really are.

## Adolescents Are Not Simply Shorter or Less Mature Adults

A daring and socially conscious high school senior I once taught—a budding health educator, actually—took it upon herself to survey teenagers sitting near her on the beach about their sexual decision making. One of her questions concerned condom use. "Do you or would you always use condoms?" she asked. She heard some pretty interesting answers, but one really stuck out in her mind. "Absolutely," said one young man, "but only with people I know really well."

Now, if ever a "safer sex" strategy made no sense whatsoever, that was definitely it, our class agreed. But, of course, almost all decisions and all behavior make sense if only the observer can step back far enough to take in the bigger puzzle into which a particular behavioral piece fits. So, we tried hard to come up with reasons: Maybe he didn't care enough about people he didn't know well to protect them; maybe situations of this type (i.e., with people he didn't know well) occurred more spontaneously and left him unprepared. Maybe he was more anxious and nervous with people he barely knew and was afraid he'd fumble putting on a condom or even have trouble keeping an erection. Though none of those explanations adequately explained the obvious—he should either have abstained, or chosen to use a condom, anyway—at least we'd perhaps found some sort of logic.

The truth is, adolescent sexual decisions often seem to make no sense to an outside observer, even though at the time, and to the individual, they may make complete sense. This is the "almost logic" of adolescence, to which I referred in an earlier chapter. It reminds us that adolescents are not simply shorter, less knowledgeable, or less mature adults. How they think about themselves, others, and the world around them is not just *quantitatively* different but *qualitatively* different from adult patterns of thought. I've enumerated below some of the more common developmental influences that can put adolescents at risk for unwise sexual decision making. It's a pretty overwhelming list, but keep in mind as you read it that, once forewarned, you will have the ability to ameliorate most of them.

**Overwhelming, Conflicting, or Unresolved Emotional Feelings.** As with the boy on the beach, the sexual situations in which teenagers find themselves can generate intense and conflicting emotions. Some degree of insecurity, confusion, guilt, or performance or peer pressure is practically inevitable, and the resulting need to save face—or to reduce anxiety—may easily overshadow the need to think about and follow through with physical precautions.

American teenagers grow up in a society that continually transmits diametrically opposite messages about sexual behavior—that it is cool, essential, fun, easy, and carefree, *and,* that it is wrong, sinful, difficult, and dangerous. Caught in this do-don't double bind—especially when there have been no adults in their immediate lives to help them think through the contradictions—adolescents often come into sexual situations carrying a very heavy load of ambivalence. The internal discord, or "cognitive dissonance," that results can be acutely uncomfortable, so much so that it's easier simply to avoid thinking about the conflict altogether, thereby allowing things to "just happen." As a consequence, adolescents too often *do* have intercourse, but *don't* use protection. Their dissonance is partially alleviated by the lack of planning or forethought, a throwback, no doubt, to the age-old notion that premeditated sin is even worse than ordinary sin. However, the remedy comes at the high cost of having to agree to unprotected intercourse.

Remember, too, that adolescents are fundamentally here-and-now-oriented and that they are primarily concrete thinkers. They're much more likely to heed a sure, clear, and present danger, such as the fear of being embarrassed, of looking uncool, of not measuring up to self- or peer-imposed standards, than an invisible physical risk or abstract, hypothetical consequence. To us adults, therefore, what looks like totally unacceptable and risky behavior, to them may seem like a logical and sound risk-avoidance strategy.

**The Imaginary Audience.**     Psychologist David Elkind has written extensively about a very useful psychological construct that he calls the adolescent's *imaginary audience.* In explaining the enormous self-consciousness so characteristic of early and middle adolescents especially, Elkind explains that being this age is a lot like being on the stage—all the time. Acutely insecure about who they are and who they are becoming, young adolescents are constantly focused on the perceived judgments of others, partially as a way of knowing how they should judge themselves. Obsessed with issues of self-definition, self-worth, and public image, they simply assume, quite unconsciously, that others are equally as concerned with them as they are; hence the unremitting feeling of being watched and evaluated, especially by one's all-important peers. They forget that others, of course, are equally as self-conscious and therefore are themselves just as constantly worried about the judgments of *their* own "audience."

When one of my sons was about twelve, I made the awful mistake of telling him during dinner at a neighbor's house that he was wearing his pullover shirt on backward. Knowing that he would be mortified to discover this when he got home, even though the difference between the front and back was so subtle it would have been noticed by no one, I whispered this piece of information discretely into his ear. With a look of sudden terror, he scanned the entire room, certain that everyone knew about this grievous faux pas and was staring at him that very moment. He managed this inspection so deftly, it was as if his eyes had actually circled all the way around his head.

All this fuss over an inconsequential tab on the front of a shirt! I could only imagine a typical day at school, and I didn't even want to think about what it might be like for him at a party or mixer. Later, I thought of the older teenagers I teach, and pictured them in any number of social and sexual situations that would likely be fraught with self-judgment and the projected judgments of others. In the midst of all of that psychic vulnerability, and without an awareness of this normal tendency to distort one's social environment, finding the mental energy to think, plan, and protect oneself might be next to impossible.

**The Perceived Irrelevance of Personal Risk.**   Elkind writes about another crucial psychological dynamic, the adolescent's *perception of personal inviolability*. As he and other developmental psychologists point out, the central task of adolescence—separating oneself from the safety and security of one's family of origin—is so fundamentally terrifying, yet so developmentally essential, that a powerful defense mechanism takes hold. In this unconscious psychic maneuver, adolescents convince themselves that despite the big, scary world that awaits them, they are still very much in control. Whereas *other* teens may be at risk for pregnancy, STI, HIV, date rape, drunk driving accidents, and so forth, these vulnerabilities do not apply to *them* personally. Elkind explains this attitude as a kind of irrational, self-protective grandiosity, an internal voice that convinces them that they alone share a unique relationship with the surrounding universe that magically keeps them immune to danger.

Adults who know teenagers well or who still vividly recall their own adolescence will recognize this distorted perception of self in other kinds of behaviors so characteristic of the age. Who, for example, has not heard a teenager proclaim, with an excruciating sense of aloneness and total frustration, that no one else could possibly understand his or her feelings or experiences, because no one before has ever experienced them! It is as if, out of the terrifying prospect of separating from parents, adolescents must overcompensate by overseparating, and overdifferentiating self from others. That is, they decide to believe, "I am totally unique." It is this overcompensation that affords the myth of inviolability. This psychological trap becomes, for highly risk-taking teens especially, the Catch-22 of adolescent development: They cannot grow up without this perceived sense of personal invulnerability, yet they might take life-threatening risks because of it.

**Cognitive Immaturity.**   Although it does involve thought process, magical thinking is fundamentally an emotional rather than an intellectual dynamic for teenagers. It has nothing to do with being "smart," capable, or responsible; the class president, school newspaper editor, or class valedictorian is just an susceptible as anyone else. Nor can it necessarily be ameliorated with life experience, as any counselor who has seen a teen for pregnancy testing months or even weeks after she's had an abortion can attest. Not uncommonly, a girl in that situation will readily explain that she still can't understand why she got pregnant the first time, so she thought certainly it would never happen again! It is a worldview—a way of looking at oneself and the surrounding environment—that adolescents simply outgrow at some point when their levels of emotional, social, and intellectual maturity eventually converge again and realign. Moreover, getting past it can't really be rushed; as with a first period or first ejaculation, each adolescent's pace of development is dictated by her or his unique developmental clock.

Cognitive ability—as well as learning—does play a major role, however, in determining an adolescent's fundamental ability to assess risky situations and to take preventive action. After all, we can readily teach even much younger children to identify potentially dangerous behaviors (e.g., crossing the street) and to develop a plan for minimizing the risks (going to the corner, looking both ways, etc.). As is the case with younger children, however, adolescents have a much easier time with risk management when the potential risks and dangers are concrete and the available prevention strategies are clear.

In the realm of pregnancy and STI prevention, unless we present information skillfully, the potential risks and dangers remain anything but concrete, and the prevention strategies anything but clear. Most of the principles involved in the prevention of communicable diseases, for example, are abstract. In regard to sexually transmitted infections (STI), basic concepts such as probabilities of infection, undetermined incubation periods, asymptomatic carrier status, and even the whole notion of microscopic organisms are exceedingly difficult to grasp for minds that reason primarily in the concrete. Pregnancy risks are no easier to comprehend than STI: Sperm, eggs, and internal organs are totally invisible, and the whole concept of the menstrual cycle is a nightmare of illogic and inconsistency. Add to these challenges the hodgepodge of methods of pregnancy and disease prevention currently available, and no wonder the issue of curbing teenage pregnancy and STI is often, at best, a matter of damage control.

**Projected Gender Roles and Stereotypes.**   Despite profound changes in American attitudes toward sex and gender, sexist and stereotypical beliefs persist and exert a powerful influence on the dynamics of prevention behavior. For example, consider the contradictory cultural messages about the female role in prevention: girls are supposed to be less interested in sexual intercourse yet more responsible regarding its potential consequences. Therefore, they are more likely to be condemned should an unwanted consequence occur, but also more likely to be judged if they are the ones to come to a sexual situation with condoms or contraceptives in hand (or pocketbook). This no-win emotional and social bind is a setup for inaction and unhealthy reliance on male control in situations in which the girl may well be the one with the most to lose.

Stereotypes of adolescent boys, on the other hand, are just as muddled. Although they are supposed to seek out and want sex at every possible opportunity, they're also not supposed to appear too eager about it—lest a girl think that he thinks she is perceived as "easy" or that he is "only after one thing." From either person's perspective, the notion of preplanning or even the appearance that preplanning has occurred becomes anathema and thereby may preclude itself from happening.

**Ignorance, Misinformation, and Miseducation.**   Despite the near absence of comprehensive sexuality education in our schools, young people today receive information about sex and reproduction constantly from television, movies, books, magazines, newspapers, the Internet, adults, older siblings, and, of course, peers. That's good news, and it's also bad news. Adolescents are often very well informed about these topics—meaning they have lots of pieces of information—but they are rarely well educated, since those pieces are seldom organized or retrievable in a meaningful or useful way. Accumulated haphazardly from here, there, and everywhere, most of what they know has been absorbed in totally random fashion, in much the same way as a sponge soaks up water; little distinction is made between information that is correct or incorrect, unimportant or essential, complete or incomplete. With no way to recognize which pieces are which or even that they are all mixed up with each other, adolescents end up thinking they know a lot but have no way of assessing what it is they *really* know.

**Poor Methods of, and Poor Access to, Prevention.**   The perfect contraceptive for an adolescent age group would be easy to get, easy to use, easy to transport, easy to conceal, easy to reverse, easy to understand, and hard to forget. It would be highly effective against both pregnancy and disease, be inexpensive, cause no serious side effects, be physically and emotionally comfortable to use, and be capable of use independent of partner motivation or control. In short, it doesn't exist.

Each of the available methods falls short along one or more of these important dimensions. Pills, for example, though highly effective when used correctly, require a gynecological visit, vigilance about use, and ongoing prescription refills; they also provide no protection from STI and indeed may even increase susceptibility to some types. Condoms provide excellent prophylaxis against STI, have no side effects, and are more accessible (though picture the imagined audience in the mind of an adolescent needing to purchase them in a very public place). They also require forethought, planning, interruption of sexual activity, and exceptionally careful use every time they are needed. Sponges (due back on the market soon, as of this writing) can be bought without prescription, but come with complex written instructions and without the help or guidance of a trained health-care provider. Diaphragms do come with professional counsel and also require an exam that will include STI screening, but involve touching the genitals in ways that make many adolescent girls feel keenly uncomfortable. And so on.

In addition to the motley assortment of available products, the access to information and services, especially those that specifically cater to the special needs of adolescent populations, is another serious barrier to effective use. The Alan Guttmacher Institute estimates that nearly 40 percent of teenagers in United States who need contraceptive advice and services are not currently served by local pharmacies, doctors, hospitals, health departments, or clinics.

**Alcohol and Other Drugs.** The relationship between alcohol and other drug use and unprotected sexual intercourse is well documented. Studies of adolescents who have experienced unintended pregnancies have found that up to half had been drinking, using drugs, or both before the act of intercourse that resulted in the pregnancy. Other research has documented that among adolescents who combine alcohol, other drugs, or both with sexual activity, 16 percent use condoms less often after drinking, and 25 percent after other drug use.

Alcohol and other drug use is also implicated in the problem of acquaintance rape. Surveys of college students have determined that at least 75 percent of the males and at least 55 percent of the females involved in a rape incident had been drinking just prior to the act.

The direction of causality in situations involving the combination of sex and drugs is not clear: Is it the drinking or drug use *itself* that leads to the sexual behavior? Or, does the desire come first? That is, do teenagers deliberately use alcohol or drugs to facilitate having less guilt or anxiety about sex? Or perhaps the general tendency to engage in one type of risk-taking behavior is correlated with the likelihood of engaging in others. Regardless of the explanation, the combination of sex and drugs for any reason impairs judgment and places adolescents at increased risk for pregnancy, rape, and sexually transmitted infection.

A related concern is the incessant use of sexual messages and imagery to sell alcoholic beverages. Practically all these advertisements picture very sexy couples simultaneously enjoying each other and whatever it is they are drinking. In fact, the copy often makes an explicit statement about the similarity between sexual arousal and the taste and feel of alcohol in the body. The use of alcohol for the purpose of seduction is also a common theme, and perhaps the most potentially dangerous are beer ads encouraging the combination of large quantities of alcohol with sexual activity. (My least favorite example: a six-pack of beer featured beneath the words "The Joy of Six.") Alcohol companies would not be allowed to encourage drinking and driving (although beer ads often flaunt pictures of revved-up sports cars painted with the same colors and graphics that appear on the particular brand being advertised), but they *are* allowed to promote drinking and dating. Clearly, based on research as well as common sense, "*Don't* drink and date" is the message teenagers need to hear.

**Counterproductive Media Messages.**   In addition to these and other advertising messages, Americans witness thousands upon thousands of other sexual scenarios each year on television and in the movies. Most of these encounters depict situations in which sex is portrayed as essential, simple, impetuous, impersonal, and consequence-free. For young viewers, for whom sexual intercourse can be dangerously premature, these messages are the developmental equivalent of encouraging young children to play in the street, never brush their teeth, or speak freely with strangers. These kinds of endorsements, of course, would never be permitted over the airwaves, but because the sexual seduction to which our children are exposed is so much more "subtle," it remains a pervasive yet unchallenged influence.

Psychologist William Fisher points to another powerful and insidious influence of media. American adolescents view a nearly unending stream of imagery that promotes sexual activity, yet provides practically no imagery or reference at all to pregnancy or STI prevention. Consequently, it is very easy for teenagers to fantasize elaborate strategies for seduction (e.g., sexy dress, talk, music, eye contact), but nearly impossible for them to imagine parallel prevention strategies (e.g., going to a clinic or a drug-store, talking to a partner about STI or contraception, putting a contra-ceptive product in or on their bodies). In fact, research studies of young women's written fantasies of enacting sexual seduction found that contra-ception was never mentioned; in young men's scenarios, it is imagined by some, but often in the context of a botched seduction. In other words, we need to concern ourselves with what our children don't see in the media about sex, as well as what they do see.

**Social Inexperience.**    American teenagers, overexposed as they are to so-phisticated sexual images and to adult-oriented sources of sexual informa-tion, can easily manage to look and sound convincingly grown up when they speak about sexual matters. In sometimes intimidating or off-putting ways, they often give or try to give adults the impression that they are knowledgeable, confident, experienced, and without need of adult help or input.

No matter how much they may know factually and how skilled the adults who parent and teach them, teenagers are by definition amateurs at making independent choices and taking responsibility for their lives. They find themselves constantly in novel situations that require careful judgment and quick action and for which they have no reserve of experi-ence, no fund of trial-and-error mistakes and successes to draw on. Their abilities to assess true feelings and values (their own and others'), to evalu-ate alternatives, to predict and prevent consequences, to communicate as-sertively, and to follow through consistently and responsibly are fledgling at best. The task of learning to manage their sexuality is no different, only in that the stakes may be higher and the cultural and social supports less available.

## Matching Interventions to Developmental and Cultural Hurdles

The risk factors described above make it painfully clear that the idiosyn-crasies of normal adolescent development, combined with the incon-gruities of contemporary American sexual mores, can beget a prescription for calamity. It would be hard to identify an adolescent sexual experience in which one or more of these ten factors is not operational to some degree, and even one alone may lead to disastrous consequences. Typically several apply at once, and they are often interconnected and mutually reinforcing. Given their weight and complexity, it seems a wonder that *any* children make it through adolescence sexually unscathed. (Despite the apparent potential for difficulty, remember that most children do.)

With the exception of the myth of inviolability—in which case *time itself* provides the only real solution—there are many available strategies to remedy these potential hurdles. Forewarned is forearmed: The more that adults comprehend the unique ways in which adolescents commonly think and react, the more we can intervene with the right amount and kinds of anticipatory guidance.

*Our ultimate, collective goal is to slow our teenagers down*, by encouraging them to become more thoughtful, direct, and deliberate in their decision making and their relationships, and by discouraging or diminishing the factors that set them up for premature experimentation. And, as we've said, research has told us consistently that it is aware and communicating parents who are the first line of defense in slowing kids down.

**Cultivate Your Child's Emotional Intelligence.**   Many books written for parents and educators have emphasized a trait that psychologist Daniel Goleman was the first to popularize: "emotional intelligence." The acute interest in this subject has been stimulated by research demonstrating that emotional intelligence—much more so than mental facility—is one the most consistent predictors of success, happiness, and fulfillment in adult life.

One of the hallmarks of emotional intelligence is the capacity both to "read" the feelings of others and to recognize and clearly express your own. Encouraging our children to develop these important life skills will also enable them to be more in charge of their emotions, rather than at their mercy, in stressful or pressured situations. If we help them anticipate situations in which strong emotions may make them prone to choose saving face over safety, and actually rehearse with them how to say no or "No, thanks" firmly and nonconfrontationally, we'll enable them to handle themselves assertively. And if we can help them think and speak clearly about their personal code of (sexual) values, they'll be less likely to experience moral ambivalence and inflated vulnerability to pressure situations. Together, all these various skills and strategies are potent antidotes to negative peer pressure and popular culture values to which inevitably they will be exposed.

**Help Adolescents Demystify Their Own Development.**    I was a young adult when Gail Sheehy published her classic book, *Passages*. At the time, adulthood stretched ahead of me like a vast and unpredictable monolith; I remember finding comfort and a sense of control in her descriptions of the various stages of adult development and in being able to forecast some of what I might experience.

We can do the same for our adolescents, as parents and also in specially designed courses on adolescent issues in middle and high schools. By helping them hold a mirror to their own experiences, we can minimize some of the confusion and isolation of the age and also help diffuse some of the barriers to healthy decision making. If we can help them to see their own imaginary audience, for example, and understand why and how they've created it, they'll be better able to distinguish personal projections from objective reality. When we prepare them to expect mood shifts and identity confusion, we can also remind them that for a time they'll be prone to underestimate situations involving risk taking and danger. If they're stubbornly stuck in an adolescent brand of logic that only goes so far, we can help them by withholding our criticism or impatience and stretching their thinking skills: "Yes, but, I'm wondering if you've thought about? . . . " or "Yes, but, what do you think you would you do if? . . . " As their personal cultural interpreter, we can teach them how to deconstruct distorted media images about sex, gender, and alcohol and explain that since they're "just kids," the media count on their being vulnerable enough—and stupid enough—to fall for the hype. (They won't like that idea at all.)

**Systematize Our Children's Sexual Learning.**    As discussed, adolescents' capacity to make complex sexual decisions is compromised both by their relatively immature (though developmentally normal) thought processes and by a history of formal sexual learning that is haphazard and inappropriately delayed. Aside from the ability to understand and process sophisticated cognitive information, engaging successfully in any kind of prevention behavior also requires high-level thinking skills. To prevent pregnancy and STI, for example, one must be able to mentally project oneself into the future ("I might possibly have sexual intercourse"); think about the possible consequences of one's actions ("If I do, I might be exposed to pregnancy or STI"); and decide on preventive steps ("Therefore, I'd better purchase condoms or other contraceptives, or rethink the idea of having intercourse"). These steps in logic and logistics all require sophisticated abstract reasoning—including the ability to predict future events, assess complex probabilities, and engage in what psychologists call "reverse operations."

Reverse operations is a difficult cognitive skill and one of the last to emerge developmentally; a person must not only be able to think far ahead, but then capably perform the mental gymnastics of reversing possible future events—by abstractly working backward from the future to the present—in order to devise a preventive plan. The fledgling ability to think in these terms begins to appear in a sizable number of teens as they near sixteen, an age by which many have already initiated risky sexual behaviors. Younger teens are simply unable to anticipate or engage in these intellectual steps in any kind of complex situation, including sexual ones. Adults can help by making these abstract mental steps more concrete as they talk with children and adolescents about their present and future decisions, in other words, by proactively "walking them through" the requisite thinking processes involved in planning and prevention.

In addition to these developmental concerns, we must be aware that unless the teaching of sexual health information is timely, targeted, and systematic, dangerous misperceptions will result. A clear case in point is the widespread confusion I hear constantly regarding the methods of pregnancy prevention versus the methods of disease prevention. I read once about a study in which 50 percent of teenagers polled believed that birth control pills also protect users against the spread of STI. The results didn't surprise me at all. Virtually all teenagers have heard at some time that condoms are a method of birth control, and they've heard as well that condoms also protect against STI. I think they simply mis-connect these two pieces of information, overgeneralizing to other contraceptives, and decide that birth control and disease control are one and the same issue. Without skilled, explicit, and systematic instruction, they won't get the crucial distinction: Although both pregnancy and STI result from the same behavior, namely, sexual intercourse, pregnancy prevention is a matter of stopping sperm-to-egg contact, whereas disease prevention involves the entirely different matter of preventing certain kinds of body-part-to-body-part contact.

By the way, we've also totally misled and confused young people and everybody else with the stupid phrase "Don't share body fluids," a leftover from the early days of the epidemic, when sexually explicit language was not permitted in the public domain. First, the issue of body fluids only applies to HIV, not other STIs. Second, even in the case of HIV, the virus is present infectiously only in *some* body fluids (i.e., blood, semen, vaginal lubricating fluid, and breast milk), not all. In my experience, most adults can't even confidently name these implicated fluids, because education and public information are rarely specific enough. Moreover, there is absolutely no reason to separate teaching about HIV from instruction about all other STIs, as is common practice: The fundamental information we need to communicate about transmission (and protection) is almost always the same. Here's the clearest and most complete message to deliver: People acquire STIs (including HIV) by engaging in mouth-to-genital, genital-to-genital, and genital-to-anal contact with an infected partner.

The fact that the media are doing most of the sex education in the United States—even when the education is sound—means that our kids are continually receiving a distorted picture. Even at their best intentioned, the media are ultimately about getting attention (and dollars); it's the "sexy" stories about sex that sell. HIV/AIDS commands enormous attention—and that's good—but the near exclusive coverage of that one STI has dwarfed our children's (and our own) understanding of other sexually transmitted infections that are not only serious but in reality much more prevalent in teenage populations. Even in the relatively well educated communities where I teach, no more than half of my students or their parents can name the two most common STIs (genital warts and chlamydia) off the top of their head. We've got to make sure that they and we are getting our information from right sources.

**Teach the Lifesaving Concept of Relative Risk.**   Grab a pencil, and without looking ahead at the next few paragraphs, take a minute to write out an answer to the following question: "What are three things an individual can do to lower his or her chance of getting or spreading a sexually transmitted infection?"

What if I had added, as you were almost finished, "but none of your answers can be 'remain abstinent, practice monogamy, or use condoms'"? How many items would you have left? How many more could you think of?

Now suppose I had asked, "What are three important things an individual can do to lower his or her chances of having a car accident?" Would your top three answers have been (1) don't ever drive; (2) only drive up and down on your driveway; and (3) practice using the brakes, *a lot?* And how many total items could you have listed in this case?

Before we cut our children loose in an automobile by themselves, we teach them dozens of strategies for avoiding a car crash; we don't just make sure they know how to slam on the brakes in the last seconds before impact. Our goal is to teach them everything we possibly can—every piece of knowledge, judgment, self-awareness—to maximize the chance that they'll be nowhere near an impact in the first place. We know that the street is a very risky place, but if they develop the right mind-set, learn all the rules, and master all the skills, they can lower those risks to practically zero. That's why we're willing to let our young people go, because we know that their level of risk is relative to the number of things they know about protecting themselves.

The difference between how we prepare young people for the dangers (or the pleasures) of sex and how we prepare them for the dangers of driving is that most of us unequivocally want our children to drive. We don't really want them to have sex—or at least not intercourse—until they're ready, or older, or married. So we don't really prepare them. In reality, of course, we don't get to control when or whether they have sex (of any kind); we can only help enable them to handle their sex life morally, respectfully, and carefully.

We're not doing a great job. Over the years, I've asked thousands of young people and their parents the question about STI that opened this section. Once I've told them they have to eliminate condoms, abstinence, and monogamy, they're pretty much stuck. Surely, we had better think of a few more strategies than that, since regardless of our wishes, the vast majority of young people will not choose the strategies of abstinence or monogamy. And the biggest irony of all: One reason they won't is because that's all we teach them about.

The key is to remind ourselves that children are not walking, talking body parts that might get themselves into trouble. Until we realize this, we'll continue to admonish, "Don't share your sexual parts with anybody, but if you do, make sure they're covered." Instead, we need to take into account who our children are, not simply what we're afraid they might do. And who they are, as I'm constantly reminding my students, are thinking, developing, feeling, valuing, decision-making, problem-solving, relationship-building *people*—who happen to have sexual body parts.

With this in mind, we'll realize that the most important messages we need to give are not about body parts, but about inner parts. Not about semen and viruses, but about courage and communication. Not about condoms and contraceptives, but about forethought and caring, choices and feelings, honesty and self-esteem. And the more we teach them about all those things—and how inextricably they connect to our sexual health—the safer they will be.

Here's an alphabetized list of sixteen additional answers to my question, compiled by a typical group of students who had studied the concept of relative risk (many items apply to other risk-taking situations that teens face, as well):

- *Accept* that you are personally susceptible to STI.
- *Be brave* enough to confront potentially embarrassing situations.
- *Communicate* assertively.
- *Decide* to wait as long as possible before engaging in high-risk sexual behaviors.
- *Engage* in a healthy lifestyle.
- *Feel* good enough about yourself to take care of your health and safety, even if it means displeasing others.
- *Get* periodic STI testing, and if infected, follow the doctor's regimen and abstain from risky behaviors until the infection is clear.
- *Hold off* on high-risk behaviors until both partners are tested, then practice monogamy.
- *Insist* that you and your partners be honest with each other about past sexual, drug use, and medical history.
- *enjoy* low-risk behaviors whenever in doubt about yourself or a partner.
- *Know* (in advance) your sexual values and beliefs.
- *Limit* the number of your sexual partners.
- *Match* the levels of emotional and physical intimacy in your relationships.
- *Never* mix sex with alcohol or other drugs.
- *Observe* symptoms of STI in yourself and others.

- *Pride* yourself on being a person who continues to educate herself or himself about all aspects of STI prevention, detection, and treatment.

Another clear and essential application of the concept of relative risk concerns date and acquaintance rape prevention. All young people need to understand that the vast majority of rapists do not fit the stereotypical image of a crazed stranger who jumps out the bushes and attacks someone who just happens to be in the wrong place at the wrong time. Most rapes occur between people who know one another, in isolated locations where the victim has agreed to go—precisely *because* the two are acquainted.

We've done a good job in recent years convincing people that rape is about power and dominance, not sex. (In fact, to a degree we've *overdone* it; for the rapist, rape is certainly also about sex.) What motivates and excites the rapist fundamentally is not the opportunity for sex, but the opportunity to hurt, demean, humiliate, and overtake another person *by means of sex*. In other words, when the other person says no, that's the real turn-on for the rapist. It's important for us to help young people understand that this is the one and only cause of rape: the conscious decision made by the rapist to overrule and overpower another person sexually. Since, by definition, the victim has absolutely no power or control over that decision, he or she is never responsible in any way for having been raped.

However, although there is only one cause of rape, there are multiple contributing factors that can increase the chance that date or acquaintance rape will happen. Rape and assault prevention depend on how well young people can enumerate and understand these risk factors, since to a large degree their chance of being victimized is relative to how well they are able to avoid them.

First of all, every teen should understand the potentially grave risks of socializing while under the influence of alcohol and other drugs. Drug use not only leads to impaired judgment and lowered capacity for self-defense, but can also alter personality and induce aggressiveness. Second, girls need to thoroughly understand the psychosocial factors that may cause them to become a target. Although it is always wrong to assume that the way a person dresses or acts signals sexual availability, others may mistakenly think so nonetheless. Girls also need to be especially wary of

boys who are excessively jealous and controlling and conscious of the criteria they use to judge another person's trustworthiness. Moreover, they
must know in advance of any given situation what they are willing to say
yes and no to sexually, since ambivalence often leads to giving mixed and
confusing signals. If a girl happens to be alone in an isolated location with
someone who has been trained to think that girls don't really mean no
when they say so or that girls who "tease" deserve what they "get," she
may be especially vulnerable. Under any circumstance, girls are wise to
have first dates with groups of friends or in public places.

Parents of boys need to be vigilant about these issues as well. Young
men must realize that in today's world, they are much more at risk socially
and legally to charges of sexual harassment and assault. Protecting themselves and the young women in their lives is a matter of self-awareness,
mutual respect, clear values, and careful, direct communication—values
emphasized throughout this book. Parents must make it explicitly clear
that it is never acceptable to force sexual activity of any kind, and they
must actively challenge the rampant gender stereotypes in our society that
promote disrespect of girls and women.

**Become an Advocate for Adolescent Sexual Health.**   We can also help
our children—and everyone's children—by helping our communities and
government face up to their responsibilities to young people and their
needs. I know of no parent groups organized for the sole purpose of lob-
bying *for* comprehensive sexuality education in schools, only those that
lobby *against*. These groups—many with presumptuous and self-congrat-
ulatory names like "Parents Who Care" and "Citizens for Parental
Rights"—portend to speak for *all* responsible parents. Caring, concerned
parents can and do hold widely disparate views about the best strategies
for educating their children; the vast majority of American parents surveyed in the 1980s and 1990s prefer a comprehensive approach. It's time
for the real "silent majority" to actively and vocally lend support to their
local schools and to ask for the same back. Parents should not have to do
this job on their own; they need their immediate community to deliver
the same kind of realistic, relevant, and comprehensive messages that they
attempt to give at home. By the same token, teenagers need to know that
there are many adults—in the family, at school, and within area clinics
and service organizations—who are willing and able to address their real
concerns.

## A Post Test of Sorts

As a check on yourself, take a few moments to revisit the parenting situations first presented in Chapter 8. For each example, write out which one or more of the five core needs is being expressed by the child, and place a star next to the need that seems most pressing. Explain how you think you would respond to each need. I've replaced two of the situations for which possible responses were given earlier.

1. You find that your twelve-year-old has been watching R-rated movies at the home of a friend.
2. A parent walks in on two five-year-olds playing "doctor."
3. A fifth-grader wants to go to the movies on a "date."
4. Your college freshman son or daughter wants to bring a boyfriend or girlfriend home for the holidays. They want to sleep in the same bedroom.
5. Your sons are playfully calling one another "fags."
6. A fourth-grader wants to know what a "blow job" is.
7. Your ninth-grade daughter is very level-headed and mature for her age, but the kids in her grade seem to be in the fast lane socially.
8. You have been dating a new person for several months, and you'd like him or her to move in on weekends. You have three children, ages nine through fifteen.
9. Your fifth-grade daughter refuses to discuss puberty with you, even in the most basic of terms, and seems very anxious about the whole subject.
10 Your very good-looking son receives constant phone calls from girls in his grade. This seems to make him very uncomfortable.

# Sexual Orientation: Why and How It's Everyone's Business

Walk through the hallways in almost any school building—middle, high school, even elementary—and within a very few moments you'll hear one of the universal epithets of choice among American youth: "That's *so* gay."

Should you ask or confront the students about their language, they'll often look at you as if you're from another planet. "Oh, gay doesn't mean *gay*" (the words "you idiot" are implied in their tone as they say this). "It just means *stupid* [or *nerdy* or *clueless* or *loser*]. We don't mean anything by it. It's just a word that we use, just a harmless expression."

"Harmless, eh?" I usually say at this point. The follow-up conversation typically goes something like this:

"You've just put down an entire group of people, but you didn't mean anything by it?"

"No, of course not. We don't have anything at all against gay people. Honest we don't."

They catch each other's eyes and nod earnestly.

"So the fact that you're using the word *gay* as a substitute for *stupid* or *loser* is a simple coincidence?"

"Right. Besides, there aren't any gay people around here, so even if we did mean something negative, we're not really offending anybody."

"OK," I say, "let's look at this another way. I'm Jewish. Suppose I walked into a school in an area of the country where there were hardly any Jews. Suddenly I heard kids saying stuff to one another like, 'Oh, that's *so* Jewish," or, 'You're such a Jew! I can't believe what a Jew you are!' Then suppose I walked over to them and said, 'Hey, listen. I happen to be Jewish and that comment really offended me.' What if they tried to convince me that they didn't *really* mean 'Jew' as in *Jew*—or that they didn't *really* hold Jews in a negative light, or that I certainly shouldn't take what they'd said personally. Would I be likely to believe them? Would you?"

"OK, you made your point. But there *really aren't* any gay people around here."

"How do you know? And if there were, do you think they'd let on, given the way people around here talk? Maybe that's precisely why there don't seem to be gay people—kids or adults—in our school. Besides, do you have to be gay to be offended by antigay put-downs? Who else might be hurt or upset by your language?"

It's a long and hard conversation. Sometimes I feel I get through, sometimes I know I don't; the older the kids, the harder it becomes. In fact, unless adults consistently intervene *much earlier,* once kids have reached middle adolescence, this manner of speaking will have become deeply and thoughtlessly embedded in their youth language and culture. From that point on, they'll often resist adult interference on developmental principle (even if they happen to agree with the adult point of view).

Since homosexuality is a forbidden topic in most schools at the age when antigay name-calling begins to surface (in some places as early as first grade), the kind of adult intervention required to extinguish these insidious attitudes and behaviors before they become entrenched rarely occurs. It is, of course, a lack of adult intervention that has caused the problem in the first place; kids know that *gay* is one of the few remaining epithets they can get away with, because adults won't—or don't know how to—call them on it. Unless and until schools begin to take a more active role, it is parents who will have to take the lead if this destructive cycle is to be reversed.

## The High Costs for Sexual Minority Youth

As destructive as their attitudes and behavior may be, the students I just described really do not harbor intense hatred or disapproval toward sexual minorities. However, many other students (and school personnel) do. The unwelcoming if not outright hostile school environments in which sexual minority youth (gay, lesbian, bisexual, and transgender, or "GLBT") typically find themselves exact a high toll. In comparison to their peers, for example, they are five times more likely to report skipping school because of feeling unsafe, three times as likely to be threatened with a weapon at school, twice as likely to report having seriously considered suicide, four times as likely to report having attempted suicide, twice as likely to be a teen parent, three to ten times as likely to report having tried cocaine, and twice as likely to report bingeing on alcohol at least once in the past month.

It is difficult to imagine another situation in which such intolerant attitudes would be allowed to exist inside a school building. Yet, in many school communities, these behaviors go unaddressed, even unnoticed. It is incumbent upon us as responsible educators, parents, and caring adults to ask how and why this outright discrimination—and the resulting emotional, physical, and educational costs for sexual minority youth—are allowed to persist.

And persist they do. Youth risk behavior surveys in Massachusetts, Washington, and Vermont in the 1990s have provided convincing data about the extent of bias against sexual minority youth in U.S. schools. For example,

- 97 percent of students in public schools report hearing homophobic remarks from peers.
- 53 percent of students report hearing antigay remarks made by school staff.
- 80 percent of prospective teachers report negative attitudes toward sexual minority youth.
- two-thirds of guidance counselors harbor negative feelings toward GLBT (gay, lesbian, bisexual, or transgendered) people.
- 77 percent of prospective teachers would not encourage a class discussion on homosexuality.
- 85 percent oppose integrating gay and lesbian themes into their existing curricula.

Not surprisingly, these same surveys find that 80 percent of gay and lesbian youth report feelings of severe social isolation. Remember, too, that for ethnic or racial minority youth, home and community outside of school usually provide an oasis of understanding and sympathy—and shared minority group status—as a buffer against prejudice or mistreatment at school. Gay youngsters, on the other hand, may feel just as isolated and rejected in relation to family and community as to peers or other adults.

## How Homophobia Hurts Everyone

Although the pressing needs of sexual minority youth in schools are deserving of our most immediate consideration and response, it is vital to remember that the targeting of any particular group of students ultimately affects the health and well-being of an entire school community. Wherever the overt victimization of any minority group is permitted, students understand intuitively that all other individuals and groups are thereby potentially vulnerable, and a highly charged and threatening environment for every student results.

Moreover, the targeting of this particular minority group, unlike others, creates an additional vulnerability. Since one's sexual orientation is an invisible attribute, essentially anyone potentially may be relegated to sexual minority status—by virtue of stereotyping, perception, rumor, scapegoating, public name calling, and the like. The written testimony of one young high school graduate at a safe schools legislative hearing in the late 1990s makes the point poignantly:

I experienced hateful verbal attacks often in high school, most likely because of my passion for theater and musical theater. Quiet and reserved socially in my freshman year, I finally began to feel successful and happy sophomore year when my opportunities to act and sing took off. As soon as I began to expose that passion, the attacks began.

Actors and singers, especially those who were proud of that identity, were "fags." It became a popular and acceptable thing to assign that label to me as I had no method of self-defense. After all, how do you respond to such claims? "No, I am not a homosexual!"

How can you substantiate such a response? Others certainly can choose not to believe you. It's not as if you can hold up a card or a license stating your sexual orientation.

And, of course, being more firm with statements like, "I believe it is wrong for you to use those kinds of labels with me or anyone else," only fuel the fire. My own strong belief in the validity of homosexuality as an identity only added to the hurt I was feeling. I felt hurt and I felt the hurt of those close to me who are homosexual.

It is vital to understand that in schools where hostility toward sexual minorities is especially acute, virtually everyone is caught in the dynamic: students who are GLBT; students who are not GLBT, but who are perceived to be; and students who are in neither group at present, but who are worried that unless they distance themselves sufficiently, often by participating in various forms of GLBT bashing, they might well be. Thus, everyone in the building potentially becomes involved, either as victim, potential victim, perpetrator, or bystander.

## Why the Reluctance to Intervene?

Many factors explain the reluctance of schoolteachers, administrators, and guidance personnel to intervene against blatant bias against sexual minorities. Prejudice, stereotyping, lack of awareness, and sheer discomfort with the topic of homosexuality and transgender (and the subject of sexuality in general) certainly play a role. In addition, many school personnel are genuinely confused or conflicted about these issues because of their own deeply held moral or religious beliefs, and others may truly want to intervene but lack the skills and training to know how. Lack of leadership at local and state levels is also a paramount ingredient; only a small minority of districts and states explicitly mandate equitable treatment of sexual minority youth. Furthermore, mandates that do exist do not necessarily guarantee adequate funding or specific directives for enforcement and staff training. Moreover, organized opposition groups, most notably the Family Research Council, lobby heavily on local and national levels against equity-oriented changes in school policies and practices, charging that these are tantamount to promoting homosexuality and other "alternative life styles."

## Two Remarkable Events

Two unrelated but remarkable events in late 1999 may help lay the groundwork for progress in making schools emotionally and physically safer places for sexual minority youth. In November, a historic weekend-long summit transpired between two hundred gay and lesbian civil rights advocates and two hundred associates and followers of the Reverend Jerry Falwell at the reverend's church in Lynchburg, Virginia. Falwell, previously an indefatigable source of negative rhetoric about homosexuality, agreed to the meeting in response to the high-profile killings of two gay men, Matthew Shepard and Billy Jack Gaither, and the massacre of seven Christian youths at a Baptist church in Fort Worth, Texas. Reportedly, the targeting of Christians and the brutality of the Shepard and Gaither murders persuaded Falwell to concede the potentially destructive power of hateful language.

As Falwell told the press, "You don't know what it means to be targeted until you have been a target yourself." He vowed that in the future he and his staff would avoid any "statements that can be construed as sanctioning hate or antagonism against homosexuals." While still maintaining his conviction that homosexuality is morally wrong and continuing to oppose legislation guaranteeing civil rights protections to sexual minorities, he asserted unequivocally that calling off the rhetoric was an essential step in preventing further bloodshed.

The second watershed event was the publication of the booklet *Just the Facts about Sexual Orientation and Youth*, an eleven-page document distributed to each of the 14,700 public school districts in the United States and officially endorsed by the following medical, mental health, educational, and religious organizations: the American Academy of Pediatrics, American Counseling Association, American Association of School Administrators, American Federation of Teachers, American Psychological Association, American School Health Association, Interfaith Alliance Foundation, National Association of School Psychologists, National Association of Social Workers, and National Education Association. Subtitled *A Primer for Principals, Educators, and School Personal*, its preface puts forth its fundamental message:

Controversies in our society about homosexuality are increasingly involving schools. As principals, educators, and school personnel, you need good information that will guide you through these controversies. This fact sheet has been developed by a group of education, health, and mental health, and religious organizations that all share a concern for the health and education of all students in schools, including lesbian, gay, and bisexual students. We know you also share this concern—that all students deserve an opportunity for learning and healthy development in a safe and supportive environment.

Among the booklet's central points is the emphatic assertion that "the idea that homosexuality is a mental disorder or that the emergence of same-gender sexual desires among some adolescents is in any way abnormal or mentally unhealthy has no support among health and mental health professional organizations." Stating unequivocally that homosexuality is not an illness requiring a "cure" (the booklet also debunks claims made by proponents of "reparative therapy" that homosexuality is a mental disorder), the publication describes sexual orientation as an integral component of a person's total identity, like one's culture, ethnicity, and gender. In a final section, "Relevant Legal Principles," it reminds policy makers that lesbian, gay, and bisexual students are entitled to equal protection under the law, citing recent Supreme Court and lower court decisions requiring that school districts protect students from harassment, including antigay harassment.

## Foundations for Change

Together, these two events—combined with the increasing body of data documenting the near universal health and safety hazards for GLBT youth in our schools—provide school policy makers with a compelling factual and moral rationale to cut through existing barriers to school change.

### Common Ground

Schools have a moral and legal obligation to provide a safe learning environment for all students. Children and adolescents who come to school and feel targeted, labeled, stereotyped, and marginalized because of who they are—or who their family members happen to be—are in effect denied a level playing field in the academic arena. It is unreasonable to expect them to learn and to participate effectively in school life if they are constantly feeling threatened or abused. Student safety and the principle of equal access to education are core values inherent in the American tradition of schooling. Any school board member or school superintendent who advocates programs and policies designed to promote these values stands on high moral principal, if not squarely on his or her fiduciary or fiscal responsibilities, given the successful litigation of recent student-on-student harassment lawsuits. Promoting a safe and equitable school environment does not mean that the school is acting to promote any particular sexual orientation or gender identity any more than maintaining a safe and equitable environment in relation to race, ethnicity, gender, or religion means promoting a particular race, ethnicity, gender, or religion. To the contrary, by insisting on a level playing field for all students, schools demonstrate that specific aspects of an individual's personal identity are essentially irrelevant to the learning environment and therefore not open to endorsement (or condemnation) in any way.

## Absence of Cause to Discriminate

Groups opposing equitable treatment of gay and lesbian youth in schools often argue that the homosexual "lifestyle" is inherently unhealthy or pathological. Therefore, to support gay and lesbians students in any direct way is perceived as dangerous to children, a betrayal of the community at large, and an abdication of proper adult responsibility. The Just the Facts Coalition, publishers of *Just the Facts about Sexual Orientation and Youth*, have provided a powerful source of rebuttal information for school personnel who find themselves confronted with these inaccurate assertions. Although the coalition's views may be deemed controversial by some, the medical and mental health associations that support and endorse its work are indisputably credible. School officials—who are impelled ultimately to base decisions affecting student life and health upon the most reliable clinical and scientific information available—now have this data at their immediate disposal.

## Protected Category Status

The contention that homosexuality is a lifestyle choice, not an inherent component of identity, provides another forcefully articulated justification for denying equal protection. Opposition groups often charge that the concept of equal protection is inapplicable to homosexuality, because sexual behavior is a personal choice presumably under individual control. Therefore, gays and lesbians are depicted as asking unfairly for "special treatment" based on their individualized sexual preferences. By stating emphatically that sexual orientation is a matter of individual identity, not personal choice, the coalition has provided school personnel with an additional rationale for extending equal protection policies to include minority youth. Moreover, as *Just the Facts* points out, the Supreme Court (*Romer v. Evans,* 1996) has ruled that "public officials may not impose discriminatory burdens or unequal treatment on gays and lesbians because of the public's animosity toward them."

## Religious Tolerance

The Reverend Falwell has reminded us of the true meaning of religious tolerance. Religious tolerance does mean simply "to tolerate" or "to put up with." It is founded on the mutually respectful acknowledgment of a moral principle basic to American government and culture: All people have the absolute right to private judgment in matters of faith. Tolerant individuals agree to disagree with each other when they hold differing views—without condemnation or mistreatment. (Some might argue that Reverend Falwell has agreed to disagree without condemnation, but not without mistreatment, since he does not favor legal protections for gays and lesbians.)

Schools officials must understand that tolerance is always a two-sided equation: Just as students have the right to be who they are and to receive an education free of condemnation or mistreatment regardless of their sexual orientation, students (and parents) have the right to believe what they believe about homosexuality according to their own conscience or religious faith, without experiencing condemnation or mistreatment because of those beliefs. Schools must actively and equitably seek to protect the rights and ensure the physical and emotional safety of individuals on both sides of the equation, just as they must insist that all points of view along the spectrum be presented respectfully.

Policy makers must also recognize that although all individuals have an absolute right to hold and to respectfully state their religious beliefs, no specific religious group can be allowed to determine or dictate school policy about matters that significantly impact student life—either directly, by pressuring administrators to take sides, or by default, by insisting that they sidestep issues entirely to avoid offending a particular faith community. For administrators to do either is to risk violating the rights of other

faith communities that may hold different views; jeopardizing the principle of separation of church and state; and ignoring the immediate and
pressing needs of targeted youth. School policy in public and non-
parochial school settings must remain focused squarely upon real student
need, sound educational principle, shared community values, and available factual data, not the particular interpretations of any one religious
faith.

School officials must also differentiate between religious beliefs, which
are based on faith (and in some cases particular scriptural interpretations)
and cultural beliefs, which are based on perceptions or interpretations of
facts. The role of schools in relation to these two very different kinds of
beliefs is not the same. As indicted above, schools have a responsibility to
protect the right of all individuals to respectfully state their faith-based
beliefs. However, they also have the responsibility, as educational institutions, to challenge non-faith-based beliefs known to be inaccurate and
potentially damaging. *Cultural stereotypes of gay and lesbian individuals as
inherently evil, abnormal, inferior, perverted, unhealthy, dangerous, contagious, or predatory are based in prejudice and myth.* Just as schools would be
required to refute false and reprehensible remarks about any other minority group in our society, they are obliged to actively work to dispel un-
truths and vicious stereotyping of lesbians and gays as well.

Individuals who oppose homosexuality on religious grounds often resent the use of the label *homophobic* to describe them or their point of
view, and rightfully so. The term *homophobia* refers specifically to bigotry,
prejudice, or discrimination based on an *irrational fear* of gay and lesbian
individuals. For some individuals, homophobic attitudes or behaviors
constitute a deep-rooted defense mechanism, used either to ward off one's
fear of their own potential homosexuality (psychological homophobia) or
the fear that they will be perceived as homosexual by others (social homophobia). A person who holds faith-based views opposed to homosexuality
(or transgender) is not necessarily homophobic or disapproving of homosexuality in any way other than theological.

## Growing Up Gay

Throughout this book—and at the risk of oversimplifying—I've attempted to write about children and adolescence as generally and universally as possible, without reference to particular racial, ethnic, or

socioeconomic groupings. I've also been very mindful of how and where I've introduced or interjected the issue of sexual orientation, so as not to accentuate sexual minority youth as different but rather the same in most respects. For example, the fundamental psychosocial tasks of adolescence, a subject addressed repeatedly, embody the same set of universal stresses and challenges, irrespective of the adolescent's particular sexual orientation.

All teens, sexual minority youth included, struggle continuously with five core developmental issues—identity, integrity, individuality, independence, and intimacy. They do so to discover their own answers to some of life's most profound questions: Who am I? How am I the same but unique and separate in regard to family and peers? How can I best make my own way in the world? How can I create close, healthy, and satisfying relationships with others on an increasingly adult level? As they endeavor to construct and incorporate this emerging sense of a more grown-up self, they'll need to master complex social skills, explore new roles and experiences, expand their social and intellectual worlds, develop more sophisticated and mature decision-making and coping skills, and identify and pursue career and occupational goals.

That's a tall order indeed for all adolescents, gay or straight. In one hugely important respect, however, gay and transgendered youth are different: *Through no fault of their own*, they must come of age within a society, a school, a group of peers, and often a family, an ethnic community, and a religious tradition that are overtly hostile to who they are. Cruelly and coldly relegated to an invisible, isolated, and stigmatized minority, they are obliged to cope, often on their own, with untold vulnerabilities and stresses on top of the universal developmental challenges of adolescence.

## How Are Gay Kids Different?

Read through once more the lists of psychosocial tasks and developmental questions identified above. Now picture yourself (or your child) attempting to mount these challenges while constantly having to bear a huge, dark secret. Imagine that to become a healthy grown-up, you must explore and integrate a positive identity and self-concept, but must do so in the face of pervasive and damning stereotypes about the very person you are becoming, and without modeling from parents or other important adults. Think about getting up every day for school and having to brace yourself to endure yet another day of rejection or humiliation or to watch, silently, while others like you endure them, with no one to help you learn the coping behaviors or survival skills you need to protect yourself and others from abuse or exposure. Contemplate your social life: How would you meet other sexual minority youth, begin to experiment with dating and sexual behavior in safe ways and with adult guidance, build the social skills you'll need to create healthy intimacy in future relationships? Imagine trying to envision your future—job, family, religion, community—against the backdrop of discrimination and intolerance that you read and hear about constantly in the media. Caitlin Ryan and Donna Futterman, in *Lesbian and Gay Youth: Care and Counseling*, say it powerfully:

> The social and emotional isolation experienced by lesbian and gay youth is a unique stressor that increases vulnerability and risk for a range of health and mental health problems. From a very early age negative attitudes about homosexuality are reinforced through social institutions and the media. Children learn to think that being "gay" is "deviant," "unnatural," and intolerable. They learn from a variety of credible sources—their families, teachers, religious leaders, friends—that being lesbian or gay means living alone, being rejected and ostracized, foregoing a meaningful career or satisfying intimate relationships, and not being accepted or integrated into the broader society. Through a variety of deprecating stereotypes they learn that being lesbian or gay means living a half-life; by the time they enter early adolescence, when social interactions and sexual strivings coincide with formulating an adult identity they have learned to hide same-sex feelings, attractions, and behaviors from others and often from themselves. Prejudice, fear and hatred of homosexuals (or *homophobia*) are also internalized. As adolescents struggle to reconcile societal myths about homosexuality with a growing sense of dread they might be lesbian or gay, these internalized feelings of stigma and self-hatred increase existing vulnerabilities.

> The dangerous consequences of these societally induced vulnerabilities—depression, fear, anxiety, self-blame, self-loathing, hampered identity development, poor school performance, truancy or dropping out, abandonment of career or educational aspirations, alienation from family and peer groups, alcohol and drug abuse, participation in risky sexual be-

haviors, suicidal thoughts and attempts—are well documented by Ryan and Futterman and others. Singly or in combination, these vulnerabilities can foreclose on a young person's life and future before they even start, sometimes forever. Knowing that children live and suffer silently and often invisibly in our midst—for some of us in our very own homes and for all of us in the homes of our neighbors, family, friends, associates, and co-workers—requires us as moral and caring adults to work to create safer communities and to model compassion and understanding to all our children.

## Coming Out

Despite a society that remains fundamentally hostile, the average age of *coming out*—or acknowledging or disclosing one's homosexuality—has decreased steadily in recent years, from sometime in the early twenties to age sixteen. Presumably, the drop has resulted from the increasing openness throughout all levels of our society about the general topic of homosexuality. Most young people are aware of same-gender attractions by the age of ten or twelve, or even earlier—just like their heterosexual peers—and even may have engaged in same-gender sexual experiences. However, the process of *consciously* self-identifying as lesbian or gay typically occurs later.

Coming out, first to oneself and then to friends, family, and others, is a gradual process, and for most people, it is a double-edged proposition. For youth especially, disclosure may increase the risk of being rejected or verbally or even physically abused, but it may also be the only hope of their accessing supportive heterosexual peers and adults, connecting with a caring and informed gay and lesbian community, and experiencing opportunities for affirmation and socialization. It can also increase the prospects for a healthier and more fully integrated adolescent and adult life.

For many young people, internalized homophobia and fear of hostile reactions deter them from coming out. Others are coping with home and school situations in which the wisest and safest course of action is to remain closeted. Some lesbian and gay teens, however, have become outspoken activists for their cause. They have begun to write about their own personal life experiences; to organize, especially by establishing or attempting to establish gay-straight alliances within their schools (extremely controversial in some communities); and to speak out as panelists at safe-schools conferences and before local and state legislative and school board hearings. Their voices are powerful and real, and these brave and eloquent young people have become a vigorous force for change.

## The Good News for Lesbian and Gay Teens

As researchers and youth-serving agencies have discovered, the dangerous effects of stigma and marginalization on sexual minority youth are in large measure reversible. I vividly recall a stunning presentation I heard in the early 1980s by an administrator at the Hetrick-Martin Institute in New York, a community-based facility for gay youth. "Given our success, people think we must be doing amazing things here. But, basically, what we do is provide a safe place where these kids can hang out and play cards with one another and just be normal kids. It's the stigma and isolation that's their major problem on the outside." For sexual minority youth who are fortunate enough to have access to these kinds of peer support groups and positive adult role models, most of the stressors and vulnerabilities connected with sexual minority status eventually resolve.

People opposed to the movement to create safer schools and communities for sexual minority youth often accuse its advocates and those seen as their heterosexual "allies" of having hidden motives—of wishing merely to promote a so-called homosexual agenda. What is implied in the rhetoric is that lesbian and gay adults deliberately choose to exploit disaffected youth in order to further their own selfish political goals, or even worse, that their real aim is to get into our schools so they may "recruit" children and adolescents into their "homosexual lifestyle." Appealing to powerful and deep-rooted cultural stereotypes, this kind of blatant and hateful fear mongering has succeeded in depriving many young people of desperately needed adult support.

One of the most important roles that adults play in children's lives is to provide healthy models for behavior. Adolescents look to adults both consciously and unconsciously as models of healthy relationships and as guides-by-example of life and career options. Interaction and conversations among sexual minority youth and adults help lesbian and gay adolescents learn that there is a broad range of diversity within the homosexual community, just as in all communities. They become aware through firsthand experiences that the narrow and loathsome stereotypes to which they have been exposed are wrong and grossly inadequate, and that they, too, will eventually find a comfortable "fit" and place for themselves in adult society. And they learn, perhaps most importantly of all, that gay adults can be happy, fulfilled, and successful people.

Adults—gay and straight—can also provide important anticipatory guidance to lesbian and gay youth in many practical ways. They can

- help them devise effective strategies for dealing with harassment and potential violence and for deciding when, how, and if to disclose one's sexual orientation.
- assist them in examining ideas of what it means to be lesbian, gay, or bisexual, and teach them about the process of sexual development.
- explain the benefits of abstinence and postponement of sexual behavior and help them understand that learning about and coming to terms with one's sexual orientation does not require participation in particular sexual acts.
- encourage them to explore sexual behaviors gradually and safely, and help them focus on developing a personal code of sexual ethics and enhancing the quality of their interpersonal and intimate relationships.
- counsel them about risky sexual practices and about STI/HIV and pregnancy prevention (many will have heterosexual experiences as well), and caution them against mixing sex with alcohol or other drugs and having multiple or anonymous partners.
- warn them about the potential for abusing alcohol and other drugs as a tempting but false means of dealing with isolation, rejection, or internalized homophobia.
- help them recognize, talk about, and cope with the unique stresses in their lives that make them particularly vulnerable to depression, suicide, substance abuse, and other risky behaviors.

Perhaps most important of all, adults can locate or help create support groups in their area for sexual minority youth, where they can socialize, find empathy and understanding, and share feelings, experiences, and strategies. The most powerful medicine for all young people is to have opportunities to normalize their adolescent experience.

How frightening and tragic that when these kinds of supports are un-available, sexual minority youth must make their way through some of life's most daunting developmental challenges—and through the extra burdens imposed on any stigmatized minority—without the crucial input from caring and understanding adults that all young people need and de-serve.

## The Coming-Out Process for Families

The discovery or disclosure that a son or daughter is gay typically will throw an entire family into crisis. In fact, parents and other family mem-bers may experience the same powerful and potentially paralyzing emo-tions—denial, fear, stigma, disappointment, helplessness, isolation, shame, self-blame—as the youth himself or herself. Each family member will need time to adjust and to process her or his individual reactions. Sometimes, having sensed for a while that something was wrong because of the child's secrecy, evasiveness, or difficult behavior, parents may actu-ally experience relief to know that he or she is not in serious trouble with another problem such as drugs. For others, worry and concern for their child's physical and emotional safety will be paramount. In any case, ac-cess to accurate information about homosexuality and to other families that have experienced and surmounted similar challenges is crucially helpful. The national organization PFLAG (Parents, Families, and Friends of Lesbians and Gays) is an excellent resource and has chapters throughout the United States.

Tragically, some families never get the help they need to move past the initial crisis and emotion generated by the discovery or disclosure; they remain so unaccepting that the relationship can never be repaired, or they may even expel the child from their home. (Estimates of homeless lesbian and gay homeless youth vary but are thought to be as high as 40 percent in some areas of the United States.)

As Ryan and Futterman explain, the coming-out process for families of sexual minority youth can be a lengthy, multistage ordeal. Typically, it be-gins with denial ("maybe it's just a phase") and eventually involves a pe-riod of painful grieving over the loss of the child's perceived heterosexuality. Families may also need to comes to terms with, and ulti-mately relinquish, long-held fantasies about the child's future prospects for heterosexual marriage and family. By educating themselves, families will of course discover that many lesbian and gay couples live together in long-term, committed relationships and that an increasing number are choosing to become parents through adoption or medically assisted conceptions. Families that are most successful in remaining physically and emotionally intact eventually learn to work through and let go of negative and distorted attitudes and beliefs about homosexuality to which they may have ascribed in the past. They are then able to recast their remaining sense of lost expectation into a newfound understanding and appreciation of the positive, gratifying, and accomplished lives that all individuals, heterosexual or homosexual, are capable of leading.

Other families will learn to accept a child's homosexuality to varying degrees. For parents, siblings, or extended family whose deeply held religious beliefs proscribe homosexuality absolutely, the experience can be extremely gut-wrenching. (Patricia Miller's book, *Sex Is Not a Four-Letter Word*, is a particularly helpful resource for parents struggling with religious conflicts regarding a child's homosexuality.) In any case, what the child most needs to know is that on some fundamental level, he or she is still loved and accepted *unconditionally.*

## Teaching about Gay and Lesbian Issues in Schools

Teaching about homosexuality in schools is one of the most controversial issues in American education today. Aside from objections raised by some religious groups (see the discussion earlier in the chapter), there exists great misunderstanding of its purpose. Just as many people misinterpret sexuality education as being focused literally on sex, they are apt to think that education about homosexuality education is intended to focus literally on homosexual sex. Particularly at the elementary school level, therefore, they may be mystified at how the topic of homosexuality could be in any way age-appropriate. No wonder they may think that someone else's agenda is in play. Moreover, as with the misguided beliefs and fears about the process of sex education we've discussed earlier, they may worry that "knowing will lead directly to doing" if their children are exposed to the subject.

The fact of the matter is that classroom teaching—almost at any age—in no way *introduces* the subject of homosexuality to children or adolescents. In today's world, lesbian and gay issues are ubiquitous in children's lives: From TV talk shows, news stories, movies, and other programming they watch, to the playground chatter they overhear, to the "in-group-out-group" language of their peer group, the topic of homosexuality is already in their thoughts and experiences. Homosexuality is simply a reality of modern American life that is ever-present in media and current events, in families and friendships, in laws, politics, religion, and youth culture. Schools that attempt to grapple with the topic—by providing accurate information and by allowing children to talk about what they already know or think they know and to clarify and learn from the views of others—are not in any way "putting ideas in children's heads." Rather, these schools are fulfilling their responsibility to help kids understand the world as it is.

Conversely, when schools or parents deny, ignore, or run from this or any other important issue in children's lives, they may implicitly communicate or teach various destructive messages: that adults are too disinterested, uncomfortable, or uninformed to care; that they lack the courage to stand up to controversy or conflict, even when the education, health, and emotional and physical safety of young people may be at stake; that they are clueless or in utter denial about what exists right before their very eyes and ears. As we have emphasized in this book, uninvolved adults will end up both undercutting themselves as credible adult resources and abdicating their all-important roles and duty to affirm, give information, clarify values, set limits, and provide anticipatory guidance. And they will virtually assure that culture and peers will step into the void.

Lessons in school about homosexuality are not intended to promote anything but education, understanding, and safer school environments. They do not advocate that people become gay, only acknowledge that some people are gay; they are not about describing sexual practices—although certainly the topic may come up and be addressed—but about clarifying the reality of people's lives. For example, talking about the topic of homosexual families (i.e., families headed by gay and lesbian couples) is no more about the subject of sex than is talking about life in families headed by heterosexual individuals. The topic at hand is not the mechanics of sexual behavior, but the fact that some people love, desire, live and have sex with one another in same-gender relationships.

Almost always, the most important topics that arise in such conversations are not about sex, or even sexual orientation, but about issues of bias and discrimination, respect and tolerance. The learning typically goes way beyond "gay sex" or even the "gay issue" to discussions of ethical and kind treatment of others. And, because children of all ages understand name calling and mistreatment—and how very much they can hurt—the topic can be handled in an age-appropriate fashion at almost any age. It is never too early for children to talk about respect and to learn about differences among people.

Conversations in school also allow students to learn many new facts and to critically examine the myths, misinformation, confusions, and stereotypes about homosexuality to which they are constantly exposed. They will learn to identify and analyze images of lesbians and gays in the media and clarify crucial distinctions regarding biological gender, gender roles, gender identity, and sexual orientation. They'll explore theories of how people develop heterosexual, homosexual, or bisexual orientations (thought to be a combination of biological and environmental factors) and learn that people do not *choose* their particular orientation but rather come to *discover* it. They'll hunt for current events in the fields of religion, law, politics, science, health, and family life that pertain to sexual orientation, intersexuality, and transgender. They'll learn that lesbian and gay individuals are part of a highly diverse population of people who defy narrow and often derogatory stereotypes regarding physical appearance, mannerisms, occupation, and lifestyle.

Almost all young people question their sexual orientation, if only at some brief point, and some continue to question their place on the sexual orientation continuum for considerable periods of time. (In fact, facilities and programs that serve sexual minority youth more and more commonly refer to their clientele as GLBTQ youth, for Gay, Lesbian, Bisexual, Transgendered, and Questioning.) It is helpful for young people to understand that individuals can experience different patterns of development: Some will know or sense their orientation long before pubescence, most will find that their orientation solidifies around or by the time of puberty, whereas others will discover it more gradually. By age eighteen, most (95 percent) know with certainty. Full awareness and acceptance of bisexual orientation, interestingly, appears to be significantly delayed in comparison to heterosexuality or homosexuality, occurring commonly in the middle to late twenties.

Adolescents also need to appreciate crucial distinctions between the sexual orientation, sexual attraction, sexual fantasy, and sexual behavior. Many people who are fundamentally heterosexual (or homosexual) in orientation will at some time in their lives experience fantasies about same-gender (or other-gender) sexual encounters or find themselves romantically or sexually attracted to particular members of their same (or other) gender. They may or may not act on those fantasies or attractions, but even for those who do, individual experiences will not *change* or determine fundamental orientation.

It is not at all uncommon for heterosexual (or homosexual) adolescents to experience same-gender (or other-gender) attractions or "crushes," even to the point of physical experimentation. If they do not comprehend the relatively transitory nature of these experiences—or the differences between attraction, fantasy, behavior, and orientation—they may draw inaccurate conclusions or place inappropriate labels on themselves or others. By the same token, they need to understand that pressuring themselves to engage in particular sexual acts with particular individuals will not establish, confirm, or deny sexual orientation. One's sexual orientation simply is what it is; people can "have" a sexual orientation without engaging in any sexual behavior at all.

## Making Change Happen

As mentioned earlier, in the upper-level courses that I teach, students use the local paper and a daily national newspaper as their text. One of the most dramatic trends I've noticed over the decades is that each year, a higher percentage of the articles relate to aspects of homosexuality and to gay and lesbian issues in our society. This topic is not going away, and the opportunities and pressures for schools and families to change will mount. Many changes will evolve gradually and unconsciously as gay culture and gay youth continue to move, in the words of Ryan and Futterman, "from the margins to the mainstream." The pressures on schools, no doubt, will often involve acrimonious conflict and debate. All of it will take time. As Kevin Jennings, executive director of the Gay Lesbian Straight Education Alliance, continually points out, change is a process, not an event.

Unfortunately, while time passes, another generation of youngsters—gay and straight—will suffer the consequences of our adult silence, confusion, conflict, and inaction. In some schools, every child is affected by homophobia every single day. For gay youth and adults and for all of us who know, love, care about, parent, or are parented by people who are lesbian or gay, the effects are immediate and deeply painful. Surely, there is common ground enough in our compassion for one another and for our children to make change happen more quickly, one event at a time.

# Notes

## Chapter 1

1. Page 4, Catherine Russell, "'The Talk' with Kids Should Occur Early, Often," *Washington Post,* April 6, 1999.

2. Page 4, *European Approaches to Adolescent Sexual Behavior and Responsibility* (Washington, D.C.: Advocates for Youth, 1999, fact sheet).

3. Page 5, "Parent–Child Communication: Promoting Healthy Youth" (Washington, D.C.: Advocates for Youth, 1999, fact sheet).

4. Page 7, Pamela Wilson, *When Sex Is the Subject: Attitudes and Answers for Young Children* (Santa Cruz, Calif.: Network Publications, 1991).

5. Page 8, National Guidelines Task Force, *Guidelines for Comprehensive Sexuality Education, Kindergarten–Twelfth Grade,* 2nd ed. (New York: SIECUS [Sexuality Information and Education Council of the United States], 1996).

6. Page 8, Debra Haffner, "What's Wrong with 'Abstinence-Only' Sexuality Education Programs," *SIECUS (Sexuality Information and Education Council of the United States) Report* (New York: SIECUS, April/May 1997).

7. Page 9, *European Approaches to Adolescent Sexual Behavior and Responsibility* (Washington, D.C.: Advocates for Youth, 1999, fact sheet).

## Chapter 2

1. Page 30, Anne Bernstein, *Flight of the Stork: What Children Think (and When) About Sex and Family Building* (Indianapolis: Perspectives Press, 1994).

## Chapter 4

1. Page 94, Richard Eberst, "Defining Health: A Multi-Dimensional Model," *Journal of School Health* 54, no. 3 (March 1984): 99–104. Eberst was the first to sug-

gest using the idea of the Rubik's Cube as a model for understanding wellness. Sexuality educator Carol Flaherty-Zonis was the first to apply it to the concept of sexual decision making.

## Chapter 6

1. Page 110, Erik H. Erikson, *Identity, Youth and Crisis* (New York: Norton, 1968).

2. Page 111, Mildred L. Brown and Chloe Ann Rounsley, *True Selves: Understanding Transsexualism—for Families, Friends, Coworkers, and Helping Professionals* (San Francisco: Jossey-Bass, 1996).

3. Page 111, Anne Fausto-Sterling, *Sexing the Body: Gender Politics and the Construction of Sexuality* (New York: Basic Books, 2000).

4. Page 113, Melissa Hendricks, "Is It a Boy or a Girl?" *Johns Hopkins Magazine,* November 1993.

5. Page 114, Anne Fausto-Sterling, "The Five Sexes: Why Male and Female Are Not Enough" *The Sciences,* March-April 1993.

6. Page 114, William O. Beeman, "What Are You: Male, Merm, Herm, Ferm, or Female?" *Baltimore Sun*, March 17, 1996.

7. Page 121, Lisa Maurer, "Transgressing Sex and Gender: Deconstruction Zone Ahead?" *SIECUS (Sexuality Information and Education Council of the United States) Report* (New York: SIECUS, October/November 1999).

8. Page 121, Dallas Denny, "Transgender in the United States: A Brief Discussion," *SIECUS (Sexuality Information and Education Council of the United States) Report* (New York: SIECUS, October/November 1999).

9. Page 131, Mary Pipher, *Reviving Ophelia: Saving the Selves of Adolescent Girls* (New York: Ballantine, 1994).

10. Page 132, Dan Kindlon and Michael Thompson, *Raising Cain: Protecting the Emotional Life of Boys* (New York: Ballantine Books, 1999).

11. Page 132, William Pollack, *Real Boys* (New York: Henry Holt, 1998).

12. Page 134, Jackson Katz and Sut Jhally, "Why Violence? Why Boys?" *Boston Globe,* May 2, 1999.

13. Page 135, Frank Pittman, *Man Enough: Fathers, Sons, and the Search for Masculinity* (New York: G. P. Putnam's Sons, 1993).

14. Page 136, Michael Gurian, *The Wonder of Boys* (New York: Tarcher/Putnam, 1996).

15. Page 136, Michael Gurian, *A Fine Young Man* (New York: Tarcher/Putnam, 1998).

## Chapter 7

1. Page 146, SIECUS/Advocates for Youth, *Survey of Americans' Views on Sexuality Education* (Washington, D.C.: SIECUS/Advocates for Youth, 1999, report of a national poll by Hickman-Brown Research in February and March 1999).

2. Page 152, American School Health Association, *Sexuality Education Within Comprehensive School Health Education* (Kent, Ohio: American School Health Association, 1991).

3. Page 152, Clint Bruess and Jerold S. Greenberg, *Sexuality Education Theory and Practice,* 3rd ed. (Dubuque, Iowa: William C. Brown Communications, 1994).

4. Page 156, David J. Landry, Lisa Kaeser, and Cory L. Richards, "Abstinence Promotion and the Provision of Information About Contraception in Public School District Sexuality Education Policies," *Family Planning Perspectives*, November/December 1999.

5. Page 154–156, Haffner, "What's Wrong with 'Abstinence-Only' Sexuality Education Programs."

## Chapter 9

1. Page 189, Mark Schoen, *Belly Buttons Are Navels* (New York: Prometheus, 1990).

2. Page 190, Debra Haffner, *From Diapers to Dating: A Parent's Guide to Raising Sexually Healthy Children* (New York: Newmarket Press, 1999).

3. Page 192, Pipher, *Reviving Ophelia.*

4. Page 195, Susan Golombek and Robyn Fibush, *Gender Development* (New York: Cambridge University Press, 1994).

5. Page 196, Barrie Thorne, *Gender Play: Girls and Boys in School* (New Brunswick, N.J.: Rutgers University Press, 1997).

6. Page 200, "The Truth About Tweens," *Newsweek,* October 18, 1999, 62–72.

## Chapter 11

1. Page 237, Sidney Simon and Sally Olds, *Helping Your Child Learn Right from Wrong* (New York: McGraw-Hill, 1976).

2. Page 238, Adele Faber and Elaine Mazlish, *How to Talk So Kids Will Listen, and Listen So Kids Will Talk* (New York: Rawson, Wade, 1980).

3. Page 241, Thomas Gordon, *PET: Parent Effectiveness Training* (New York: Peter H. Wyden, 1970).

## Chapter 12

1. Page 264, "Parents Are Alarmed by an Unsettling New Fad in Middle Schools: Oral Sex," *Washington Post,* July 8, 1999.

2. Page 264, "Our Children and Their Sex Games," *Dublin Times,* July 17, 1999.

3. Page 265, "The Face of Teenage Sex Grows Younger," *New York Times,* April 7, 2000.

4. Page 267, "Youth Risk Behavior Surveillance: United States, 1999," *Morbidity and Mortality Weekly Report* 49 ( June 9, 2000) (SS–5).

5. Page 267, Parents Television Council, "What a Difference a Decade Makes: A Comparison of Prime Time Sex, Language, and Violence" (Los Angeles: Parents Television Council, March 1999, special report). Report also available at www/parentstv.org.

## Chapter 13

1. Page 279, Jackson H. Brown, *Life's Little Instruction Book* (Nashville, Tenn.: Rutledge Hill Press, 1991).

2. Page 285, David Elkind, "Understanding the Young Adolescent," *Adolescence* 13 (1978): 127–134.

3. Page 289, Alan Guttmacher Institute, *Contraceptive Needs and Services 1995* (New York: Alan Guttmacher Institute, 1997).

4. Page 290, National Center on Addiction and Substance Abuse at Columbia University, *Dangerous Liaisons: Substance Abuse and Sex* (New York: National Center on Addiction and Substance Abuse at Columbia University, 2000).

5. Page 290, William Fisher and Deborah M. Roffman, "Adolescence: A Risky Time," *Independent School* 51, no. 3 (spring 1992): 25–32.

6. Page 292, Daniel Goleman, *Emotional Intelligence* (New York: Bantam Books, 1995).

7. Page 293, Gail Sheehy, *Passages: Predictable Crises of Adult Life* (New York: Bantam Books, 1977).

## Chapter 14

1. Page 303, Centers for Disease Control and the Massachusetts Department of Education, *The Massachusetts Youth Risk Behavior Survey: 1997* (Boston, 1997); Safe Schools Coalition of Washington, *Seattle Teen Health Risk Survey: 1995*; Vermont Department of Health, *Vermont Youth Risk Behavior Survey: 1997* (Burlington, 1997).

2. Page 306, Frank Rich, "Has Jerry Falwell Seen the Light?" *New York Times*, November 6, 1999.

3. Page 306, Just the Facts Coalition, *Just the Facts About Sexual Orientation and Youth: A Primer for Principals, Educators, and School Personnel* (Washington, D.C.: National Education Association, 1999).

4. Page 312, Caitlin Ryan and Donna Futterman, *Lesbian and Gay Youth: Care and Counseling* (New York: Columbia University Press, 1998).

5. Page 317, J. C. Gonsiorek, "Mental Health Issues of Gay and Lesbian Adolescents," *Journal of Adolescent Health Care* 9 (1988): 114.

6. Page 317, Patricia Miller, *Sex Is Not a Four-Letter Word* (New York: Crossroad Publishing, 1995).

7. Page 319, Haffner, *From Diapers to Dating*.

8. Page 320, Kevin Jennings, "Silence Is the Voice of Complicity," *Independent School* (winter 1999): 54–59.